I0952458

THE DRAGON
EXTENDS
ITS REACH

Also by Larry M. Wortzel

China's Military Modernization: International Implications (1988)

The Chinese Armed Forces in the 21st Century (1999)

Class in China: Stratification in a Classless Society (1987)

Dictionary of Contemporary Chinese Military History (1999)

Related Titles from Potomac Books

Dismantling the West: Russia's Atlantic Agenda
—Janusz Bugajski

*Iran's Revolutionary Guard: The Threat That Grows
While America Sleeps*
—Steven O'Hern

Israel vs. Iran: The Shadow War
—Yaakov Katz and Yoaz Hendel

Red Rogue: The Persistent Challenge of North Korea
—Bruce E. Bechtol, Jr.

*Socrates in Sichuan: Chinese Students Search for Truth,
Justice, and the (Chinese) Way*
—Peter J. Vernezze

THE DRAGON
EXTENDS
ITS REACH

Chinese Military Power Goes Global

LARRY M. WORTZEL

Potomac Books
Washington, D.C.

© 2013 by Larry M. Wortzel
All rights reserved
Potomac Books is an imprint of the University of Nebraska Press

Library of Congress Cataloging-in-Publication Data
Wortzel, Larry M.
   The dragon extends its reach : Chinese military power goes global / Larry M. Wortzel. —
First edition.
       pages cm
   Includes bibliographical references and index.
   ISBN 978-1-61234-405-8 (hbk. : alk. paper)
   ISBN 978-1-61234-406-5 (electronic)
   1. China—Armed Forces. 2. National security—China. 3. China—Defenses. 4. China—
Military policy. I. Title. II. Title: Chinese military power goes global.
   UA835.W672 2013
   355'.033051—dc23   2013003518

Printed in the United States of America on acid-free paper that meets the American
National Standards Institute Z39-48 Standard.

Potomac Books
22841 Quicksilver Drive
Dulles, Virginia 20166

First Edition

10 9 8 7 6 5 4 3 2 1

CONTENTS

ILLUSTRATIONS

FIGURES

TABLES

MAPS

PREFACE

In 1988 I was a U.S. Army major on my way to China to assume the position of assistant army attaché at the U.S. embassy in Beijing. One step in the preparation for this assignment was to attend a conference on the People's Liberation Army (PLA) that featured some of the best-known and established experts on the Chinese military in academia, the foreign policy community, and the U.S. government. At the conference, a highly experienced scholar painted a view of the PLA as a military that lacked the capability "to be anything more than a nuisance." China's military equipment was characterized as obsolete, and its ability to operate beyond its borders was described as minimal.

Even then it struck me that this characterization was wrong. Certainly whatever forces and equipment the PLA mustered on the battlefield had been more than a nuisance to the U.S. and UN forces in the Korean War. In 1962 the PLA had soundly defeated the Indian Army over disputed border areas. The air defense, armor, and engineering forces that the Chinese military deployed to Laos and North Vietnam had been far more than a "nuisance" to American pilots during operations in Southeast Asia in the 1960s and 1970s. Also, as a military intelligence analyst, I had observed the Chinese military's preparation for and the conduct of its 1979 "self-defensive counterattack" on Vietnam, really a full-scale invasion designed to convince Vietnamese leaders that China was the major power on the Asian continent.

The Chinese military is a "party army"—that is, one controlled by the Chinese Communist Party (CCP)—with limited missions. It was primarily designed to keep the CCP in power, to control or suppress the populace, and to protect China's borders. But to call it a mere "nuisance" minimized its history and capabilities.

Once I saw the PLA up close as a military attaché, it was clear that my disagreement with the characterization of China's military at the academic conference was correct. Some of the equipment was old, but the soldiers were tough and their leaders were quite capable. The PLA did things differently than the U.S. Army and the U.S. Marine Corps, in which I had experience, but it was effectively organized, led, and equipped for its primary missions. I had the opportunity to go into one of China's national training areas with an artillery division for a few weeks, and had the opportunity to visit and make a parachute jump with a unit from its airborne forces, the Fifteenth Group Army (really part of the PLA Air Force). Meanwhile, its strategic missile forces, then a smaller arm of the PLA, had adequate nuclear forces and delivery systems to deter the Soviet Union, India, and the United States. Yet experienced "China watchers" and senior academics routinely dismissed the PLA as an ineffective fighting force.

Almost twenty years later, at a major conference on the PLA at the U.S. Army War College, I presented a paper on China's advances in command, control, communications, computers, intelligence surveillance, and reconnaissance (C⁴ISR). In that presentation, I described how the PLA had begun development of a major new ballistic missile variant that it thought could successfully attack a U.S. aircraft carrier with a maneuvering warhead. Dozens of Chinese military research papers made it clear that PLA developers thought they were on the cusp of such a capability. But U.S. Navy officers at the conference scoffed at the thought that China could achieve such capabilities. That C⁴SIR paper has been updated as chapter 2 in this book. And the U.S. military has had to devise an entirely new operational concept, "AirLand Battle," to counter China's "antiaccess/area-denial" capabilities, including the DF-21D antiship ballistic missile.

It is that professional experience that led me to write this book. Over a couple of decades the PLA systematically, if slowly, modernized its equipment, focused on training its personnel, and changed its mission to meet the challenges of new times. The PLA is turning into a modern armed force with its own unique operational doctrine. PLA doctrine developed in response to requirements set down for it by the CCP central leadership to fulfill expanding national interests but also in light of China's history. As China's national interests expanded significantly beyond its immediate borders, its military was required to expand its capabilities and scope of operations. China is now part of a global supply chain and economic system, and is dependent on energy and food that must be imported from all around the world. And China depends on air and sea transportation to ship out its products. This book seeks to explain the new role the Communist Party envisions for the PLA in securing China's global interests and how the PLA is structuring, equipping, and modernizing itself to meet this role.

In December 2004 Hu Jintao, simultaneously Communist Party general secretary, Central Military Commission chairman, and president, set the parameters
for the PLA to "go global." In a speech on "the historic missions of the PLA," Hu
made it clear that China's military must be able to help safeguard China's expanding national interests and to incorporate increased maritime, space, cyber, and other
forms of operations into its missions. When Hu was replaced by Xi Jinping, a
process that began in November 2012 and was completed in 2013, Xi's first major
encounter with the PLA was with the strategic missile forces. This implies that a
robust nuclear and conventional missile force will develop further.

To be candid, however, as much progress as the PLA has made in some of
these areas, it still has many weaknesses. Although China's ballistic missile capabilities have modernized and its entire missile force is mobile, the PLA has struggled to field a submarine-launched ballistic missile (SLBM). This book describes
these failures; even though China has the necessary submarines to employ an
SLBM, the Navy does not seem to be able to produce the missile. Although the
PLA Air Force apparently has tested two different versions of a stealth fighter aircraft and successfully copied advanced Russian fighters, China's defense industries
have struggled for decades to make a highly durable jet engine. There seem to be
some major problems with quality control and metallurgy in China's industrial
system. For both fighter jet engines and turbine engines for tanks and other
armored vehicles, the PLA still has to rely on foreign sources. Through a long
process of subterfuge, the PLA Navy acquired an aircraft carrier, but it is strug-
gling to develop the aircraft that would fly from its deck and to develop the arrest-
ing gear to help the aircraft land.

The move toward a global military force is most successful in strategic missiles,
cyberwarfare, and space operations, but is slower in other areas. The Navy was the
priority for some time, and current emphasis seems to be on air forces. China's
ground forces, however, have not seen the same emphasis on developing global
capabilities. One objective of this volume is to present a balanced picture of PLA
development.

Another objective of this book is to add a bit of realism to the debate about
whether China is an ally or friend of the United States. Many Americans, inside
and outside of government, have a romantic and idealized view of China as a true
ally. Going back to the days of the Office of Strategic Services (OSS) mission to
China during World War II, American military officers have tried to treat the
People's Liberation Army as an ally. However, alliances depend on fundamentally
shared values, which are missing from an army that is run by a communist party

and has the fundamental mission of keeping in place a "people's democratic dictatorship."

There have been periods of cooperation between the United States and China, which included cooperation with the PLA. The two countries worked together to confront the Soviet Union after its invasion of Afghanistan. That cooperation included a program to sell advanced weapons to the PLA to improve its capabilities against Soviet forces. The PLA, however, never romanticized this cooperation. China's military and Communist Party leaders kept their focus on exploiting cooperation with the United States to steal technology, reverse-engineer military equipment, and learn about how the U.S. military trains and operates.

When the PLA was used as the main instrument of repression to quell prodemocracy and anti-Party demonstrations in 1989, the period of military cooperation between China and the United States changed. President George H. W. Bush stopped all military technology sales and transfers to China in response to the Tiananmen Massacre of June 4 of that year. Still, there were other forms of contact between the U.S. military and the PLA.

Earlier the PLA had observed the way the British military handled the Falklands War with Argentina and began to study the value of the capacity to conduct operations at long distances from one's homeland. The PLA was transfixed on how the United States and its coalition partners used new technology, satellite and airborne surveillance systems, space communications, and stealth technology against Iraq in the Gulf War. Academic institutions and operations officers of the PLA studied these conflicts to see what lessons could be applied to China's military. China developed its own new weapons and surveillance systems to enable the PLA to develop similar capabilities or at least to counter the U.S. capabilities that the PLA saw as threatening. After all, China still threatened war against Taiwan, supported North Korea, and had territorial disputes with U.S. allies.

To address how the PLA is developing and just how far it has come toward becoming a global military power, the book draws on China's own military literature to outline how the PLA describes its own future. It also examines Communist Party documents and statements from CCP leaders. In writing this book, I drew on a series of monographs I developed for the U.S. Army War College, as well as my personal experience in China. On my first trip to China in 1979, I began to acquire PLA publications, and over the years I built that personal library, focusing on such issues as missile forces, command and control, space operations, and information warfare. On each trip into China, an almost annual occurrence, I updated that collection, which was invaluable in writing the book.

Instinctively, having spent much of my life studying the history of the PLA, I have tried to incorporate into this book how the organization sees itself. The Chinese armed forces have their own unique military culture, the product of starting out as an insurgent guerrilla force. After World War II, as the PLA transformed itself from a collection of guerrilla bases and columns into a large maneuver army, it quickly adapted itself to a different form of warfare, incorporating weapons it had captured from the Japanese and from Nationalist (Guomindang) forces. I have tried to explain how that history and military culture affect the PLA today and the lessons the PLA takes from its own history.

I believe *The Dragon Extends Its Reach* has sufficient military and technical rigor to make it useful to professional military personnel and students of strategy and warfare inside government, in academia, and in the policy or intelligence community. However, its target audience is broader than that. By putting military doctrine into the context of China's history and of the PLA's military culture, the book also serves the student of military sociology and military history. I also have attempted to explain how some of China's military doctrine and developments affect foreign affairs and U.S. interests, in the hope of making it useful to students of foreign affairs.

Chapter 1 is the introduction to the book and to the People's Liberation Army. It explores China's expanding global interests as a major world power with economic interactions and investments in every hemisphere. The chapter discusses the ways that the PLA's own unique military culture developed from and is grounded in recent Chinese history, as well as in China's ancient military classical literature. Chapter 1 also examines the geopolitical context of the PLA's modernization, including China's resource needs, overseas investments, and the regional security environment in Asia. It puts this discussion into the context of the CCP's response to twenty-first-century conditions as articulated through policies from the Central Military Commission and the Politburo Standing Committee. Finally, chapter 1 introduces the structure, organization, arms, and branches of the PLA.

Chapter 2 examines the creation of a nationwide and increasingly global C^{4}ISR structure for the PLA. Advances in technology and changes in the way other nations engage in war in the information age stimulated change in China. The chapter discusses how the PLA examined the responses of other modern militaries to recent warfare and the lessons the PLA drew for itself in creating its C^{4}ISR system. Finally it outlines how China's responses remain grounded in earlier military doctrine and show where adaptations have been made more suitable to the nature of China's armed forces. All subsequent chapters of the book take the developments in C^{4}ISR and explain how they affect other domains of war and the arms and services of the PLA.

Chapter 3 explores China's naval modernization and its security policies in the maritime domain. This chapter examines new ships and systems (e.g., submarines, the aircraft carrier program), the approach China is taking to the areas in the East China Sea and South China Sea where Beijing claims sovereignty, and concepts being explored by China's strategists to secure distant sea lines of communication. The chapter also addresses the sea-denial and antiaccess strategies being adopted by the PLA and the American reaction to them.

Chapter 4 explores the transition from an air force that focused primarily on coastal and land air defense to one with expanding global reach. It discusses concepts of offensive and defensive air operations and how aerospace activities are becoming integrated with ground, naval, and other military capabilities.

The ground forces of the PLA are the focus of chapter 5. It explores their structure and organization and the limits on the resources being put into ground force modernization. It discusses the domestic context for maintaining a large ground force in China—the CCP's deep concern for maintaining internal stability and ensuring its continued rule. And this chapter examines regional contingencies for which the ground forces could be called upon, especially in Central Asia and Southeast Asia.

Chapter 6 discusses the modernization of the strategic missile forces and the integration of both conventional and nuclear missiles into the Second Artillery Corps (another name for the strategic missile forces). It also explores the uses of cruise missiles as strategic weapons and how short-range missiles affect Taiwan and Japan. This chapter will discuss the new antiship ballistic missile program and how the missile forces will work with the Navy to implement an antiaccess strategy. Finally, chapter 6 examines the debate inside China over the utility of adhering to the CCP's stated "no-first-use" policy on nuclear weapons.

The PLA's concepts for and approach to space warfare has been debated in the United States, Japan, and Europe since China intentionally shot down one of its own satellites in a test in January 2007. The antisatellite test also sparked a debate about whether the PLA was operating independently of civil (i.e., CCP) control. Chapter 7 discusses space policy, concepts such as space control, and the use of satellites for reconnaissance and communications. The chapter also explores PLA doctrine for the integration of space and cyberwarfare into its military operations.

Chapter 8 discusses the PLA's approach to modern information warfare in the electromagnetic spectrum. This chapter examines China's approaches to cyberwarfare and the way that China's military doctrine is evolving to take advantage of cyber-warfare as a tool of espionage, as well as a strategic weapon. It also explores how the PLA has taken old Soviet radio-electronic combat doctrine on combining electronic warfare and strike warfare to create "integrated network electronic warfare" (INEW).

What seemed to be an anachronism in the PLA, the General Political Department and its political commissars, is the topic of chapter 9. It discusses the department's missions in conducting information operations and psychological operations, and its doctrine of using the international legal system to achieve ends in warfare and conflict.

Chapter 10, the concluding chapter, discusses what to expect from China's military and its political doctrine over the next two decades, as well as how the PLA's modernization affects international security and military affairs. It examines where the PLA has made large strides in its evolving military development and where it falls short of its own objectives. The chapter also discusses the implications of PLA developments for the United States and makes a few suggestions on U.S. responses to China's military development.

There is no doubt that some readers will find the book deficient in one area or another. Admittedly, it does not delve deeply into the organization, structure, and allocation of equipment for each part of the PLA. These topics are addressed in general and in the context of how these matters affect broader security doctrine and politico-military affairs. Other volumes are available for readers who want precise details on each piece of equipment in the PLA inventory.

1 The PLA's Role in China's Foreign Policy

This book addresses the future of the Chinese People's Liberation Army (PLA)—how it is evolving and gaining strength to meet China's regional and global interests. However, the PLA's military culture, or ethos; its organization; its traditions; and the operational concepts it employs are embedded in the history of its establishment. This chapter will first look at how the PLA got its start as the military arm of the Chinese Communist Party (CCP). Then it will introduce the reader to the PLA's organization. Finally, the chapter will discuss in broad terms how China's military is evolving to address China's foreign policy interests.

The PLA traces its birth to an armed resistance against Nationalist forces on August 1, 1927.[1] "August" and "1" (eight-one, or *ba yi*) are the two ideographs that appear on the PLA flag and military insignia to signify its origins. Before the Nanchang Uprising, Communist military forces were part of the Nationalist (Guomindang) Chinese Army of the Republic of China (ROC) that moved from Guangzhou, in southern China, northward to take on northern warlords.[2] The Guomindang commander, Jiang Jieshi (Chiang Kai-shek),[3] renamed the force the Northern Expeditionary Army. On the way north, in order to suppress what it saw as growing Soviet influence in the Nationalist Party and Army, the Guomindang government began a purge of CCP members.[4]

This began a period of "white terror," a murderous purge of Communists from the Guomindang. The CCP responded by organizing an independent armed force that eventually focused on organizing the economy, society, and populace in rural areas. The CCP leaders later became the senior leaders of the PLA and, in 1949 after the revolutionary war, the most senior officials of the People's Republic of China (PRC).[5]

In response to the Guomindang purge, the Communist Party (or Gong-chandang) organized an uprising in Nanchang and seized the Nanchang Arsenal in

1

rebellion against the Guomindang.[6] They held out at Nanchang until August 5, 1927, when they withdrew and moved southward into the Jinggang Mountains (Jinggangshan) in a remote area of Jiangxi Province. The rebellious Communist forces reconstituted themselves there as the First Workers and Peasants Army (or Red Army) and conducted a series of guerrilla actions against the Guomindang known as the Autumn Harvest Uprisings.[7]

The reference to "workers and peasants" is homage to the influence of Soviet leaders from the Communist International in Moscow, which called for organizing the proletariat, or workers, in urban areas. Mao Zedong and other CCP leaders, however, had much more success organizing the peasantry against the landlord class in the countryside. Thus the PLA became an army that depended on the peasantry and had the most success in rural areas.

In 1928 the forces of Zhu De joined Mao Zedong's in the Jinggang Mountains, creating a military base area for a Communist revolution.[8] They established a series of "CCP soviets," and by 1931 the region became a military zone housing the Communist revolution against the Nationalists.[9] The Communists organized the peasants in the area, managed land distribution, established a military organization, and maintained relations with foreign Communist parties and nations. The PLA and the CCP leadership remained in the Jinggang Mountains until 1934, holding off a succession of encirclement campaigns and attacks from the Nationalists.

In 1934 the CCP, surrounded and out of contact with the Soviet Union, faced annihilation by Nationalist forces. Communist forces abandoned the Jinggang Mountains and began the "Long March" (Changzheng) out of Jiangxi, seeking to break free from Guomindang attacks and pressure in the Jiangxi-Hunan area. The goal was to establish a new and more secure base in a remote region of China. They passed through Hunan, Guilin, Guizhou, Yunnan, Sichuan, and Gansu Provinces, eventually arriving in Yan'an, in Shaanxi Province. The Long March took thirteen months, during which the continually shrinking Red Army moved across eight thousand miles before consolidating in Yan'an in October 1935.

The Long March had started with the Communist forces at strength of 102,000. By the time they reached Zunyi in Guizhou Province in January 1935, their strength had dwindled to about thirty thousand, and fewer than that eventually reached the new base area in Yan'an in 1935.[10] Of approximately 3,000 women who took part in Long March, only 149 survived.[11] From the new strategic base area, with other forces distributed in central and western China, the CCP waged primarily a guerrilla war against the Nationalists and Japanese forces until

1945. As the surrender of Japan became imminent, they mounted a revolutionary war against the Nationalists. On October 1, 1949, having beaten Jiang Jieshi's Nationalist Army, Mao Zedong and his fellow Communist leaders proclaimed on the walls of the Forbidden City in Beijing the establishment of the People's Republic of China.

This revolutionary history of guerrilla warfare, endurance, and reliance on the peasantry in a "people's war" informs the military culture and traditional operational approaches of the PLA today. Before the split between the Communists and Nationalists that culminated in the Nanchang Uprising, the military systems of Japan, Germany, and the Soviet Union influenced the way the Nationalists and Communists organized and fought. The PLA modeled itself along German and Soviet lines with a general staff system.

Today's PLA[12]

As constituted in the nation's 1997 Law on National Defense, China's armed forces have three components: the active and reserve forces of the PLA, the People's Armed Police (or PAP, as they are often called), and the militia, which are local, part-time military units spread all around China.[13]

The PAP is part of China's armed forces, although it is not actually part of the PLA according to the Law on National Defense. The PAP was formed in 1983 out of China's border control forces, internal security units, and units of the Ministry of Public Security.[14] Control of the PAP falls on two organs: the State Council, through the Ministry of Public Security, and the Chinese Communist Party Central Military Commission (CMC). The State Council also has responsibility for the local militia units working through local government bodies known as people's armed departments. The active and reserve PLA are under the firm and exclusive control of the CMC. Still, there is a duplicate organization to the CMC in the national government, although its members are the same. As Ellis Joffe, a well-known Israeli scholar on the PLA pointed out, "The institutional framework for the exercise of political controls [of the PLA] has in theory not changed since the early 1950s. It consists of Party Committees, political commissars, and political departments which run parallel to the military chain of command and are activated through supervision, education, and [ideological] campaigns."[15]

Including its reserve units, today's PLA is a force of about 2.3 million people. Approximately 510,000 are in the reserves.[16] Ground force strength is 1.6 million personnel. The PLA Navy (PLAN) is about 225,000 strong, the PLA Air Force (PLAAF) has around 400,000 personnel, and the PLA Second Artillery Force (PLASAF—the strategic missile force) has approximately 100,000 people.[17] The PAP is 660,000 strong, and the militia numbers around 10 million members.[18]

The Law on National Defense charges the active and reserve units of the PLA to be a standing army responsible for the national defense. But the PLA also has responsibility for maintaining public order. The PLA's reserve units have the same combat missions as the active units and can be mobilized by the state to become active in wartime or national disasters, as well as to help maintain public order. Like the PLA, PAP and militia units also may be called upon to help maintain public order.

There are chapters in this book devoted to in-depth coverage of the PLA Navy, the PLA Air Force, the Second Artillery Force, and the ground forces, or the PLA Army (PLAA).[19]

Political Control of the PLA

It is important to understand that the Chinese Communist Party is fixated, above all else, on maintaining its control of the country. The PLA is a "party army," and as such it is controlled by the Central Military Commission of the CCP.[20] China's constitution defines the nation as a Communist state—a dictatorship of the proletariat—under the leadership of the CCP. That relationship is part of the historical legacy of the PLA's formation as the armed component of the CCP. As set out in the State Council white paper *China's National Defense in 2010*, "the armed forces of China undertake the sacred duty of resisting foreign aggression, defending the motherland, and safeguarding overall social stability and the peaceful labor of its people. To build a fortified national defense and strong armed forces compatible with national security and development interests is a strategic task of China's modernization, and a common cause of the people of all ethnic groups."[21] It is the mission of "safeguarding overall social stability" that ensures that the PLA and the other two elements of China's armed forces remain the ultimate guarantors of CCP control.

The supreme command and leadership organization directing China's armed forces is the Central Military Commission.[22] This is a Communist Party organization that, according to the CCP constitution, is selected by the party's Central Committee. The party's general secretary is almost always the CMC chairman, and one of the senior members of the party's Politburo Standing Committee (PBSC) is generally also a member. In 2011 the vice chairmen were the minister of defense, the chief of the PLA General Staff Department, the heads of the other general departments (Political, Armaments, and Logistics), and the heads of the PLA Navy,

Air Force, and Second Artillery Force. The number of members on the CMC is not fixed and has varied over time. Also, there is a parallel but matching state organization, the State CMC, but its membership is identical to that of the party.[23]

The CMC sets broad policy and direction for the PLA and has control of China's nuclear weapons, with the CMC chairman as the "supreme Command authority."[24] However, the CMC is not always fully integrated with the leadership of the state. For example, after the earthquake that struck Sichuan Province in 2008, Wen Jiabao, China's premier, was put in charge of the state's disaster response effort. A number of PLA officers assert that Wen asked Gen. Guo Boxiong, vice chairman of the CMC, to accompany him to Sichuan and subordinate the PLA's action to Wen's response as vice president. The rumor in the PLA is that Guo responded by telling Wen that since Wen was not a member of the CMC, he (Guo) worked for CCP Chairman and President Hu Jintao. Therefore, Guo reportedly refused to travel and subordinate his actions to Wen.[25] The CMC also has been a major power base during political transitions in the CCP. Deng Xiaoping retired from all his official duties but retained the position of CMC chairman for two years. Once Deng turned the CMC position over to Jiang, Jiang Zemin was both CMC chairman and CCP general secretary. And Jiang did the same thing to Hu Jintao, holding on to the CMC chairmanship for two years after retirement from all other state and CCP positions. In the CCP transition in November 2012, however, Hu Jintao yielded both the general secretary and CMC chairmanship to Xi Jinping.

Another perennial problem affecting coordination among the PLA, the CMC, and the state leadership is that China has no organization analogous to a national security council. From time to time situations arise where the CMC and Politburo Standing Committee go ahead with some action, and the other elements of the government, such as the Foreign Ministry, have no idea what may have transpired. This appears to be the case with the 2008 kinetic antisatellite test China conducted (see chapter 6). The CMC was fully informed, as was President Hu Jintao, but the foreign minister, who is on a CCP–State Council foreign affairs leadership group, was reportedly not even consulted since he was not a member of either the PBSC or the CMC.

The armed forces are formally charged with four main "goals and tasks" in the white paper *China's National Defense in 2010*:

> Safeguarding national sovereignty, security and interests of national development. China's national defense is tasked to guard against and resist aggression,

defend the security of China's lands, inland waters, territorial waters and airspace, safeguard its maritime rights and interests, and maintain its security interests in space, electromagnetic space and cyber space. It is also tasked to oppose and contain the separatist forces for "Taiwan independence," crack down on separatist forces for "East Turkistan independence" and "Tibet independence," and defend national sovereignty and territorial integrity.

Maintaining social harmony and stability. The Chinese armed forces loyally follow the tenet of serving the people wholeheartedly, actively participate in and support national economic and social development, and safeguard national security and social stability in accordance with the law. Exercising to the full their advantageous conditions in human resources, equipment, technology and infrastructure, the armed forces contribute to the building of civilian infrastructure and other engineering construction projects, to poverty-alleviation initiatives, to improvements in people's livelihood, and to ecological and environmental conservation.

Accelerating the modernization of national defense and the armed forces. Bearing in mind the primary goal of accomplishing mechanization and attaining major progress in informationization by 2020, the People's Liberation Army (PLA) perseveres with mechanization as the foundation and informationization as the driving force, making extensive use of its achievements in information technology, and stepping up the composite and integrated development of mechanization and informationization.

Maintaining world peace and stability. China consistently upholds the new security concepts of mutual trust, mutual benefit, equality and coordination, advocates the settlement of international disputes and regional flashpoint issues through peaceful means, opposes resort to the use or threat to use of force at will, opposes acts of aggression and expansion, and opposes hegemony and power politics in any form.[26]

Broad policies to carry out these responsibilities are within the purview of the CMC.[27] The Ministry of National Defense, which is a structure under the State Council, serves primarily as a means to interact with other militaries and governments. The minister of defense invariably is a CMC member, and it is through the CMC that real power is exercised. The defense minister has no operational control over PLA forces. Execution of CMC policies is carried out by the four general headquarters departments of the PLA.

The General Staff System[28]

The General Staff Department, or GSD, of the PLA is led by the chief of the General Staff (*zong canmouzhang*), roughly a counterpart of the chairman of the Joint Chiefs of Staff in the United States. The GSD is responsible for military operations, training, mobilization, intelligence, electronic warfare, communications, training, cartography, meteorology, military affairs, and the foreign affairs of the PLA. It runs the national command-and-control system and a network of alternate command centers. The GSD also acts as the service headquarters for the PLA Army. In the experience of this author, however, when it came to counterpart relations visits between the PLA and the U.S. armed forces, the chief of the PLA General Staff has been treated as the counterpart to the chairman of the Joint Chiefs of Staff, while the senior-most deputy director (chief of the General Staff) of the GSD has been treated by the PLA as the counterpart to the U.S. Army chief of staff. The GSD deputy director responsible for intelligence matters is generally treated as the counterpart of the director of the U.S. Defense Intelligence Agency.[29] The GSD also oversees the Army's aviation, artillery, engineer, air defense, chemical defense, intelligence, and electronic warfare forces, training, and programs. While the GSD director is known as "the chief of the General Staff," the other general staff department heads are known as "directors" (*zhuren*).

The General Political Department (GPD) is responsible for the PLA's political and ideological education, the personnel system, and the political reliability of soldiers and officers.[30] It carries out these functions through a system of political commissars and political instructors in staffs and units throughout the military. Unit commanders at all levels in the PLA have counterpart political commissars who have similar ranks and share responsibility for the performance of units and personnel. The political commissar system keeps the personnel dossiers on all troops and manages promotions. Party committees at all levels of the PLA, in its schools, and in all its organizations participate in morale boosting, ensuring consensus on Party policies among the troops, and collective decision making. The GPD also runs the PLA's newspapers, journals, magazines, websites, television stations, sports teams, and dance troupes. Its functions are pervasive in such areas as internal security and discipline. The GPD has responsibility for all propaganda matters and, with the United Front organization of the Communist Party, for activities directed at Taiwan. When the PLA deals with the militaries of other Communist nations, such as North Korea, Vietnam, Laos, and Cuba, the GPD usually takes the lead.

As an example of the General Political Department's scope of responsibility, an article in the PLA's online newspaper recently discussed cooperation between the administration of Beijing Municipality, China's capitol, and the GPD for providing care and assistance to injured or sick demobilized soldiers in the municipality. This covered not only Beijing Military Region PLAA personnel, but personnel from the PLA Navy and Air Force. The GPD arranged for assistance to demobilized soldiers and their families living in the area. Thus the GPD, in addition to its political and propaganda roles, also provides for personnel and retirement services.[31]

The General Logistics Department (GLD) runs the PLA's supply, finance, and quartermaster systems; hospitals and health services; transportation; petroleum and lubricants supply systems; barracks and facilities construction; and accounting and auditing.[32] Although the national system of PLA farms and factories is smaller today than it was up until the 1980s, the GLD still runs several national-level factories, depots, and farms. The majority of PLA units below the level of brigade or regiment produce their own vegetables and livestock on farms in the vicinity of their bases; the GLD oversees this system. The GLD also runs approximately fifty national-level depots for various types of military equipment and uniforms. And the GLD produces food and beverages for the PLA. Its responsibility ends there, however; weapons, major equipment end-items, and ammunition are produced by the General Armaments Department (GAD).

The General Armaments Department evolved from the Equipment Department of the GSD.[33] The GAD formed as a separate, new, national-level department of the general staff system in April 1998, taking over some of the responsibilities of the Commission of Science, Technology and Industry for National Defense (COSTIND) and some responsibilities that traditionally were placed on the GLD and GSD. The GAD runs the system of weapon production and repair, ammunition production and storage, research institutes, and weapon test centers, and maintains a system of military representative offices at civilian factories that produce military equipment and weapons. China's space program, including its satellite launch and tracking facilities, are GAD responsibilities. The GAD's responsibility for weapon testing and production extends to nuclear weapons, so it runs the nuclear test base at Lop Nor.

The Headquarters of the Arms and Services

The PLA Army, Air Force, and Navy are separate services, although only the Air Force and Navy have their own service headquarters. As discussed above, the headquarters of the PLAA (ground forces) is the General Staff Department. The Second Artillery Force (PLASAF), China's strategic missile force, is a separate branch, or *bingzhong*. The PLAN, PLAAF, and PLASAF each have their own separate national headquarters in Beijing and their own commanders.

Each of these organizations has its own political commissar system and its own logistics and training system. But these still function under the direction and control of the GSD, GPD, GLD, and GAD. The situation gets more complicated at the regional level, where each of these organizations is part of the structure of the military regions.

Military Regions and Theaters of War

The People's Republic of China is divided into military regions (called "military area commands" in some PLA English-language translations). The military regions are large areas comprising two or more provinces. Today there are seven military regions; in the past there were more military regions (MRs, or *da junqu*).[34] Each MR comprises several provinces, provincial-level, centrally administered cities (such as Beijing, Tianjin, or Shanghai), or autonomous regions. And each MR has two or more group armies[35] assigned to it, as well as PLAAF, PLASAF, and in most cases PLAN forces. The military regions in 2013 were structured this way:

- Shenyang MR: Liaoning, Jilin, and Heilongjiang Provinces (each province is a military subdistrict or district);
- Beijing MR: Hebei and Shanxi Provinces, Nei Menggu (Inner Mongolia) Autonomous Region, and the centrally administered municipalities of Beijing and Tianjin (centrally administered municipalities are garrison districts);
- Lanzhou MR: Shaanxi, Gansu, Qinghai, Ningxia, and Xinjiang Provinces or autonomous regions;
- Jinan MR: Shandong and Henan Provinces;[36]
- Nanjing MR: Jiangsu, Zhejiang, Anhui, Fujian, and Jiangxi Provinces, as well as the Shanghai Municipality (garrison district);
- Guangzhou MR: Hunan, Guangdong, and Hubei Provinces; Hainan Island; and Guangxi Autonomous Region;
- Chengdu MR: Sichuan, Guizhou, and Yunnan Provinces; Xizang (Tibet) Autonomous Region, and Chongqing Municipality (garrison district).[37]

Each military region has its own commander and political commissar, as well as a full staff. The Army units in an MR are organized into group armies, although there are independent brigades, regiments, or divisions in some MRs that have a direct line of command and control from the MR headquarters. Each military region commander has his own regional Air Force commander, and the coastal MRs (Nanjing, Jinan, Shenyang, and Guangzhou) have a Navy commander.

The MR is usually commanded by a lieutenant general or a general, and the political commissar is one of the same two ranks. In each MR there are several deputy commanders. Generally there is one deputy for each of the separate services represented (Navy and/or Air Force), as well as deputies responsible for operations, training, and/or logistics. There is also a chief of staff leading the MR Headquarters Department, with several deputies. The other departments in an MR parallel the general departments: political, joint logistics, and armaments.[38]

The primary combat forces assigned to a military region are group armies (*jituan jun*) and PLA Navy and Air Force units. The PLA had eighteen group armies (GAs) in 2011. The exact size and composition of a GA varies around China depending on the mission of the MR to which it is assigned, but there are generally two or three infantry divisions or brigades, an armored division or brigade, an artillery division or brigade, an antiaircraft artillery brigade, an engineer regiment, and various combat support units such as communications, chemical, and reconnaissance forces.[39] In addition to the GA subordinate to the MR headquarters, there are independent divisions, brigades, or regiment-size units. GAs have some twenty-five thousand to forty thousand personnel. There also is one airborne GA in the PLA; however, it is part of the PLA Air Force, even if it is a ground fighting unit. The strength of the Fifteenth Airborne Army is approximately thirty-five thousand personnel.[40]

In the MR's effort to become a "joint" organization, its staffs have been augmented by joint political, logistics, and armaments department staffs. Second Artillery Force staff elements also augment the military region, but it is not clear whether they have a coordinating function for their headquarters or if they operate under the direct control of the MR commander.

We have some indications of how and under what conditions the PLASAF supports MRs and GAs. The Chinese military press has reported, for instance, that on June 10, 2011, during an exercise in the Tengri Desert of Lanzhou Military Region, the MR formed itself into a theater of war (*zhanqu*). A GA from the MR worked jointly with elements of the PLASAF, the PLA Air Force, the People's Armed Police, and Army aviation units to attack an enemy force.[41] According to the description of the exercise, when the GA commander, He Qingsheng, called for support from the PLASAF, it fired missiles on request from the supported Lanzhou Military Region GA. Unfortunately, this description did not clarify whether the missile units operated in direct support of the engaged Lanzhou unit responding to his immediate command, or if in the exercise scenario the missile forces had to go back to a higher organization in the PLASAF to get approval for the fire mission.

In peacetime the military region headquarters prepare, train, and exercise the forces under their control. But in wartime or time of emergency, a designated MR headquarters converts into a theater of war, and other MRs may be subordinated to it or designated to support combat operations.[42] There are precedents for combining more than one military region into a front with a geographic mission. For instance, during the Chinese attack on Vietnam in 1979, there were two fronts—one on the eastern portion of the Sino-Vietnamese border and one on the western—each of which comprised more than one military region. And the General Staff Department operational headquarters in Beijing, as well as the PLA Air Force, deployed operational forward command staffs to augment the theater of war.[43] According to a PLA Academy of Military Science book on command and control of joint campaigns, theaters of war are organized to perform specific theater or wartime strategic missions. Theaters of war can be based on the geographic boundaries of one military region or can be comprised of multiple military regions, depending on the mission and geographic requirements. Theaters of war are designed to provide the commander with access to all required military and civilian resources in the theater, but they also can be augmented with forces or control headquarters from around China. An integrated command and control network supports a theater of war and the network is part of the national command and control system.[44]

Military Districts[45]

Each of China's military districts administers and commands the forces in a single province or autonomous region. The military districts are known by the name of the province. Military regions, on the other hand, take their name from the city in which their headquarters is located. It is in the military districts (MDs), under MD commanders and their staffs, that the active force, reserve, and militia units of the PLA come together for mobilization, training, and other preparations. Like the military regions, the MDs have a full range of staff from the four general departments (GSD, GPD, GLD, and GAD) to assist the commander. At the district level, PLA leaders often have close relationships with the local government and local People's Armed Police units.

China has four centrally administered cities: Beijing, Tianjin, Shanghai, and Chongqing. There the military garrison commands (*jingbeiqu*) are the equivalent of military districts, and commanders report to their respective military region commanders.

The provincial-level military districts are further subdivided into military sub-districts (or military subcommands). These MSDs, as they are known, correspond to and take the name of the county, prefecture, or city where they are located. The commander has a headquarters and a staff to administer the forces under his control, as well as the mobilization offices and the People's Armed Forces departments (PAFDs), which monitor and administer conscription for the PLA and the militia in the subdistrict. These military subdistricts are also the loci of PLA recruiting and conscription. At the local level, MSDs and PAFDs address issues related to demobilized soldiers and localized material support for PLA, reserve, and militia units, and organize training for the militia. The PAFDs are unique in that the officers assigned to them wear PLA uniforms but with different insignia. The PAFD officers are deeply embedded in their communities, which may lead to corrupt activities, including the diversion of resources or accepting bribes for conscripting (or not conscripting) people into the different arms and services of the PLA.

Bribery in People's Armed Forces departments involved in the conscription process has been a persistent problem for the PLA. It is a difficult one to address. As Dennis Blasko has documented, the balance of volunteers and conscripts in the PLA is adjusted regularly, and the PLA relies on the People's Armed Forces departments in military districts to manage its conscription once quotas are levied.[46] There are ample opportunities for families or individuals to pay their way into service, avoid service, or seek a particular arm of branch of the military. PLA blogs also have entries complaining that promotions were secured through bribes. Thus, despite regulations on the conscription process, when you get down to military subdistricts these practices persist.

According a 2010 article in the CCP Propaganda Department–controlled newspaper *Global Times* (*Huánqiú Shíbào*), the CMC has "issued a new regulation outlining the responsibilities of military supervision authorities assigned the task of weeding out corruption." Senior officers in the PLA were warned not to "pursue a luxuriant lifestyle" and admonished to live a "simple life." The article reported such problems as bribing senior officers with presents and constructing luxurious facilities for the PLA, as well as the consistent complaint that officials in People's Armed Forces departments in the military districts seek bribes from potential recruits.[47]

National Mobilization[48]
The PLA maintains a national defense mobilization system designed to activate military units, as well as the militia and parts of the state government, in the event of

national emergency or war.[49] It has used this mobilization system to respond to natural disasters, such as the 2008 Sichuan earthquake and the serious flooding in southern China in 1998, and it has used it in war.[50] At the national level, the premier of the State Council is chairman of the National Defense Mobilization Committee system, established in 1994.[51] Vice premiers of the State Council and vice chairmen of the Central Military Commission serve as the vice chairmen of the National Defense Mobilization Committee. There are other members, however, including the leaders of government ministries and commissions, as well as leaders from the general departments of the PLA. Dennis Blasko, in *The Chinese Army Today*, explains that "a deputy chief of the General Staff Department is assigned the position of Secretary-General of the state NDMC (National Defense Mobilization Committee) and is primarily responsible for overseeing mobilization work in the PLA."[52]

This national mobilization system extends right through the military regions, districts, and subdistricts. The operating concept is to ensure that local civilian and military leaders, working together, are able to catalog and bring together all the resources in their area to address emergencies or contingencies. The system is designed to mobilize the necessary manpower, economic resources, supplies, and transportation assets to respond to crises or war.[53] The national defense mobilization system also is designed to activate civil air defense and conduct general defense education for the local populace.[54] For specialized forms of military operations such as cyber warfare or information warfare, the PLA has activated a series of information warfare militia units.[55] Establishment of these specialized militia units was endorsed in an article published by the PLA Academy of Military Science.[56] Such units are apparently available for mobilization or support of the government in counties around the country; one Internet security research firm in the United States identified thirty-three probable units of this type.[57]

As an example of the effectiveness of China's national defense mobilization system, the senior of the deputy chiefs of the PLA General Staff Department, Ge Zhengfeng, pointed out in a 2005 interview with Hong Kong's monthly magazine *Chien Shao* the way that the nation had mobilized in response to widespread flooding in 1998. Ge noted that the response was an "all-around national mobilization" drawing on units from across the PLA and local forces.[58] The PLA also includes members of the reserves and the militia, as well as local civilian authorities, in some of its military exercises.[59] Generals Liu Chengjun and Liu Yuan, then commandant and political commissar of the PLA's Academy of Military Science, respectively, summed up the mobilization system as "depending on the masses and developing people's war," the traditional strategy on which the PLA has relied from the time of its establishment.[60] People's war was characterized by extended guerrilla warfare and conventional warfare relying on help from the civil populace for logistics and even militia.

The national mobilization system is grounded in PLA history, going all the way back to the way the Red Army depended on and worked with local people in the Jinggang Mountains from 1927 to 1934.[61] It depends heavily on the local military departments and the activation of militia. In a Xinhua News Service report in December 2010, Liang Guanglie, then China's defense minister, put the "total number of primary militiamen in the whole country" at 8 million and the size of the reserve PLA force at 520,000.[62]

Converting from Designation as a Military Region to a Theater of War[63]

A military region may be designated a theater of war in time of conflict or military emergency.[64] The formation of a theater of war is usually temporary, and one or more MRs may be combined into a theater with a specific geographic orientation. The theater of war may then be augmented with forward staffs from the other services and arms of the PLA or from one of the general departments.[65] The formation of theaters of war is grounded in PLA history. The PLA used its revolutionary base areas as theaters during the revolutionary war period (1927–1949).[66] Depending on strategic considerations, geography, and the battlespace, forces from other military regions generally augment an MR when it becomes the headquarters of a theater of war.[67] In the Korean War (1950–1953) when PLA forces crossed the Yalu River into North Korea during their first campaign against United Nations (UN) forces, that theater of war was subdivided into eastern and western sectors.[68]

From a broad strategic standpoint, the PLA has formed geographically oriented theaters of war to respond to anticipated hostilities in case of a conflict, as well as to conduct combat operations. In recent times, during the Sino-Vietnamese War of February 17 to March 17, 1979 (what the Chinese significantly term its "self-defensive counterattack against Vietnam"), the PLA created two theaters of war. The Northern Theater of War was on the Sino-Soviet border. Formed in anticipation that the Soviet Union might react to China's incursion into Vietnam, it comprised forces from the Shenyang, Beijing, Jinan, Lanzhou, and Xinjiang Military Regions. However, some divisions and group armies from the Northern Theater were transferred southward to support operations against Vietnam.[69]

The Southern Theater of War was further subdivided into two subtheaters (*fenqu*). The Guangzhou Military Region commander, Xu Shiyou, was given responsibility both for the entire Southern Theater and for the eastern subtheater, comprising Guangxi Province and Guangzhou Province, in the event the conflict spread into the Gulf of Tonkin or South China Sea. The western subtheater was under the command of Yang Dezhi, who was the Kunming MR commander. Geographically it was centered in Yunnan Province.[70]

Tradition, Structure, and Political Culture of the National Security Decision-Making Process

The tradition in the Chinese Communist Party and the People's Liberation Army is "committee-based" (or "collective") decision making, command, and control.[71] This process dates all the way back to the establishment of the party and the PLA, according to one authoritative PLA text. In fact, at that time—the mid-1920s to 1930s—the party and the Army were one entity. This introductory section will examine the history and tradition of the defense decision-making processes of the People's Republic of China from the establishment of the People's Liberation Army. Even at lower unit levels, where there is a political commissar, the commissar and the unit commander work out consensus decisions.

The primary source for this section is a study on command, control, and the national security decision-making process in the PLA published by the Academy of Military Science in 2006, *The Study of Operations Command and Control* (*Zuozhan Zhihui Xue*). The purpose of this effort is to make clear the way that CCP political culture has evolved and how that culture will affect future national security decision-making processes. This section, therefore, forms a basis for judgments made later in this book.

From the time of the establishment of formal command-and-control structures in the PLA at the Jinggang Mountains revolutionary base area, the Communist Party made its decisions collectively, in a series of meetings attended by senior party members and representatives of the Communist International.[72] The CCP established its central military department in 1928 with a staff section and a political department but vested command and control at the highest level in the CCP Central Committee, which was the highest body of the party responsible for relations with other parties, directing political work in the party, and establishing party organizations.[73] From that time forward, especially because of the dispersed nature of the "revolutionary base areas" distributed around the country, the Central Committee and its Central Military Commission relied on discussion and consensus at the highest central levels for overall guidance in military operations but decentralized command and control in the units.[74] A committee managed the separate revolutionary bases, and the strategic leaders of a base area were the operational directors of its combat forces.

The PLA's Supreme Command Department (*Zuigao Tongshuai Bu*) was committee-based and relied on radio broadcasts, messengers, and telephone to communicate. The committees of the separate base areas listened to broadcasts and formulated their own operational orders. This process continued for some years during a series of PLA organizational meetings (at Gutian, Lianghekou, Ningdu, Maoergai, and Zunyi) during the Long March and until the CCP stabilized its headquarters and developed a formal staff in the Yan'an base area in 1937.[75]

By 1937 a more mature command-and-control structure developed as the PLA focused on independent guerrilla operations. Mao Zedong was the chairman of the CMC, with Zhu De as vice chair. Xiao Jingguang was chief of staff. This is noteworthy because Xiao and Mao had been removed from leadership positions at the 1932 Ningdu Conference.[76] The consolidation of the PLA at the revolutionary base in Yan'an resulted in the establishment of the training and matériel departments of the PLA and the creation of a "basic command post (jiben zhihuisuo)" for the conduct of the war. Also during this period, units and dispersed base areas established formal staff systems and systems of staff procedures.

By 1940 the first set of formal staff and command regulations came out for the PLA. The CMC set military strategic missions and sent them to the dispersed units and base areas.[77] The PLA also established a centralized communications department at the Yan'an headquarters with a nationwide communications network, a logistics network, and a set of broadcast radio stations responsive to the CMC.

As the PLA fought the civil war, between 1946 and 1949, specialized staff functions were added to the command-and-control system to facilitate CMC coordination of the operations of army groups, corps, and military arms and services. In very short order, the PLA converted from an essentially guerrilla force into a large army able to engage in large-scale combined arms operations. It was during this period that the CMC established the General Staff Department, the General Political Department, and the General Logistics Department. Formal staffs were established in columns, divisions, corps, and armies. Moreover, under each field army, separate commands were set up for special troops, arms, and services. The CMC established a "forward general command committee" (*zong qian wei*) and a deployed rear-area general logistics headquarters department to support the forces. Still, the authority for decision making was centralized at the CMC, but commanders were to exercise initiative in response to situations in the field.[78]

At the time of the Korean War, the large deployment to North Korea of "Chinese People's Volunteers" (that is, PLA troops, the euphemism having been created to avoid an official war with the United States) in dispersed corps required better command and control. According to *The Study of Operations Command and Control*, this was the "biggest transformation in the command-and-control system of China."[79] The CMC established a major headquarters for the Chinese People's Volunteers in Korea. It functioned like the *zong qian wei* in the civil war. Forward command headquarters for the Air Force, artillery, air defense, armored, engineer, and railway forces were established and put under centralized command and control. This system of forward command and control incorporated the ability to conduct "skip echelon command and control" (*yueji zhihui*), bypassing intermediate headquarters when necessary. Thus, the CMC or GSD could communicate and direct operations down to forward commands, deployed service commands, groups, or divisions.[80] This development formed the basis of modern command and control in the PLA.[81] Another important feature for the PLA command, control, and decision making was that, for the first time, China's forces needed joint international headquarters and command-and-control structures.[82]

After the Korea War the two highest political structures in the CCP, the Politburo Standing Committee and the CMC, focused on national interest considerations in military decision making. In addition, a unified headquarters system developed, formalizing procedures and command relationships among the CMC, the GSD, and military region headquarters.[83] The PLA institutionalized the basic relationships and the reliance on "skip echelon command and control." This allowed the CMC, or an intermediate headquarters to skip an echelon of command in a crisis situation and directly contact and control a subordinate unit, providing greater flexibility to higher-level commanders. These processes and structures were evident in the Sino-Indian War, the Sino-Vietnamese War, and the gathering of PLA forces around Beijing before the Tiananmen Square massacre of 1989.[84]

The internal battles among members of the leadership in the revolutionary base areas started out with zero-sum politics. At various times between 1928 and 1935, senior military and political leaders were in or out of leadership positions, most especially Mao Zedong. However, partially because of military campaign pressures but also because of pressure from the Communist International, CCP elite politics evolved into a form of power sharing between factions.[85] Mao, Peng Dehuai, Lin Biao, and Ye Jianying supported a more open management style and a guerrilla-based army. Zhang Guotai, Zhu De, and Liu Bocheng, among other leaders, believed that the Army should develop along the lines of the Soviet (and German) general staff systems, with a strong staff, rank structure, and mutually supporting arms and services.[86] In the early stages, leaders were in or out, but by the time the PLA established its base in the "Anti-Japanese War" at Yan'an in 1937, a system of power sharing and collective decision making on military and national security issues prevailed. Without question, there were departures from the established processes. The purge of Peng Dehuai at the Lushan Conference in 1959, for criticizing Mao and the "Great Leap Forward," is an example of such a departure. Indeed, the whole "Cultural Revolution" period was characterized by massive zero-sum political actions by which some of the leading figures of the Chinese Revolution were imprisoned or persecuted. For the most part, however, the CCP and the PLA showed an amazing ability to accommodate differing factions in the leadership. Thus, as this book investigates other questions such as leadership factions in today's China and national security decision making, the reader should keep in mind the institutionalized political culture.

To reinforce what seems to be a tacit agreement among CCP elites to "share power" among factions, it is important to remember the way that Deng Xiaoping rehabilitated many of the persecuted Cultural Revolution figures after 1978. When I visited the Eighth Route Army Liaison Office (a museum) in Xian in 1979, no picture of Liu Shaoqi was on display. Liu was a major leader in the civil war and former head of state, but he was purged by Mao in the Cultrual Revolution. By 1982, when I next visited the museum, the curator had put his photo back on the wall.

Moreover, to continue the discussion of Liu Shaoqi: once Deng posthumously rehabilitated him, his family prospered and moved up in party ranks. Liu Yuan, a PLA general and in 2012 the political commissar of the PLA General Logistics Department, is Liu's youngest son. Another son, Liu Yunzhen, is a senior commercial banker. A daughter, Liu Pingping (aka Wang Qing), is a senior domestic trade official and has a doctoral degree from Columbia University. Liu Tingting, another daughter, is in business. Thus, the sins of the father can be erased with rehabilitation.[87] Thus the Party takes care of its "princelings."

In the opening minutes of his speech at the eightieth anniversary of the PLA, Hu Jintao, concurrently CMC chairman, CCP general secretary, and Chinese president, made special mention of all of the leading PLA figures from 1927, including some of the founders of the PLA that the party had persecuted or "erased" from its history at times.[88] Still, some bad blood remains in the CCP. In a speech celebrating the thirtieth anniversary of the founding of the PRC on September 29, 1979, Ye Jianying failed to mention Liu Shaoqi or Peng Dehuai.[89] However, he castigated

Lin Biao and the "Gang of Four" for their excesses in the Cultural Revolution. Hu Jintao made no mention of Lin, who has still not been rehabilitated.

Another institution to which the CCP and the PLA are devoted is the tradition of collective decision making, where there is room for discussion. The party is a monolith, devoted to "democratic centralism." However, internally for decades there has been a surprising flexibility and willingness to tolerate discussion and dissent from major decisions in the military sphere. Zhu De's conduct of the Hundred Regiments Campaign in 1940 departed from the agreed approach by the CMC and supported by Mao favoring guerilla warfare over conventional military battles.[90] Zhu instead conducted a series of conventional battles against Japanese forces. Mao's approach prevailed because of the high number of casualties incurred by Zhu's forces and those of Liu Bocheng, He Long, Peng Dehuai, and Nie Rongzhen. Nonetheless, all of these other leaders stayed at the center of PLA and Chinese national security decisions through the establishment of the PRC and during the Korean War.

In the speech at the eightieth anniversary of the founding of the PLA, Hu Jintao put great emphasis on collective leadership:

> While waging arduous struggles over the past 80 years, the PLA has relied firmly on the people under the leadership of three generations of the Party's collective leadership with comrade Mao Zedong, comrade Deng Xiaoping, and comrade Jiang Zemin at its core, and the collective leadership of the Party since the 16th CPC National Congress, and has made great contributions to the nation's independence and the people's liberation, the country's prosperity and strength and the people's well-being.[91]

Note, however, that there is no mention of former CMC chairman Zhao Ziyang, still erased from party history because the party blames him for bringing on the Tiananmen Square massacre.

To reinforce this willingness to listen, and react, to strong dissent from collective decision making, it is useful to recall that the CMC accommodated Su Yu's dissent from the CMC war plans and orders he received in PLA operations leading up to the Huai-Hai Campaign. In January 1948 the CMC, by message from its base area headquarters in Xibaipo, instructed the East China Field Army to detach three corps and send them far to the south of the Yangtze River to conduct independent operations.[92] Su, acting commander of the East China Field Army, immediately and directly objected to this course of action.[93] He fired a message back to the CMC objecting to its orders and essentially reminding them of Mao's operational principles. Instead, Su suggested keeping the forces together, suddenly concentrating them, and then rapidly dispersing them at critical junctures to fight battles of annihilation against the Nationalists. This strategy was consistent with the operational principles outlined by Mao.[94] Su followed this with another message in April seeking to keep the East China Field Army forces in reasonably close proximity and coordinating operations with the forces of the Central Plains Field Army in the area that later was the focus of the Huai-Hai Campaign.[95] In the end, Su's approach and his objections to the CMC's instructions put the PLA in a position to conduct the Jinan Campaign on the Shandong Peninsula, setting the stage for the Huai-Hai.[96]

Why focus on this early Communist Party history and the history of PLA command and control? An eye toward history is important because the People's Republic of China and the PLA institutionalized a political culture that evolved from those experiences. The way that the CCP and the PLA make national security decisions and handle leadership conflict today reflects this political culture.

The PLA's Role in Addressing Foreign Policy Interests

For decades the PLA was essentially an insular organization focused primarily on China's immediate periphery. From 1927 to 1937, the PLA focused on its "Soviet base areas" (*suqu*), growing their strength, building up forces, and defending against the Nationalists.[97] The PLA had no air force, no navy, and no capacity to project power beyond China's shores. China's long history, however, reinforced a tendency to create buffer zones free from foreign intervention where China's leaders could dictate terms to nearby states or maintain coercive power over them.[98]

China has traditionally been a continental power. Of course, in addition to undertaking land expeditions, the Chinese explored the region by sea centuries ago in order to conduct trade along maritime routes. They had commercial sea routes out to Africa as early as the tenth century AD. Foreign economic and trade interests expanded for China during the Song dynasty (960–1279 AD), when China had a "powerful and technologically sophisticated navy."[99] During the Yuan Dynasty, between 1405 AD and 1433 AD, Zheng He made seven voyages around Southeast Asia, South Asia and reaching Africa. His mission was to increase commerce, although his fleets had thousands of armed personnel. The Korean Peninsula and parts of Vietnam became "vassal states" (*shuguo*), coerced to do the emperor's bidding. But China's reach tended to focus on waters near its nine thousand miles of coastline and the six thousand islands along that coast. As John Garver puts it, "various Chinese dynasties collapsed, . . . sometimes to be followed by long periods of political disunity, but a new dynasty always arose to reunite the vast cultural area of China. . . . Educated Chinese generally accepted the idea that lands populated by Chinese and making up the Chinese cultural area ought to be unified under a single ruler."[100]

The nineteenth century began a period during which stronger foreign powers, including Japan, took advantage of the weakness of the Qing dynasty and dictated terms of trade and jurisdiction over parts of China's territory. This lasted through to the time that the People's Republic of China was established. The period that began with the Opium War in 1839 through the establishment of the PRC is characterized in Communist Party histories as a "century of national humiliation."[101] Central to the way that the Chinese Communist Party frames its security orientation, this period saw the following:

- China lost the Opium War to Great Britain and was forced to open a number of concession areas (treaty ports) along the coast and on the Yangtze River, and cede control of them to Britain, as well as other powers.
- In 1860 an Anglo-French force burned the emperor's Summer Palace in Beijing.
- China lost the Sino-Japanese War of 1894–1895 and was forced to cede control over Taiwan and Manchuria to Japan (which also took control of the Korean Peninsula).
- A foreign expeditionary relief force from eight nations (the United States, Great Britain, Russia, Germany, France, Japan, Italy, and Austria) forcibly entered China to relieve their legation areas in Beijing and protect their citizens from attacks by the "Boxers United in Righteousness" during the Boxer Rebellion.[102]
- The Qing dynasty and the imperial system collapsed and were replaced by a weak republican government that could not control large areas of the country.
- Japan established a puppet state, Manchukuo, in China's northeastern area of Manchuria.
- An eight-year war against Japan was fought throughout most of China.
- The Chinese Civil War was concluded after three decades of conflict between the Nationalists and the Chinese Communist Party.[103]

Once the People's Republic of China was established, the PLA had to defend a nation. Not only did it need to consider how to finish off the remnants of the Nationalist Army that had escaped to Taiwan, but suddenly there were coasts and airspace to defend. And there were constant attempts to penetrate or destabilize the PRC from the outside.[104]

Initially the PLA was oriented toward a "people's war" strategy that focused on organizing the masses of China's population into a broad, guerrilla-based defensive posture if China were invaded. To achieve the mass of personnel to execute the strategy, for the most part the people's war strategy focused on mobilizing militia units. The period during which this strategy was employed lasted from about the end of the Long March in 1935, until the PLA conducted its "self-defensive counterattack," occupying a zone across northern Vietnam in 1979.

Even though the PLA's broad posture and orientation focused on strategic defense, its military planners did not ignore offensive action. And for portions of the period in question, the PLA was still active in combat. During the Korean War, the Chinese People's Volunteers streamed into North Korea to fight United Nations, South Korean and U.S. forces. In 1962 the PLA fought a border conflict with India, seizing broad areas of disputed territory and then withdrawing to what China claimed were the appropriate boundaries. During the U.S. involvement in Vietnam (1956 to 1975), fifty thousand PLA active personnel came to the assistance of North Vietnam, with Chinese units stationed there, as well as in Laos. In 1969 the PLA engaged in regiment-size battles with forces of the Soviet Union over a boundary conflict. And on February 16, 1979, the PLA began a broad offensive along the entire length of the Sino-Vietnamese border, culminating in a unilateral withdrawal by the PLA a month later.

After sustaining heavy combat losses in the attack against Vietnam, the PLA revised its broad military posture and shifted its doctrine from people's war. This change amounted to the PLA's acknowledgement that modern technology, better connectivity, and improved command and control were necessary if the PLA were to prevail in modern war in the latter part of the twentieth century. Observations by Chinese military strategists of other conflicts, particularly the British defeat of Argentine forces in the Falkland Islands in 1982, contributed to the perceived need to modernize military doctrine in China.[105] At about the same time, the PLA started to experiment with mobile, integrated warfare and the establishment of large-scale geographic theaters of war (*zhanqu*).

By 1985, however, the PLA's broad defense doctrine had shifted again. Military thinkers in China assessed the geostrategic situation as changed. Their expectation was that by the latter part of the twentieth century, large-scale "total war" (*zongti zhanzheng*) was less likely and that the PLA should instead be prepared to fight "limited wars" (*youxian zhanzheng*) or "local wars" (*zhubu zhanzheng*).[106] These views characterized PLA doctrine until 1991.

With the Gulf War (1990–1991), PLA military planners got a shock when they saw the way that the United States and its allies used high-technology weapons, mobility, and joint operations to collapse and defeat Iraq's armed forces.[107] As David Shambaugh points out,

> PLA analysts had predicted that U.S. forces would become bogged down in a ground war. . . . Nearly every aspect of the campaign reminded the PLA high command of its deficiencies: electronic warfare; precision guided munitions; stealth technology; precision bombing; the sheer number of sorties flown; campaign coordination through airborne command and control systems; the deployment of attack aircraft from half a world away using in-flight refueling; the use of satellites in targeting and intelligence gathering; space-based early warning and surveillance; the use of command centers in the United States to coordinate operations; . . . the maintenance of high tempo operations, etc.[108]

The shock produced a major shift in thinking in the PLA. The PLA already had begun an examination of what the United States called the "revolution in military affairs (RMA)." This concept involved improving battlefield awareness with better sensor systems, linking sensors, weapons systems and command and control, the use of precision weapons, increased lethality, a faster operations tempo, and better identification of the location of friendly and enemy forces. What had been a broad theoretical examination of the RMA inside PLA academic centers was quickly converted into a military-wide effort to modernize the force and field the capabilities the PLA was seen to lack. The ensuing new doctrine for the PLA was broadly called "limited war under high-technology conditions" (*gao jishu tiaojian xia de jubu zhanzheng*).[109] This new approach initially depended on military theories developed from the PLA's examination of the U.S. military's manuals, doctrinal writing, and operational techniques. Over time, however, through training, experimentation, and continued internal research, the PLA adjusted to create doctrine that better fit its own equipment, institutional culture, and operational style. This approach generated the range of new systems, equipment, and information-age approaches to warfare discussed in subsequent chapters. For example, the PLA introduced "smart weapons," developed a more robust space-based communications and intelligence architecture, integrated satellites and precision guidance into its weapons and weapon platforms, and expanded its own awareness of joint operations across the domains of warfare.

Modernization did not end there, however. The latest phase of operational experimentation and doctrinal change in the PLA involves coordinating integrated operations by all arms and services across the domains of war—that is, ensuring that the PLA can operate effectively in a coordinated manner in the battlespace on the ground, in the air, on the sea, in outer space, and in cyberspace or the electromagnetic spectrum.[110]

Ultimately, however, the PLA must be able to respond to what the CCP leadership requires of it to secure China's expanding national interests in a "new century and the new period (*xin zhiji, xin jieduan*)." Hu Jintao identified them as:

- Continuing economic construction
- Completing China's unification
- Promoting world peace and common development
- Protecting traditional territorial integrity on land, in maritime areas, and airspace
- Unswervingly protecting China's security and interests on the seas, in space, and in the electromagnetic spectrum (*dianzi kongjian*)[111]

Hu made clear to the PLA in a major speech in December 2004 that the military had to prepare for a major new role in defending China's national interests.[112] As pointed out earlier in this chapter, traditionally the PLA focused on China's immediate periphery and on domestic integrity and security.

In his speech, Hu set out for the PLA what the Central Military Commission calls "the historic missions of the armed forces."[113] The CMC vice chairman, Guo Boxiong, in a week-long meeting at the PLA's National Defense University in September 2005, reinforced these as Hu's synthesis of the military theories of Deng Xiaoping and Jiang Zemin.[114] The historic missions, Guo said, are:

- To reinforce the armed forces' loyalty to the Chinese Communist Party
- To help ensure China's sovereignty, territorial integrity, and domestic security in order to continue its national development
- To help safeguard China's expanding national interests
- To promote world peace and development[115]

The "historic missions" provide broad guidance and justification for security thinkers in China to explore new approaches to military theory, roles and missions for forces, and new equipment and technology to increase China's capacity to operate as the military force of a nation with global interests. Academy of Military

Science theorist Jiang Yamin reminds China's students of warfare that Hu Jintao's charge to the PLA to provide a firm national defense for China "in the twenty-first century" means that the PLA must have a strong capability to counter attacks at long distances and defend distant lines of communication—that is, beyond China's more traditional focus in Taiwan, the South China Sea, and China's immediate periphery.[116]

These historic missions are important in the context of future PLA contingency missions, military growth, and deployments because they establish a formal framework and ideological justification for using the military in a regional and global context. They represent a significant departure for the PLA from the traditional insular and regional orientation of China's military to greater concern for external affairs.

PLA national security thinkers increasingly make reference to expanded overseas contingency and force-presence missions for the PLA. In one text for the PLA National Defense University, Senior Col. Wang Lidong expressed the view that as the PLA strengthens to carry out its external missions, it will need to develop a stronger maritime capacity as part of China's "comprehensive national security."[117] The third of the missions set out by Hu Jintao, "safeguarding China's expanding national interests," is a responsibility that requires the PLA to develop the capacity to operate and have a presence at longer distances away from continental China.[118]

After Xi Jinping replaced Hu Jintao as CCP general secretary and chairman of the CMC in November 2012, Xi's first major meeting with the PLA was with officers of the Second Artillery Force. Xi focused on the need for the PLA to maintain ideological purity and party loyalty. He also made it clear that the strategic missile forces were to be the supporting structure (*zhicheng*) of China's great power status.

2 C⁴ISR

The leaders of the People's Liberation Army understand that technology drives the modern revolution in military affairs. Technology affects how commanders organize forces and the way those forces operate and interact on the battlefield. PLA leaders and military thinkers have systematically explored new technologies to improve command, control, communications, computer systems, information exchange and data transfer technologies, surveillance systems, and reconnaissance systems (C⁴ISR) in an effort to improve military effectiveness.[1]

Military planners have taken advantage of new technologies to facilitate data exchange between weapon systems, military arms and services, and individual military units, making possible cooperative target engagement in combat, which allows multiple platforms (i.e., combat aircraft, ships, subs, missile launchers) on land, on the sea, and in the air to fire on the same target simultaneously. The PLA now has a national, redundant command-and-control system linking the senior leaders and war planners of the Central Military Commission and the General Staff Department command center in Beijing with alternate command posts, with military regions, and with subordinate units, including deployed ships and aircraft. All of this enables the PLA to conduct integrated military operations across the different domains of war: land, sea, air, space, and the electromagnetic spectrum (cyberspace and electronic warfare).

In employing the range of C⁴ISR systems available, the PLA has gained better situational awareness, facilitated the routine projection of military forces out of the region, and managed to strengthen a regional defensive perimeter that extends nearly two thousand kilometers from China's coast into the western Pacific. These capabilities have enabled what United States military thinkers call China's "antiaccess/area-denial" (A2/AD) strategy,[2] even if the PLA itself does not use that term.[3]

In China's military doctrine, the PLA calls these "resisting intervention" or "counterintervention" (*fan jieru*) strategies.[4] The A2/AD acronym appears in PLA literature in response to American characterizations.[5]

Thinking about C⁴ISR and its importance in modern military operations has been an evolutionary process in the Chinese military. In the 1990s PLA military theorists learned how to apply information technology to war by watching how the United States armed forces experimented with technology and performed in combat employing that technology.

The white paper on national defense released by China's State Council in December 2006 acknowledged that "a revolution in military affairs is developing in depth worldwide" and noted that "military competition based on 'informationalization'[6] is intensifying."[7] Since that time, the Central Military Commission has been aggressive in ensuring that the PLA incorporates new information systems. As a number of publications from Chinese military institutions of higher learning made clear after Chinese analysis of Western militaries—particularly U.S. forces and their interactions with their North Atlantic Treaty Organization (NATO) allies—the consensus was that the PLA had to adopt and employ these new technologies.[8]

Map 2.1   Western Pacific, South China Sea, and East China Sea

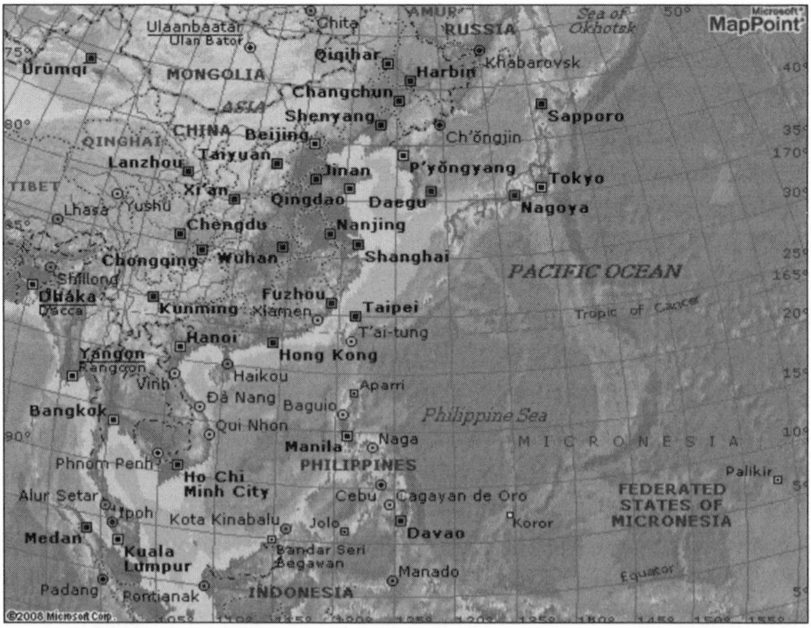

Source: U.S. Defense Mapping Agency (1986).

The PLA's long-term goal, out to the mid-twenty-first century, is to create a more modern force that can challenge (or deter) the best military forces in the world.[9] Given the presence of U.S. forces in the Pacific and the long-standing tensions between the United States and China over Taiwan, PLA military thinkers not only use the United States as the model for the force they must train to counter, but they also believe it poses China's most formidable potential adversary. Many in the PLA fear the latent power of the United States, concerned that it could use that power to coerce or dominate China.[10] One PLA strategist, Peng Guangqian, explains that as the United States "shifted the center of gravity" of its own military strategy and power eastward, with "over half of its aircraft carriers and 60 percent of its submarines" in the Pacific and new forces moved to Guam, it is only natural that China be concerned.[11]

PLA military theorists are convinced that to be successful in battle in the information age, any commander must be able to use integrated C⁴ISR systems.[12] Senior PLA leaders do more than merely discuss information operations—they incorporate them into force-on-force field exercises.[13] New purchases of equipment from Russia and technology from Europe are part of a defense architecture that depends on C⁴ISR technology. Moreover, PLA military planners are applying the new technologies and weapon systems to platforms that may be decades old.

As the PLA studies aspects of networkcentric warfare and the C⁴ISR systems that such warfare requires, its theorists see the U.S. armed forces as "the gold standard" on how to apply information technologies and automated electronic data exchange to war.[14] At the early stages of the PLA's exploration of the topic, its literature drew on American military manuals. Although there are no explicit calls from senior leaders to prepare for war against the United States, it is clear that the PLA sees American forces as presenting the greatest challenge China's military could face. More recently, the PLA has been developing its own body of military theory on C⁴ISR and is also drawing on doctrine from the former Soviet Union to develop "integrated network electronic warfare." (See chapter 8 on information operations and electronic warfare.)

Perhaps the most authoritative long-term guidance to the PLA on the subject of C⁴ISR and networked warfare architectures is from a decade ago, made by Gen. Zhang Wannian. Zhang was chief of the General Staff Department of the PLA from 1992 to 1995 and vice chairman of the Communist Party's Central Military Commission after that. He has said that the PLA "command and control systems must be 'networked' to increase the effectiveness of combat units . . . which will naturally be accompanied by a reduction in the number of layers of command and control."[15] General

Zhang noted that the U.S. armed forces, through digitization and networking, reduced the number of layers of higher command, and he predicted that the PLA can expect similar results to produce a "comprehensive system of networked forces and command and control."[16] Shortly after taking the position of chairman of the CMC in November 2012, Xu Junping reinforced the importance of networked warfighting architectures in an address to the Second Artillery Forces.[17]

PLA researchers have studied the data links that support combat systems for the U.S. military and have created a catalog of the knowledge necessary to replicate, counter, or attack them, building a how-to manual for attacking joint U.S. data-control systems and communications.[18] These researchers have carefully consulted dozens of corporate websites and tactical data-link operator guides, as well as NATO and U.S. manuals, to produce this guide for electronic warfare and jamming to disrupt critical U.S. cooperative target-engagement and C⁴ISR data links.

In a PLA National Defense University strategy text, Wang Zhongquan notes that strategic command-and-control networks "have multiple uses and systemic effects."[19] Such networks, Wang concludes, "can contribute to command and control systems, strategic warning systems, and intelligence organizations when linked together in a network. The parts of a network of this type include defense communications networks, satellite communications systems, national military command-and-control networks, and networks of strategic or regional command and control centers."[20] Wang's book provides a sophisticated analysis of the U.S. strategic warning system and command-and-control network based on a review of published literature in the United States.[21]

The U.S. effort to "harness the revolution in military affairs" was a way to take advantage of "technological leaps in surveillance, command and control, and longer range precision guided munitions" to make joint military forces more effective in war.[22] A goal of the RMA was to "see a large battlefield with fidelity," which required the United States to explore a range of force structure issues and changes that revolve around advances in technology and weapons requiring forces that were empowered by knowledge and information systems fighting in "flattened, less hierarchical organizations."[23] The U.S. Navy linked C⁴ISR with the concept of "timely, sensor-to-shooter information direct to the war fighter."[24] All the services caught on quickly in the effort to link command-and-control systems, information technologies, dissemination systems, and space assets to "strike targets with an accuracy of feet from standoff distances."[25]

This effort was not lost on the People's Liberation Army. One Academy of Military Science researcher expressed the view that to engage in modern war, the

PLA must be able to "attack the enemy's knowledge systems and such high value targets as communications, carrier battle groups, and aviation warfare units."²⁶ The goal set for the PLA by this researcher was to "destroy the enemy's ability to fight and control war."²⁷ Among other U.S. Military publications, U.S. Army Field Manual 100-6, *Information Warfare Doctrine* gave the PLA a path to developing its own doctrine.²⁸ In the book *Modern Firepower Warfare* (*Xiandai Huoli Zhan*), author Zhang Zhiwei outlines the need for the PLA to "strike crucial and strategic points to paralyze the enemy."²⁹

PLA generals working on China's military transformation have mined Western military literature and experience for ideas on incorporating information technology into military doctrine and how to build forces that can function in the information age.³⁰ In an interview with a reporter from *Outlook Weekly* (*Liaowang*), one military analyst, Maj. Gen. Zhang Ling, expressed the view that "informationized war of the future will be second only to nuclear war in terms of firepower" when modern weapons are linked to technology.³¹

Addressing the way that the revolution in military affairs has affected warfare, Li Bingyan, a major general on the editorial staff of *PLA Daily* (*Jiefangjun Bao*), pointed out that new forms of warfare involve more than massing troops or massing fires against an enemy. Instead, the introduction of high-technology warfare means that to wage a modern war, the PLA must be able to "use precision guided missiles" as a means of massing traditional fires, as well as be able "to use viruses to attack enemy computer systems, and to carry out electronic warfare to attack enemy command-and-control systems."³² This concept has been incorporated into PLA doctrine as precision-firepower missions in the book *The Science of Campaign Theory*.³³

A significant focus of Li Bingyan's is to encourage PLA officers to think in terms of traditional Chinese strategies and classics of military theory, such as *The Romance of the Three Kingdoms* and *The Thirty-Six Stratagems*, and apply their lessons to the modern battlefield.³⁴ Thus any Western military force facing the PLA must be prepared for different applications of technology to warfare than they might expect from a contemporary Western armed force.³⁵

China's military doctrine emphasizes that the PLA must focus on using C⁴ISR in warfare across the five-dimensional battlefield comprising the domains of war.³⁶ PLA military theorists believe that new technology and the development of automated systems have made strategic indications and warning, intelligence, communications, and command and control more critical in all of these dimensions of warfare.³⁷ Moreover, PLA authors express the view that "information age warfare has broken down the traditional levels and structure of command,"[38] advocating that "military forces must structure themselves around the latent capacities of information."[39]

One of the domains of war that the PLA emphasizes is space. In an article in *Outlook Weekly* cited earlier in this chapter, Maj. Gen. Zhang Ling expressed the belief that "control of space will be of tremendous significance in future information warfare. . . . The primary combat operation of future war will be the struggle for space control."[40] Zhang opined that militaries will engage in "soft strikes" against space-based information systems to control enemy satellites and "hard strikes" to destroy enemy space systems with antisatellite weapons.[41] Song Yongxin and GuoYizhing argue that warfare in space will be part of the information warfare battlefield and "whoever controls space will have the initiative in war."[42]

In a magazine interview, Maj. Gen. Li Deyi of the Academy of Military Science said firmly that "it would be inconceivable [today] if a commander in the PLA did not know how to operate a command automation system."[43] General Li opined that the PLA was behind both Russia and the United States in developing an automated command-and-control system and that the current system is "plagued by inadequate integration and coordination, as well as incompatible [foreign] imports."[44] The PLA therefore understands its problems and envisions eventually correcting them with indigenous systems.

Xin Qin, in his book *Warfare in the Information Age* (*Xinxihua Shidai de Zhanzheng*), argues that the side with the most comprehensive command-and-control system in a modern war will also have the strongest maneuver capability and be able to concentrate the greatest combat strength against the enemy.[45] According to Xin, good command-and-control systems, with good communications, facilitate maneuver and mean that a nation's military forces can exploit the strengths of mobile weapon systems.

In exercises as well, PLA commanders challenge their staffs with simulations of extended periods of combat. In one battle in an exercise in 2006 they intentionally created a "highly informationized" Blue Force that overwhelmed the PLA Red Force, which operated in the exercise scenario at a C[4]ISR disadvantage.[46] The exercise was designed to demonstrate to a PLA division the effect of the use of sophisticated reconnaissance and networked command-and-control systems. Part of the exercise was a Blue Force long-range precision strike on the Red Force. The exercise scenario timed the effects of the strike to disrupt the Red Force in its assembly areas as it was forming for maneuver operations.[47] The exercise planners included scenarios of imitative communications deception and jamming as part of the electronic warfare play to confuse Red Force commanders. Senior PLA leaders were able to demonstrate to subordinate leaders and troops the disadvantages under which the PLA operates in facing a sophisticated enemy with advanced C⁴ISR systems.[48]

At the highest levels of the PLA, senior officers understand that to increase the effectiveness of combat units, the Chinese military must digitize and network its command-and-control systems.[49] Over a decade ago, Zhang Wannian emphasized the importance of decisive action in warfare, aided by C⁴ISR systems, which can locate the enemy, estimate the effectiveness of fires, and control attacks on the battlefield.[50] In 2006, at a major military training conference, Lt. Gen. Fan Changlun made the point that an integrated combat capability requires scientific and technical training, the aim of which should be winning a war. He stressed "informatization, real war simulation, and field training" as the foci of the military region's training efforts.[51] Zhu Wenquan, commander of the Nanjing MR, emphasized networked training systems, information systems, and electronic databases in creating a modern military force.[52] By 2012, almost all PLA exercises are joint, involving two or more services, and use networked electronic systems.

Layers of Command and Control

The PLA as an institution is relatively flexible in layering its command-and-control structure. Many of its elements still reflect back on the doctrine of people's war. Contemporary military command-and-control systems routinely involve political, government, and Communist Party organizations inside the fronts or military regions in the command group organization.[53] The structure of a "joint campaign coordination organization," however, varies by the "objectives of the campaign, the scale of the campaign, and the actual conditions on the battlefield."[54]

In the English language version of *The Science of Military Strategy*, Peng Guangqian and Yao Youzhi emphasize that the PLA general staff department "functions as the 'brain' or center in the command systems of the armed forces."[55] It is a "strategic commanding authority," just as the headquarters of the Navy, the Air Force, and the Second Artillery Forces "have the attributes of a strategic commanding authority."[56] One source of confusion in PLA doctrine remains the use of the term "supreme command headquarters" (*tongshuaibu*). For the Second Artillery's nuclear forces, the supreme command headquarters is the Central Military Commission. In a theater of war, however, the theater commander is sometimes referred to as the supreme command headquarters.[57]

In wartime or crisis, the theater of war is a joint command-and-control organization. In cases where a campaign is limited to a single theater and the forces assigned to the front are sufficient for the campaign, the military and political leadership in the war zone will form a "Theater Joint War Fighting Command and Control Organization Headquarters." The commander of the theater can draw from local political, military, and Communist Party organizations. This headquarters "executes orders from the higher supreme command headquarters, the Central Military Commission, and the General Staff Department."[58]

For a third echelon of command and control in large-scale operations, the PLA may form army groups (*juntuan*) that include more than one group army (*jituanjun*) and command groups from the PLA Air Force, Navy, and Second Artillery. In a major war on a large scale, there may be two or more army groups subordinate to a theater of war. Representatives from the local political, military, and Communist Party organizations needed to support the army group would be assigned to this level of headquarters as well.[59]

Headquarters at all levels may include representatives from other military command centers, and as needed the PLA may task organize a main command-and-control center (*zhihui suo*), an alternate command-and-control center (*yubei zhihui suo*), a forward command center, and rear-area command centers for logistics purposes.[60] All of these command centers could include local political, military, and civil defense representatives, Communist Party representatives, and representatives from other PLA arms and services. The propensity to draw on the local populace and use people from local universities demonstrates the tradition of people's war being continued on the informatized battlefield.

Several points bear emphasis. First, the inclusion of local forces and local political and CCP organizations means that the traditional concepts of people's war from the 1930s to the 1970s still fit into PLA doctrine. Second, the PLA is flexible in task organizing. The commander of a theater of war can draw from educational institutions, reserve units, towns, and industries in the zone as required for the support of his forces.[61] In addition, at least the conventional and short-range missile forces of the Second Artillery are included in the structure. What is still not entirely clear is whether these forces have any nuclear weapons with them and how much authority the theater commander has to give them firing orders. For conventional missile launches, the theater commander can probably initiate fires, but for nuclear fires the order probably must come from the Central Military Commission.

Networkcentric Warfare and Offensive Action

China's military leaders believe that communications and electronic data exchange is the core of an integrated war-fighting capability.[62] At PLA academic institutions, sophisticated efforts have been under way for some time to improve joint operations and make attacks on ground targets by air and naval forces more effective.[63] Two graduate students at the PLA Naval Engineering Institute have published a paper analyzing ways to apply C⁴ISR systems in networkcentric warfare more effectively.[64]

Younger officers can be quite aggressive about the potential for using C⁴ISR systems to improve the PLA's ability to wage offensive operations. One officer from the Navy Command Academy has emphasized that "the Second Artillery is the major factor in successfully attacking an enemy naval battle group."[65] To accomplish such an attack, other analysts have said that "the PLA must use all of its electronic warfare and reconnaissance assets properly, must neutralize enemy anti-missile systems and missile sensor systems, and should use electronic jamming on the enemy fleet. Such combined kinetic and electronic attacks help the PLA attack an enemy fleet or naval base with a combination of explosive, anti-radiation and fake warheads to deceive enemy radar and sensor systems and defeat a deployed battle group or one in port."[66]

For some time, the PLA has worked on a means of keeping the U.S. Navy from operating close to the Chinese mainland. Today the PLA seems ready to use ballistic missiles to attack naval battle groups at sea. PLA officers apparently have developed and are ready to field a system, the *Dong Feng-21D*, that uses a guided, mobile trajectory during warhead reentry into the atmosphere to attack an enemy

Fig. 2.1   DF-21D Ballistic Missile Trajectory

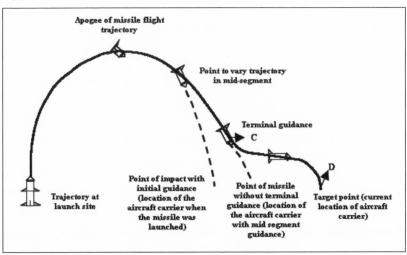

Source: Office of the Secretary of Defense, *Annual Report to Congress: Military and Security Developments Involving the People's Republic of China, 2011* (Washington, DC: Department of Defense, 2011).

aircraft carrier with ballistic missiles.[67] In one study, researchers conclude that guidance systems will allow the warhead up to one hundred kilometers of maneuverability on reentry during the terminal phase of a missile attack. They believe that a carrier "cannot effectively escape an attack within a short period of time."[68] Simulations to predict how the final attack ranges for maneuvering targets at sea would affect maneuvering reentry vehicles are also part of the research agenda for Second Artillery engineering officers.[69]

For a military force like the PLA, without a well-developed naval air arm with a long reach, few refueling aircraft, and an inventory of aircraft with limited reach, this approach makes sense. What the PLA cannot accomplish with air power can be supplemented by its missile forces. Three PLA officers from the Second Artillery Command Academy advance the idea that "guided missile forces are the trump card [sashoujian] in achieving victory in limited high technology war."[70] The keys to achieving such capabilities, in the argument of other PLA officers, lie in three areas: the use of countermeasures, the ability to achieve precision targeting, and the use of space platforms to support the effort (see chapter 7 on space systems).[71]

For a nation like China, still developing a force-projection capability, only now deploying its first aircraft carrier, with limited air-to-air refueling, and a navy that is not yet fully capable of large-scale blue-water operations, the ballistic missile concept must truly look like a "trump card." The U.S. Department of Defense (DOD) certainly has focused its attention on the concept.[72]

Building Knowledge-Based War Fighting Architectures[73]

Military theory is a great thing, especially if it is captured in doctrine that is absorbed by military forces and can be effectively employed in battle. However, the mere intellectual exploration of these capabilities is nothing but smoke and mirrors if a military does not have the forces, equipment, and systems to use the theory and doctrine in battle. The PLA has those things, albeit on a limited scale, extending its reach out into the Pacific Ocean.

The PLA is transforming itself into a modern force able to take full advantage of C[4]ISR technologies and the networkcentric war-fighting concept.[74] The sudden appearance of two U.S. aircraft carrier battle groups in the western Pacific during the 1996 Taiwan missile crisis embarrassed senior political and military leaders.[75] The PLA has since developed a data-exchange and target-locating architecture to support the PLA Navy, the Second Artillery, and the Air Force, even if some of the platforms have limited range and their numbers are still small. The national-level and regional C[4]ISR architecture gives the PLA a near-real-time regional intelligence collection capability from space that can be translated into targeting information to China's military forces.

The PLA's theater-level, automated command-and-control system is the *Qu Dian* (theater electronic) system. It is an integrated, redundant, military-region or theater of war military communications, computer, and intelligence system, linking the General Staff Department headquarters and the PLA's arms and services with regional combat headquarters and their subordinate major organizations. However, the system requires satellite data-exchange support and airborne radio and communications relay.

To be effective, the *Qu Dian* system uses many of China's seventy orbiting satellites.[76] This includes six Dongfanghong-series communications satellites, five Fengyun-series weather satellites, three earth-observation satellites, a series of military reconnaissance satellites (the Fanhui Shi, of which twenty-four have been launched but only five are in orbit; three Ziyuan satellites; and nine Yaogan satellites), and eleven Beidou global positioning, timing, and navigation satellites. Also, a pair of Zhongxing-22 (Chinasat-22) satellites provides C-band and UHF communications.[77] Along with these satellites, the *Qu Dian* system uses fiber-optic cable, high-frequency and very-high-frequency communications, and microwave systems to enable the CMC, the General Staff Department, and commanders to communicate with forces in their theaters of war on a real-time or near-real-time basis. The system also permits data transfer among the headquarters and all the units under its joint command.[78] The system has been compared to the Joint Tactical Information Distribution System, or JTIDS, a secure network used by the United States and some allies.[79]

Discussing the potential threat posed to U.S. forces by a functional tactical data, communications, and intelligence distribution system such as *Qu Dian,* Congressman Bob Schaffer of Colorado told the House of Representatives:

> Accurate ballistic missiles and the ability to observe U.S. forces from space will give China the potential to attack U.S. ships at sea and in port. This capability is being enhanced by China's development of an integrated command and control system called *Qu Dian,* which relies on its Feng Huo-1 military communications satellite launched on January 26, 2000. Qu Dian, considered a major force multiplier, is similar to the U.S. Joint Tactical Information Distribution System, or JTIDS, and boasts a secure, jam-resistant, high capacity data link communication system for use in tactical combat.[80]

In November 2012, the PLA announced that this national military command information system became a "system of systems" network, spanning all military regions and headquarters.[81] The PLA expects this national command and control system to "link equipment and the brains of man" to facilitate precision battlefield strikes as well as army-wide command.[82] The next goal, according to military theorists in the PLA, is to extend the command and control system to include "informationized logistics command systems."[83]

Other PLA combat systems have a more limited capability to act as an airborne command post and assist with combat data exchange. The enhanced Su-30MK2 fighter under development for China will improve long-range power-projection for the PLA. According to *Jane's Defence Weekly*, when equipped with a sensor system including side-looking airborne radar, the Su-30MK2 will be capable of "tasking and controlling up to 10 other aircraft on a common [communications] net."[84] The model already delivered to the PLA, the Su-30MKK, will control up to four Su-27s and, like the more advanced model under development, functions as an airborne command-and-control system with data exchange to facilitate cooperative targeting. In 2011, the PLA demonstrated its own clone of the S-30MK2, the J-16.[85] The command and control parameters of China's copy, however, are not clear at this time.

The PLA already has an airborne warning-and-control system (AWACS) built around the Russian Beriev A-50.[86] Designated the Kong Jing–2000 (KJ-2000) by China, it is equipped with Chinese-made phased-array radar and has a data-link capability, a data-processing system, an identification friend-or-foe system, and C³I capability. The KJ-2000 can exchange data with other aircraft and with naval ships equipped with compatible data links. The aircraft's loiter time on station, however, is limited by the distance it must fly to get in range of its target and can be as short as ninety minutes.

China's own Y-8 four-engine turboprop aircraft use an active electroninally scanned array (AESA) radar system, which seems to be based on a Saab design for a jointly-developed Pakistan-China AWACS.[87] The original Y-8–based AWACS apparently relied on the French firm Thales for its airborne early-warning radars and incorporated British Racal technology.[88] The PLA Air Force configured other special versions of the Y-8 (along with the Tu-154) for signals intelligence collection.[89] These aircrafts' AWACS can data-link to most of China's aircraft, helicopters, and combat ships. The system also permits data and communications transfer to at least most PLA Navy surface ships. According to *Jane's Fighting Ships*, China's *Sovremenny*-class destroyer from Russia is "the first Chinese warship to have a data systems link," which *Jane's* analysts believe is a PRC version of the NATO-designated Squeeze Box.[90] They also have the Band Stand data link to the PLA's C-802 antiship missile,[91] as well as a data link for the SS-N-22 Sunburn (P270 Moskit) supersonic antiship missile.[92] Other destroyers can take advantage of these data links: the *Luda*-class (Type 051) destroyers have been fitted with Thomson-CSF data link systems as well as Chinese developed systems, as have the *Luhai*-class (Type 051B) destroyers. These systems will link with the Zhi-9 helicopters and the surface-to-surface missiles on the destroyers.

According to *Signal*, the journal of the Armed Forces Communications Electronics Association (AFCEA), China's destroyers are all now able to data-link with AWACS, each other, their onboard helicopters, and their antiship missiles.[93] The Ka-25 helicopters that came from Russia with the *Sovremenny* destroyers are equipped with the A-346Z secure data link, and other Chinese ships have the HN-900 data link, which incorporates other foreign technologies.

The bad news for the United States and other navies in Asia is that today the PLA Navy's *Luhu*, *Luhai*, *Luda*, and *Sovremenny* destroyers are equipped with systems that function like the U.S. data-link combat information-transfer systems to

Fig. 2.2   Components of the PLA's C⁴ISR Architecture

Source: By author with assistance of the National Bureau of Asian Research.

support battle management and coordinated strikes on time-sensitive targets.[94] Chinese destroyers, and most Chinese frigates, have a system that works like JTIDS and can pass targeting data to the Su-30MKK for over-the-horizon targeting and attack vectors.[95] According to an AFCEA analyst, in some areas the Chinese ships are limited to "1940s era radar tasks of detecting and tracking air and surface targets for their own ship weapons." However, the Chinese have managed to get foreign technology, primarily from France and Russia, that allows integrated battle management and the integration of sensors, ship guns, and missiles, as well as data management of information from other ships and aircraft.[96]

Space Support for C⁴ISR

To reach and support deployed naval forces or air forces at a distance from the coast, the *Qu Dian* system needs a constellation of satellites that includes tracking and data-relay satellites, as do other intelligence-collection systems and sensors in the PLA.[97] Space, therefore, is increasingly critical to the PLA for the conduct of war, and PLA headquarters can support deployed forces with remote sensing from space and airborne platforms, and process "remotely captured images of the battlefield" in real time.[98]

Digital military mapping is part of the space architecture needed for these capabilities and supports all types of analysis, information networks, and targeting.[99] Such applications also support sophisticated combat simulations. PLA experts expect that as new, integrated "space-ground military remote sensing survey and mapping technology" comes on line, the military's processing, handling, and distribution "will be more automatic, more intelligent, and more real-time." Such improvements increase the size of the battle area in which the PLA can operate, and the PLA is working to manage forces and information in this new, expanded battlespace.[100]

Over the mainland and in close proximity to China's borders, the PLA already is able to provide real-time support for joint military operations with communications and data-relay satellites. An article in *PLA Daily* details exercises in the Guangzhou, Chengdu, Shenyang, and Beijing theaters of war using networked forces supported by satellite communications. In Guangzhou an exercise reportedly relied on a satellite-supported C⁴ISR network and fiber-optic systems to "integrate deployed military units in field locations and fixed locations." The Shenyang Military Region exercise described in the article integrated reserve units and regular PLA forces. To accomplish this, the Shenyang MR commander established communication networks with local military departments, transportation bureaus, and meteorological bureaus. In the Chengdu MR, the theater of war that was established for the exercise described in the news report incorporated the General Staff Department–run Communications Academy in Chongqing in order to support satellite communication requirements.[101] In 2012, in a live, force-on-force exercise in Nanjing MR, cadre from the army, air force, navy and Second Artillery operated jointly on line and in an exercise area to become a "multidimensional land, sea, air, space and electromagnetic system."[102]

As noted earlier, to make its C⁴ISR network operational on a real-time basis with global coverage, China needs a network, or system, of tracking and data-relay satellites (TDRS).[103] In 2008, china launched its first such satellite, the *Tianlian-1 (Skylink 1)*, a second was launched in 2011, and a third satellite in 2012.[104] The United States supports its space tracking and data transfer requirements with six TDRS in geosynchronous orbit, three of which are active at any time, but also supplements the transfer of other satellite data with other systems.[105] With its satellite network, the PLA has the ability to support manned space activities, reconnaissance, and other military missions with a common platform TRDS system in geosynchronous earth orbits. Additionally, the PLA can use mini- or microsatellites and constellations of relay satellites in low or medium earth orbit for the same purpose.[106] China has in orbit a constellation of earth environment–monitoring satellites, the Huan Jing series.[107] The HJ-1A and HJ-1B are small optical satellites, and the HJ-1C is a radar satellite. The Jianbing-5 satellite can provide near-real-time electro-optical images, and China also has in space a military remote-imaging satellite using synthetic aperture radar.[108]

As long as either the United States or Russia make such signals available to other countries in times of peace, China can use signals from the U.S. Global Positioning System (GPS) and Russia's GLONASS satellites for precision navigation. These signals support military requirements, including directing precision weapons and warheads. However, the Central Military Commission is concerned that the United States might interrupt China's ability to use the GPS system if hostilities look imminent. Therefore, over the course of several years, between 2004 and 2012, China put into orbit six of its own Beidou ("Compass") navigation satellites.[109] China's military reconnaissance capability is probably similar to the capabilities of Western sensor systems of the 1990s, a location to about ten meters in accuracy, clock geosynchronous signals to within 50 nanoseconds, and velocity to within 0.2 meters per second.[110]

Without these space systems, China cannot maintain its networked, integrated C⁴ISR architecture to support the military operations. Moreover, its space reconnaissance architecture must have the necessary tracking and data-relay satellites to be able to function on a real-time basis. China's tracking and data-relay capabilities are still limited, covering much of the western Pacific. In the future, this capacity likely will expand to cover the globe.[111] As the PLA moves to deploy a ballistic missile, the Dong Feng-21D, with a maneuvering warhead to track and target deployed naval task forces, the effectiveness of the warhead depends on the PLA's over-the-horizon radar, its space-based satellite and sensor systems, and the ability to to collect and transmit radar returns, images, and electronic intelligence reliably over extended distances on and beyond the mainland.[112] The U.S. Department of Defense projects that this anti-ship ballistic missile system will be able to engage adversaries out to 1,850 kilometers from China's coast once operationally deployed.[113]

Conclusions

The People's Liberation Army of today is not the force that the United States fought in Korea in 1950; it has modernized significantly. At the theoretical level, PLA academicians, strategists, and senior military leaders have grasped the implications of the revolution in military affairs. In the operational arena, PLA officers and leaders at all levels are being educated in these lessons in units and at command academies. In military doctrinal affairs, PLA units can now turn to manuals and a range of publications that outline how to use C⁴ISR systems in war. In training, the PLA uses these new systems in exercises. In the area of offensive and defensive operations, the PLA is heavily involved in information warfare. In addition, the PLA is building a space-based architecture to support real-time intelligence needs for its operations.

All of the command, control, and targeting architectures in development and fielded by the PLA are necessary for a major military power in the information age if that nation is to keep pace with improvements in armaments and technology. The dilemma that confronts American military planners is to estimate how the PLA will use these capabilities. Unfortunately, there is no clear road map of the intentions of the Chinese Communist Party or how the PLA will use such military power and technology. The major indication we have of China's intent with all these systems is that many of its military strategists and senior leaders clearly are targeting the United States with this new military capacity.

The PLA has solved the over-the-horizon targeting problem. It has bought and built the hardware to be a modern military force. It is also very close to fielding the systems to fight a campaign out to about two thousand kilometers from the Chinese coast. For the United States, this means that we must continue to develop and stay ahead in the areas of missile defense, kinetic- and electronic-energy

Map 2.2   Air Defense and Short-Range Ballistic Missile Ranges

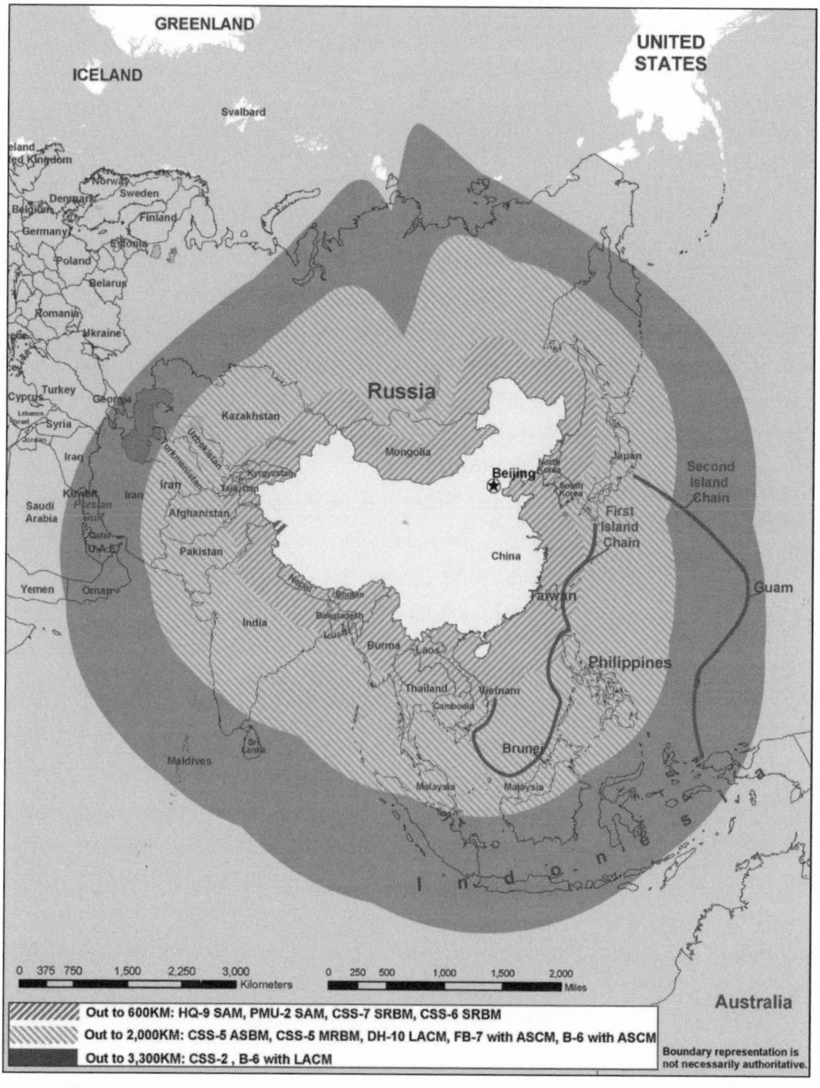

Source: Office of the Secretary of Defense, *Annual Report to Congress: Military and Security Developments Involving the People's Republic of China, 2011* (Washington, DC: Department of Defense, 2011).

weapons, electronic warfare and countermeasures, and information warfare.

China's military forces are developing dangerous capabilities—certainly more dangerous than they were a decade ago—but they are still not "peer competitors" with the United States. Even with the architecture the PLA has built, its ability to apply the systems with deployed forces at long distances away from its borders is still limited. The duration on station of its AWACS aircraft is short, their range is limited, and not all of them are capable of aerial refueling. Most of the PLA's combat ships and aircraft can engage in networked operations but can handle only a limited number of targets. In addition, not all of the weapons they carry can receive the networked combat data.

All this said, the PLA has made significant strides in less than two decades in transforming itself into a force that can engage in a modern war along its periphery and maintain its area-denial capabilities for about seventy-two hours in a radius of around fifteen hundred miles.[114] This equates to roughly the capability to defend and deny access to other forces inside the "second island chain" that Liu Huaqing conceived that China must dominate in 1985 (see the next chapter). Thus China is close to achieving a viable antiaccess strategy that, at a minimum, would impede U.S. and Japanese military operations.

Policy responses in the United States also are needed. With respect to Russia, diplomatic and economic pressure should discourage further military cooperation, or the military balance in Asia could change. European Union states apparently have accepted that their technology sales to China can threaten American forces. Legislation by Congressman Henry Hyde, the East Asia Security Act of 2005, got their attention when they were considering lifting the Tiananmen-based arms sanctions on the PLA. This legislation would have excluded European firms from participation in U.S. defense cooperation programs if they sold certain technologies to China.[115]

It is important to remember, however, that as the PLA becomes more dependent on the electromagnetic spectrum for military operations, it also becomes more susceptible to interference in that spectrum. Therefore, it is likely that strong competition in space control and information warfare will characterize the future military development of China and the United States for some time to come.

3 Naval Modernization, Strategy, Programs, and Policies

China has a long and rich history as a maritime power. Successive dynasties fought major naval battles with kingdoms up and down China's coast, tried to invade other countries by sea, and dispatched large fleets accompanied by warships and landing forces to open trade routes.[1] For the most part, China's maritime prowess declined after the seventeenth century. Often that history is not reflected in recent books on China's naval modernization, but the tradition of being a maritime power informs Chinese military thinking today. Over the last two hundred years, China has been primarily a continental power with a "brown water" navy focused on the area close to its coast.[2] In this more recent period, since the eighteenth century, China has suffered naval defeats and foreign incursions. The more recent history of foreign naval and military intervention frames China's naval modernization programs and policies in the twenty-first century.

The PLA Navy's post-1949 focus on the waters in China's immediate periphery began shifting in the mid-1980s. Today Chinese leaders recognize the Navy as a "strategic force" with responsibilities to "conduct offshore defense protecting China's territorial seas and territorial integrity, protect maritime rights and interests in the near seas, and to be able to act around the globe in support of national interests while protecting vital sea lines of communication."[3] Hu Jintao's speech to a gathering of PLA Navy political commissars caught international attention in December 2011 when the words "deeply prepare for military struggle" (*shenhua junshi douzheng zhunbei*) were translated instead as "prepare for urgent combat."[4] That translation generated much excitement in the region about China's long-term maritime intentions, and those intentions are serious. China is adopting strategies designed to counter the U.S. Navy and is developing new ships and weapons for that purpose.

This chapter examines China's naval strategies and equipment. It argues that China is in a transitional period that will produce a navy capable of pursuing maritime and trade interests around the globe. The PLA Navy's objective may not be to emulate the global posture of the U.S. Navy, but China certainly seeks the capacity to act globally, even if on a more limited scale. Further, China's naval growth specifically targets the United States, which the PLA sees as a formidable potential adversary.[5]

Historical Background

The Song dynasty saw the sea as a defensive barrier.[6] In 1132 the Song emperor established a standing navy with fifty-two thousand men.[7] It was the Yuan dynasty emperor, Kublai Khan, however, that sent large fleets and landing forces across the ocean to invade a foreign country. In 1266 Mongol emperor Kublai Khan, (his Chinese name Shi Zu), demanded that Japan's emperor submit to China's suzerainty and provide tribute, which he refused.[8] Kublai Khan established his capitol in Beijing in 1266 and began a series of attacks on the Song dynasty empire.[9] By 1271, Kublai Khan had established the Yuan dynasty, which lasted until 1368.

In the United States today, the term "kamikaze" brings to mind images of mass suicide attacks by Japanese aviators on U.S. ships in World War II. In Japan, however, *kamikaze*, or "divine wind," evokes historical memories of two major naval engagements fought against Chinese invaders. In 1274 Kublai Khan sent a force of nine hundred ships (with sailors drawn from Chinese, Mongol, and Korean ranks), forty to fifty thousand troops, and fifteen thousand horses to attack Japan at Hakata Bay in Kyushu.[10] After the Chinese landing, Japanese archers were beaten by the Chinese, but the Chinese withdrew to their ships rather than pursue their retreating foes deep into Japan's territory. With a huge storm approaching, and fearing that they would be marooned, the Chinese withdrew their ships. The storm (the "divine wind") struck the Chinese fleet, destroying three hundred ships and killing twenty thousand men.[11]

Seven years later, Kublai Khan sent a much larger fleet against Japan. Forty-five hundred ships and 150,000 men sailed from Korea to attack Kyushu again. As in 1274, the Chinese forces took a small island off Japan, seizing women and bounty. The Chinese forces then landed on Kyushu, but Japan countered by attacking the assembled Chinese fleet with small boats, setting fire to the larger Chinese ships. The Yuan forces retreated once more, as they did in 1274. Again, a "divine wind" intervened. A major typhoon struck, sinking four thousand ships and killing 130,000 men.[12]

Other Yuan fleets attacked northern Vietnam and the island of Java. But as the Yuan dynasty weakened, the military forces in China focused on continental campaigns.

During the Ming dynasty (1368–1644), China's navy reached "the pinnacle of its overseas deployments" and its maritime power.[13] A Muslim eunuch from Yunnan Province, Zheng He (1371–1433), led seven major expeditionary fleets to Southeast Asia, India, the Persian Gulf, and the eastern coast of Africa.[14] His fleets varied in size from 317 ships and twenty-seven thousand men (the first expedition) to as few as 63 ships and some ten thousand men. By the seventh expedition, Zheng's fleet was once more over three hundred ships and twenty-seven thousand men.[15] At the height of the Ming dynasty's navy, the fleet had twenty-seven hundred warships. However, a combination of threats from the north and the decision to favor domestic agriculture over science and technology saw a decline in the navy by 1474. Commerce relied on the restored Grand Canal running from north to south, and by 1503 the Ming navy was one-tenth its earlier size. By 1551 a combination of piracy along the Chinese coast and internal corruption so weakened the dynasty that the navy deteriorated further.[16]

During the seventeenth century, Taiwan began to figure in China's military affairs. The island stands a hundred miles from China's coast. Japan, Spain, the Netherlands, and Portugal had trading bases on Taiwan, but by the 1640s the Dutch became the preeminent trade power on the island.[17] Zheng Chenggong (also known as Koxinga), the son of a Ming dynasty merchant, refused to acknowledge the Qing dynasty when it conquered Ming China in 1644. Instead Zheng turned his troops and warships over to the remnant Ming dynasty, which fled to Taiwan. Zheng also conducted naval operations along the Chinese coast, fighting the Qing. The Qing finally took control of Taiwan and defeated Zheng's forces in 1683. Shi Lang, a Qing dynasty naval commander, was responsible for the successful maritime campaign. Still, the engagements took place along China's periphery.

Under the Qing dynasty during the eighteenth century, China was primarily focused on internal consolidation, and its military efforts were concentrated on continental campaigns and the nations along its periphery. Coastal trade was also a major factor in China's economic affairs. The nineteenth century, however, brought disaster to China's maritime forces at the hands of foreign powers.

In 1834, to protect and support England's opium trade with China, Lord Napier, the British superintendent of the East India Company, moved a fleet to Guangzhou (Canton). Napier died from fever, however, before any maritime conflict started. When the Chinese emperor later attempted to stop the opium trade and his imperial commissioner, Lin Zexu, seized foreign opium, the British sent another fleet under Adm. George Elliot to the area near Guangzhou. Elliot arrived in June 1840 with sixteen warships, twenty-eight transports, and four thousand troops, beginning what is known as the First Opium War. From 1840 to 1842, the British captured the ports of Xiamen, Ningbo, Zhoushan, Shanghai, and Zhenjiang, and were positioned to attack Nanjing. British forces also severed all of China's main north-south river and canal arteries.[18] Ultimately the Chinese emperor accepted the Treaty of Nanjing in 1842, ceding the island of Hong Kong to Britain; permitting the British to establish consulates in Guangzhou, Fuzhou, Xiamen, Ningbo, and Shanghai; and giving British subjects extraterritorial privileges in China.[19]

China's fate at the hands of foreign powers went rapidly downhill after that—and so did Chinese naval power. The Treaty of Nanjing proved a model for other Chinese treaties with Western powers and Japan. There was a renewed effort to build a strong Chinese navy in the late 1800s, but during the Sino-Japanese War (1894–1895), Japan defeated China's northern fleet, took possession of Taiwan, and invaded China through Korea, the Shandong Peninsula, and the Liaodong Peninsula.[20] Japan continued to occupy the Korean Peninsula and Taiwan until the end of World War II.

The start of the war, dated in China as July 7, 1937, focused the attention of the Nationalist regime on Japanese ground forces and the Communist military. The PLA, under control of the Chinese Communist Party, fought the Nationalists and Japan, but on land. It was not until the Communist forces began to consolidate power that the PLA Navy was founded during the civil war on April 23, 1949, as part of the East China Military Region.[21] Even after the People's Republic of China was established in 1949, the Navy focused primarily on the areas around China's periphery.

China's Naval Strategy Evolves

The PLA Navy's traditional missions are to "guard against enemy invasion from the sea, defend the state's sovereignty over its territorial waters, and safeguard the state's maritime rights and interests."[22] But today it is in a state of transition, widening its scope of action and expanding in size in proportion to China's expanded international interests. The Navy has submarine forces, surface forces, a coastal defense element, a naval aviation element, and a small corps of marines (two brigades).

The PLA Navy is organized into three fleets: the North Sea Fleet, headquartered in Qingdao on the Shandong Peninsula; the East Sea Fleet, headquartered in

Ningbo, Zhejiang Province; and the South Sea Fleet, headquartered in Zhanjiang, Guangdong Province.[23] For a long time it conducted occasional ship visits to foreign ports and in the 1980s deployed task forces to the southern Pacific to monitor ballistic missile experiments. For the most part, however, China's naval power has been focused on the waters in the Taiwan Strait and immediately surrounding China. When the Navy ventured out, it generally went into the South China Sea.

A major change in China's maritime orientation came in 1985 when Liu Huaqing, PLA Navy commander from 1982 to 1988, began to explore a strategy of "offshore defense."[24] He envisioned the Navy developing the capacity to move out from the coast to establish an effective defensive perimeter out to what he called "the First Island Chain." The strategy was designed to be able to control an area from 150 miles to 600 miles from China's coast. This "offshore defense" strategy included the "near seas," an area from the Kurile Islands to the Yellow Sea out to Korea and Japan, the East China Sea including Taiwan and beyond, and the South China Sea out to the Philippines and Brunei (see map 3.1). The area further into the Pacific, in the PLA Navy maritime strategy, was called the "far seas." In this area,

Map 3.1   First and Second Island Chains

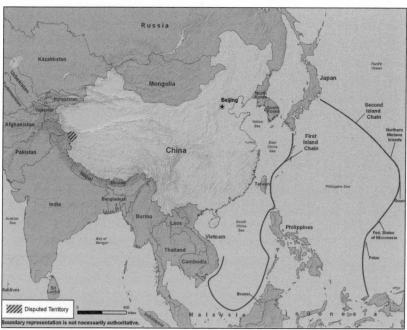

Source: Office of the Secretary of Defense, *Annual Report to Congress: Military and Security Developments Involving the People's Republic of China, 2011* (Washington, DC: Department of Defense, 2011), 23.

delineated by the "Second Island Chain," the PLA Navy was to exercise control and prevent hostile forces from enjoying unrestricted freedom of movement. The Second Island Chain extends from the eastern side of Japan out to the Northern Mariana Islands and Guam, through the Federated States of Micronesia and the island of Palau, and south to West Papua in Indonesia.[25]

Still, China's maritime strategists envisioned a phased, long-term growth in naval power, with Beijing's goals for the near seas and far seas being achieved around 2020.[26] Liu Huaqing wanted China to have an aircraft carrier but at some time in the future. And the PLA Navy was to evolve into a global force around 2050,[27] a time frame consistent with the Communist Party's long-term goals for achieving "comprehensive national power" and becoming a major world power.[28]

Over the years since the promulgation of the offshore defense strategy, the PLA Navy's geographic focus has grown. A major push for expanded naval operations could be seen in December 2004 in Hu Jintao's speech before the Central Military Commission on the "Historic Missions of the Military in the New Period of the New Century."[29] He reminded the CMC and the Navy that there are "more than three million square kilometers of maritime surface over which China has sovereignty" but more than half of that area is subject to disputes with neighboring states.[30] Hu's speech made clear to the Navy that its responsibilities were broader than just protecting China's coast and the near seas. By tasking the PLA to safeguard "China's expanding national interests," Hu required the PLA to develop the capacity to operate and have a presence away from continental China and its littoral areas.[31] The Navy has accepted this mission, and sees itself as a major component today of China's comprehensive national power and a component part of China's armed strength.[32] The Historic Missions speech is particularly noteworthy because it established a formal framework and ideological justification inside the Communist Party for using the military in a regional and global context. The speech provides broad guidance and justification for security thinkers in China to explore approaches to military theory, roles, and missions for forces, and new equipment and technology to increase China's capacity to operate as the military force of a nation with global interests.

Building a Force to Accomplish the Strategy

In order to fulfill the growing set of requirements, the PLA Navy has been expanding its forces and capabilities for years. In its report to Congress in 2009, the U.S.-China Economic and Security Review Commission (USCC) noted that from the mid-1990s, China "embarked on its largest naval modernization since the People's

Republic of China was founded in 1949." To illustrate the size and speed of that naval development, the report noted that "in recent years" China purchased or produced "38 submarines, 13 destroyers, 16 frigates, at least 40 fast-attack craft, and dozens of naval aircraft."[33] And a new aircraft carrier, *Liaoning* (the former Soviet carrier *Varyag*), was commissioned.[34] Also, for a number of years, the PLA Navy has gained experience operating task groups at long distances from the Chinese coast. It has kept a small combat force (some combination of a destroyer and a frigate or two) supported by a logistics ship in the Gulf of Aden in support of antiterrorism and antipiracy operations, providing experience in long-distance operations for naval commanders.[35]

The U.S. Department of Defense's annual report to Congress for 2011 credits the Chinese Navy with a force of seventy-five principal surface combatants, sixty submarines, fifty-five large and medium amphibious ships, and eighty-five small surface vessels equipped with missiles.[36] The International Institute for Strategic Studies gives similar numbers, although slightly lower in some cases.[37]

From Beijing's perspective, there are cogent reasons for the money it has poured into naval modernization. Increasing national pride, as China becomes an economically stronger and politically more active nation, is one reason. Obviously, there is the matter of Taiwan. Beijing wants a large enough naval force to deter or delay any decision by Taiwan to declare independence from the mainland. But if that strategy fails, the PLA needs a credible force to conduct an assault on Taiwan should the Communist Party's Politburo Standing Committee and Central Military Commission make the decision to take Taiwan by force. In the event of a PLA attack on Taiwan, Beijing is worried about intervention by the United States and even by Japan. The Taiwan Relations Act of 1979 (TRA; U.S. Public Law 96-8) requires that the United States "consider any effort to determine the future of Taiwan by other than peaceful means, including by boycotts or embargoes, a threat to the peace and security of the Western Pacific area and of grave concern to the United States." That is not a firm commitment to go to war in defense of Taiwan, but in diplomatic language the term "grave concern" conveys that it is pretty likely that if Taiwan were attacked, there would be some form of U.S. intervention.[38]

Under the TRA, the United States also is charged to "provide Taiwan with arms of a defensive character; and to maintain the capacity of the United States to resist any resort to force or other forms of coercion that would jeopardize the security, or the social or economic system, of the people on Taiwan." Taken together, these provisions of the TRA translate into a need for China to have an effective counterintervention strategy in the event the United States becomes involved should China decide to use force against Taiwan. The Chinese term for the PLA's counterintervention strategy is *fan jieru zhanlue*, which in U.S. military parlance is called an "antiaccess/area-denial strategy." In response to China, and also to contend with other potential adversaries that have similar strategies such as Iran, evolving U.S. "Air-Sea Battle," strategy is designed to ensure that even in the face of China's antiacess strategy, U.S. and allied forces will be able to operate in the western Pacific should they be required to do so.[39]

China has a number of sound reasons for its naval buildup and new strategic orientation. First, like any other nation, China must defend its coast. The experience of the nineteenth and twentieth centuries and Beijing's perception that foreign powers intervened in China's affairs during this period makes the PLA Navy more sensitive to this requirement. The need to ensure that Taiwan remains "within the fold" and responsive to Beijing's insistence that it not declare its independence also makes the naval buildup important to the Chinese Communist leadership. The PLA Navy also must be capable of defending China's disputed maritime claims and its economic interests.[40] These maritime claims are in areas rich in undersea resources and also are astride major fishing grounds. The fact that China, like many of its neighbors, gets a large percentage of its energy resources by sea demands that its navy pay more attention to sea lines of communication. Up to this point, Beijing seems to have been satisfied to leave protection of the sea lines of communication in the "global commons" (the high seas, international airspace, and outer space) to other nations.[41] Beijing also believes it must maintain a credible nuclear deterrent. For decades the PLA depended on ballistic missiles and a limited number of air-delivered gravity bombs for nuclear deterrence. That deterrent capacity is expanding so that Beijing will have a credible, submarine-based nuclear force deployed at sea.[42]

Another reason that the PLA Navy found that it needed a new strategy was to take advantage of the improvements in technology that fuses intelligence, surveillance, and reconnaissance (ISR) information, as described in chapter 2. To incorporate these new developments into its naval strategy, the PLA Navy turned to what China terms "informatization" (*xinxihua*)—that is, the ability to receive data from a variety of ISR systems, including satellites, aircraft, ships, and radar, and to ensure that data can be transmitted through a combination of satellites and other links in the electromagnetic spectrum.

China facilitated this effort by getting foreign technology. The United States even contributed to China's naval development from 1986 to 1989. The lead ship of the PLA Navy's *Luhu*–class (Type 052) destroyers was powered by General

Map 3.2   China's Energy Flows and Sea Lines of Communication

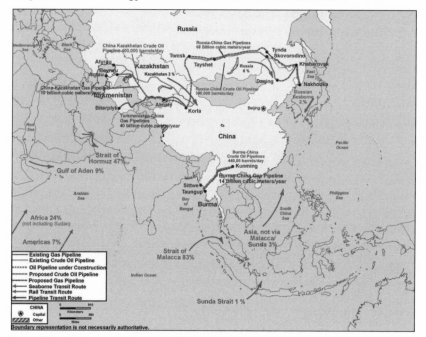

Source: Office of the Secretary of Defense, *Annual Report to Congress: Military and Security Developments Involving the People's Republic of China, 2011* (Washington, DC: Department of Defense, 2011), 21.

Electric LM2500 engines.[43] Subsequent ships are powered by engines from Ukraine or by engines manufactured in China under license from Ukraine. The same destroyers use French fire-control radars, and over a period of years PLA ships and aircraft have been outfitted with electronics from other European nations. The PLA Navy's objective was to leap ahead in the capacity to integrate battle management and take advantage of satellite information, sensors, naval guns, and information from other ships and aircraft.[44]

U.S. assistance with China's naval (and military) development ended when President George H. W. Bush put in place an embargo on arms sales to China after the PLA brutally put an end to demonstrations in Tiananmen Square on June 4, 1989. European nations also put in place a voluntary arms embargo, but some countries continued to sell defense systems and some weapons to China. France provided SA 321 Super Frelon helicopters for use in antisubmarine warfare (ASW), a variety of ASW sonar systems, naval guns, fire-control radars, search radars, and diesel propulsion systems for combatants and support ships.[45] Germany provided propulsion systems for support ships and submarines. Italy provided ASW torpedoes, fire-controls radars, and beyond-visual-range radars for PLA Navy (and Air Force) fighters.[46]

These European arms sales that strengthened the PLA Navy while it threatened Taiwan, Japan, and U.S. reconnaissance activities angered some members of Congress. Congressman Henry Hyde's East Asia Security Act of 2005 would have prohibited European companies that sold arms and defense equipment to China from participating in U.S. defense programs.[47] The Hyde bill did not pass in the House of Representatives, but America's NATO allies apparently got the message. According to Dr. May-Britt Stumbaum of the Free University of Berlin, a German specialist on security affairs in China, European companies have cut back on defense product sales to China in reaction to the Hyde legislation.[48] The PLA and China's defense industries also have improved their own indigenous systems by reverse engineering and technology transfers, and through espionage.[49]

The variation in classes of ships in China's naval inventory is a result of a continuing process of experimentation and modernization, combined with some changes in armament and fire control. Foreign help with shipboard propulsion, electronics, fire-control systems, and weapons, however, also was a factor in developing so many different classes of ships. The PLA Navy continues to experiment with hull design, propulsion systems, and onboard combat-control systems. The *Sovremenny* destroyers, purchased from Russia, were at one point the most modern in the PLA Navy. The PLA learned from what they saw on the Russian destroyers and improved China's indigenous designs, changing "hull designs, propulsion systems, sensors, weapons, and electronics."[50] At the same time, the PLA and China's defense industries work to improve air defenses and antiship cruise missiles.

Maintaining a mixed inventory of ships equipped by a variety of gun and propulsions systems from different countries and built on different specifications presents its own problems. The PLA Navy has experimented with different systems of air defense systems, shipboard guns, and antiship missiles as it developed its fleet. Once ships are in service, the Navy may change electronic packages or radar, or use existing platforms (ships) while modernizing onboard systems. Repairs and logistics, particularly for deployed ships, become more difficult. Still, the PLA Navy has managed to operate effectively in spite of these challenges as it continually experiments with ship designs and power plants.

In 2009 the chief of staff of the PLA Navy said in an address to foreign military attachés in Beijing that "the Party Central Committee and the Central Military Commission regard the navy as the priority service for force building, and continually increase naval investments."[51] This provides a perspective on how the

Communist Party views the importance of the Navy in its plans to address global security needs.

PLA Navy Aviation Forces

China's naval aviation forces are limited, focused on maritime surveillance, antiship and antisubmarine warfare, air defense, and coastal defense. Although the future could bring change, there is no doctrine in the PLA that corresponds to the way that the U.S. Navy or Marine Corps aviation assets conduct close air support of amphibious forces or ground operations.

The aviation component of the PLA Navy has twenty-six thousand personnel and 311 combat-capable aircraft. There are twenty H-5 bombers, which are copies of the Soviet Il-28 Beagle, a twin-engine aircraft carrying a crew of three. The PLA Navy also has thirty H-6 bombers, a licensed version of the Soviet Tu-16, a swept-wing aircraft with a crew of four. Both the H-5 and the H-6 can carry land-attack

Table 3.1 Principal PLA Navy Warships

Attack Submarines	59
Han (nuclear powered)	3
Shang (nuclear powered)	2
Kilo	12
Ming	20
Yuan	16
Song	4
Romeo (cruise missile test platform)	1
Golf (diesel-powered missile test platform)	1

Destroyers	13
Hangzhou (Russian Sovremenny)	4
Luyang	2
Luyang II	2
Luhai	1
Luhu	2
Luzhou	2

Frigates	65
Jiangkai	11
Jiangwei	14
Jianghu	27
Luda	13

Fast Attack Craft	76+
Houbei	65+
Huangfen	11+

Strategic Ballistic Missile Submarines	3
Xia (nuclear powered)	1
Jin (nuclear powered)	2

Source: Adapted from International Institute for Strategic Studies, *The Military Balance 2012* (London: Routledge, 2012).

and antiship cruise missiles, and some are capable of carrying nuclear bombs. Three of the H-6 bombers have been configured as aerial-refueling tankers, and H-5 and H-6 bombers also can be configured for reconnaissance missions. According to the International Institute for Strategic Studies, seven H-5 bombers have intelligence, surveillance, and reconnaissance missions, and five have antisubmarine warfare missions.[52]

The PLA naval aviation forces have a range of fighter aircraft, some of which can engage in ground attacks or attacks on ships. There are seventy-two fighters for air defense and air superiority. These are J-7 and J-8 aircraft, similar to the Soviet

MiG-21 and MiG-23, respectively. Although they have technology of the 1950s-to-1970s era, they still can be lethal. There are also a regiment of J-10 fighters (similar to the Israeli Lavi) of 1980s/1990s vintage and another of the even newer J-11. These naval aviation regiments have twenty-four or twenty-five aircraft each.[53] The J-11 is developed from and similar to the Russian Su-27. It is a fourth-generation fighter with sophisticated radar and data links that permit cooperative engagement of targets among aircraft.

PLA Navy aviation assets also include six or seven fixed-wing aircraft configured for airborne early-warning and control, as well as a similar number configured for electronic intelligence gathering. Additionally, there is range of transport, anti-submarine warfare, airborne early-warning, and rescue helicopters in the PLA Navy, which can be accommodated by a number of the PLA's ships. Early in 2013, the PLA reportedly reached an agreement with Russia to produce up to thirty-six TU-22MB bombers. The TU-22 is a 1960s vintage swept wing, supersonic bomber that the Soviet Union Russians use for strategic and maritime strike. One PLA officer interviewed about the deal speculated that the aircraft would be assigned to PLA Navy aviation forces, potentially giving the PLAN a capability to conduct maritime strikes out to the second island chain.[54]

A "New" Aircraft Carrier

For a number of years, Beijing readied its neighbors for the introduction of a PLA Navy aircraft carrier.[55] Over the years, China has purchased three decommissioned aircraft carriers, the HMAS *Melbourne* from Australia, the *Varyag* from Ukraine, and the *Minsk* from Russia. The Australian ship was exploited for design and engineering information and then scrapped, and the *Minsk* was turned into a floating hotel and casino in Macao. At that location, Chinese engineers still likely got a chance to explore its design features. After several years in dock undergoing repairs and upgrades, the former *Varyag*, put into service as the *Liaoning*, finally underwent sea trials in 2011 and 2012.[56] Having entered China's inventory in 2012, the *Kuznetsov*-class, sixty-thousand-ton ship is equipped with Shenyang J-15 fighter aircraft, which appear to be a Chinese version of the Russian Su-33, and helicopters.[57]

Operating an aircraft carrier requires a great deal of support with logistics ships for resupply and repairs and submarines and surface combatants for security. However, with India and Thailand operating carriers in the region, having a carrier in its force is as much a matter of pride for the PLA Navy as it is a way to gain experience. In the future, China will likely build its own carrier and operate more than one carrier task force. It is unclear how quickly the PLA will be able to make the transition from having an aircraft carrier and deploying it to sea, to operating an air-craft carrier battle group. Arguably one of the factors that led the PLA to move for-ward on an aircraft carrier project was the way that the forces of the United Kingdom were able to operate the light aircraft carrier HMS *Invincible* in the Falkland Islands campaign in 1982. The PLA drew the lesson from this that even limited air support deployed at sea over a long distance is critical to modern warfare.[58]

Logistics Ships

Combatant vessels aside, the PLA Navy also has made considerable improvements in its ability to support long-distance operations, as well as to conduct amphibious operations. If the PLA Navy is to conduct missions at greater distances from its coast and venture more often onto the high seas, it needs a logistics support fleet. In 2012 the PLA Navy had two *Fuchi*-class underway replenishment ships (AORs), two *Fuqing*-class AORs, and one *Nanyun*-class AOR in its inventory. One of these ships generally supports Chinese naval combatants on port calls around the world and also supported the PLA's antipiracy and antiterrorism operations in the Gulf of Aden.[59]

The PLA Navy also launched a new hospital ship, the *Daishandao* (*Taishan Island*) (Type 920), or the *Heping Fangzhou* (*Peace Ark*) as it is known when embarked on humanitarian missions. Before launching the *Daishandao*, the PLA Navy had converted some older transport or logistics ships for medical use. The new ship was designed to support both combat and humanitarian missions, giving the PLA increased international status and visibility.[60] The ship's 2010 deployment to the Gulf of Aden, which lasted ninety days, also supported the Chinese task force there and provided humanitarian assistance to four nations in the region.

Amphibious Capabilities

China's small naval infantry organization, the PLA Navy Marine Corps, comprises two brigades, both stationed in the South Sea Fleet at the naval base in Zhanjiang, at the southern tip of Guangdong Province, facing Hainan Island.[61] In total, the two brigades have ten to twelve thousand marines and are commanded by Navy officers who have spent part of their earlier careers with the Marine Corps.[62] The Marine Corps is one of China's primary rapid reaction units. The political com-missar of the marines, RAdm. Wang Guoxiang, told one Chinese newspaper that the most common missions for the marines are anti-terror operations and "non-con-ventional operations."[63] The commander of one of the marine brigades compared his troops to U.S. Navy Seals or rapid reaction units on U.S. aircraft carriers.[64]

In addition to the First Marine Brigade and the 164th Marine Brigade at Zhanjiang, the PLA has other amphibious units. There appears to be a special operations unit that is part of the PLA Marine Corps. And in two coastal military regions, Nanjing and Guangzhou, there are infantry divisions designated as amphibious units. The First Amphibious Mechanized Infantry Division, First Group Army, in Zhejiang Province, is the amphibious unit in Nanjing MR, and the 124th Amphibious Mechanized Infantry Division, in Guangdong Province, is the Guangzhou MR's amphibious division. Both divisions likely have primary missions aimed at Taiwan.[65]

Despite its long coastline and its claims on Taiwan, China does not have a long history of effective amphibious operations. In April 1949, when the PLA invaded Hainan Island during the civil war, units depended on small boats and a variety of civilian vessels. Soon after the PLA landed a large force, Nationalist forces evacuated the island, declaring it indefensible. The liberation of Hainan by Communist forces was declared in July 1950.

Attempts in August and September 1958 to take the islands of Matsu and Quemoy (now called Mazu and Jinmen), between the mainland and Taiwan, were fought off by Nationalist troops with heavy PLA losses. The PLA soldiers had used small craft and had no air support. Taiwan still has possession of the islands.

In 1974 China invaded the Paracel Islands in the South China Sea, which were occupied by South Vietnam. A task force of four PLA Navy corvettes and two submarine chasers, supported by naval air force bombers and fast patrol boats, engaged the South Vietnamese forces, damaging a destroyer and driving off four other ships.[66] A PRC infantry battalion of about six hundred men landed in the Paracels, which the PRC calls the Xisha Islands. The PLA captured forty-nine Vietnamese military personnel, who were later returned to Vietnam. There has been a small PLA garrison in the Paracels since that time.[67]

In the Spratly Islands, or the Nansha Qundao as China calls them, there have been a number of incidents involving Chinese naval vessels. In 1988 Chinese forces drove those of Vietnam off one reef, and the Chinese continue to support a naval garrison with amphibious vessels. Other parts of the Spratly Islands have garrisons manned by Taiwan, Vietnam, Malaysia, and the Philippines.[68]

The PLA Navy is building a more formidable amphibious capability, however—one that will permit it to operate more effectively in the South China Sea and in more distant, but limited, force-projection operations. China has built a new class of modern landing ships, starting with the *Yuzhao*-class landing platform/dock. With its stern well deck, the LPD will allow embarked troops to conduct assaults using amphibious craft, mechanized troop vehicles, and armored vehicles. The ship also will accommodate helicopters and carry approximately a battalion (five hundred to eight hundred troops).

China's Maritime Claims

China's territorial claims and the way its leaders interpret the UN Convention on the Law of the Sea (a.k.a. the Law of the Sea treaty) often puts it at odds with its neighbors. Currently China has maritime disputes with the Philippines, Vietnam, Brunei, Malaysia, Taiwan, Japan, and South Korea. In addition, it is constantly in disputes with the United States over the right to conduct peaceful military activities, such as air or maritime reconnaissance, in its exclusive economic zone (EEZ), which extends two hundred nautical miles from its coast or from the coastal plain.[69]

A further source of conflict between China and a number of other states is the way that China interprets the treaty's provisions on "freedom of navigation." Senior Chinese military and defense officials have for decades objected to their American counterparts about overt reconnaissance missions by U.S. aircraft and ships conducted above and in international waters but inside China's EEZ. China's military leaders often argue that such activities are not "innocent passage" or mere navigation, but are targeted military activities that should be stopped.[70] Yet China conducts similar reconnaissance off Japan, and the Law of the Sea treaty does not distinguish between warships and other types of vessels as long as those ships are not conducting an exercise that employs weapons and do not pose a threat or use of force against the coastal state.[71]

Map 3.3   China's Claims in the South China Sea and Conflicting Claims

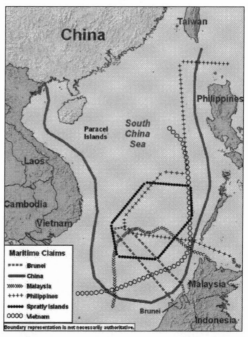

Source: *2010 Report to Congress of the U.S.-China Economic and Security Review Commission* (Washington, DC: Government Printing Office, 2010), 133.

Often these disputes have led to conflict or dangerous incidents. In 1974, after seizing the Paracels by force from Vietnam, China occupied and still controls all of the island chain. In the Spratly Islands, China has often clashed with other claimants. Here, however, China controls ten reefs or islands, while Vietnam controls twenty-two, the Philippines eight, Malaysia four, and Taiwan one.[72]

In 1988 Chinese naval forces attacked and killed a number of Vietnamese military personnel on Johnson Reef in the Spratly Islands. Also in the Spratlys, China ejected Philippine troops from Mischief Reef by force in 1995 and occupied it. A potentially volatile incident occurred between China and the United States in April 2001. A U.S. Navy EP-3 reconnaissance aircraft was operating sixty to seventy-five miles off the Chinese coast, inside China's EEZ when a Chinese fighter attempted a close intercept of the unarmed aircraft and collided with it. The Chinese fighter crashed at sea, and its pilot was lost. The U.S. aircraft was damaged and made an emergency landing on Hainan Island, where it was seized by Chinese forces, and its crew was subjected to eleven days of interrogation. Eventually the crew was released and the aircraft returned to the United States, but it had to be disassembled to be transported back.[73]

Chinese merchant, fishing, and naval ships and aircraft also have harassed U.S. and other ships in the EEZ. Between March 5 and March 8, 2009, the ocean surveillance ship USNS *Impeccable*, operating in the South China Sea, was closely approached by what the U.S. Department of Defense described as a Chinese intelligence collection ship and later by a Chinese frigate.[74] The *Impeccable* also was the subject of eleven close flyovers by Chinese military aircraft, and was told by a PRC naval officer to leave the area or suffer consequences.[75] Another U.S. surveillance ship, the USNS *Victorious*, got similar treatment in the Yellow Sea in May 2009 when a Chinese Bureau of Fisheries patrol vessel approached it and crossed its bow in darkness without warning.[76] On June 11, 2009, the USS *John S. McCain*, a destroyer operating in international waters, had its towed sonar array cut by a PLA Navy submarine while southwest of the Philippines. It is still unclear whether this was an intentional act or if the sub was conducting surveillance of the *John S. McCain* and got too close to the array. And in October 2011, after a friendly visit to Vietnam, an Indian Navy ship was challenged by PLA Navy ships.

In the South China Sea, fishing vessels and crews from Vietnam and the Philippines have been seized by Chinese maritime patrol or naval forces. And in the East China Sea, where the Senkaku (or Diaoyutai) Islands are in dispute among China, Japan, and Taiwan, there have been several incidents between Chinese fishing or maritime patrol ships and the Japanese coast guard.

The irony is that for a number of years, from 2003 to 2009, Beijing conducted a relatively successful diplomatic and politico-military strategy in East Asia. The thrust of China's "peaceful rise" (*heping jueqi*) strategy was to convince neighboring states, and the West, that China could build itself up to become a "great power" without creating a threatening military that would upset the regional order. (See the discussion of the peaceful rise theory in chapter 9).[77] Ultimately factional arguments in the Communist Party, including criticism from the PLA that the peaceful rise theory might limit PLA modernization, led party leaders to abandon that approach.[78] By 2009, however, renewed aggressive actions by the PLA Navy, the articulation of the PLA's counterintervention strategy with its antiship ballistic missiles, and urging from China's neighbors in Japan and Southeast Asia led the United States to a new tack.

On July 23, 2010, Secretary of State Hillary Clinton told attendees at the Association of Southeast Asian Nations (ASEAN) regional forum that "the United States, like every nation, has a national interest in freedom of navigation, open access to Asia's maritime commons, and respect for international law in the South China Sea."[79] This was a direct statement that the United States has an interest in the peaceful resolution of the conflicting maritime claims in the region. In October 2010, at the ASEAN defense ministers' meeting, Secretary of Defense Robert Gates repeated this position and emphasized that the United States had the right to "transit through, and operate in, international waters."[80] In 2011 the new U.S. defense secretary, Leon Panetta, voiced similar sentiments on a visit to Indonesia.[81] Thus China's sustained confidence-building campaign over a number of years ended up failing, and the United States, as it drew down from the wars in Iraq and Afghanistan, made a "turn to Asia" to reassure friends in the region of its interest.

In the East China Sea, China, Taiwan, and Japan have conflicting claims to the Senkaku Islands that could involve the United States in any conflict. China refers to these as the Diaoyu Islands. Japan has administered these islands since the 1970s based on an agreement with the United States.[82] The islands fall under the U.S.-Japan mutual security agreement, and in 2010, Secretary of State Hillary Clinton made it clear that "the United States has never taken a position on sovereignty, but we have made it very clear that the islands are part of our mutual treaty obligations, and the obligation to defend Japan."[83]

The United States Responds to China's Naval Modernization

The growth of the PLA Navy is part of a broader desire by Chinese leaders for a maritime strategy and greater "sea power."[84] That growth, combined with China's articulation of its counterintervention strategy, led the Obama administration to refocus U.S. forces on the Asia-Pacific region. Some have argued that this refocus was really a means to divert attention from the administration's drawdown of forces in Afghanistan and Iraq, but it seems clear that the Department of Defense is taking a fresh look at China's antiaccess/area-denial strategy. Among the things that alarmed Washington were the expansion of China's submarine fleet and the development of antiship ballistic missiles with maneuvering warheads.

In 2012 the United States took a fresh look at security policy in Asia, stationing more forces there. Assistant Secretary of State Kurt Campbell, in an interview at the Foreign Policy Initiative, explained that geography and national interest dictate more of a focus on the Asia-Pacific region.[85] Campbell argued that the region has developing powers other than China. U.S. military forces in Guam were reinforced, plans called for more U.S. military forces to be devoted to Asian contingencies, and new military personnel and supplies were stationed in Australia, with twenty-five hundred U.S. Marines scheduled to rotate through there.[86] The United States also would cultivate new security partnerships in the region.[87]

Before the Obama administration announced what has been called the "pivot to Asia," however, the Pentagon had begun to explore new strategic options designed to counter China's A2/AD strategy. The new U.S. strategy is often described as being relevant both to China and Iran, but it is China that is the stronger power and more pressing problem.

The PLA's own area control and counterintervention strategy focuses on degrading an opponent's technological advantages while controlling the maritime approaches to China in the western Pacific Ocean.[88] Chapter 2, on command, control, and surveillance, explained how this PLA strategy is designed to work. To accomplish its antiaccess mission, the PLA has developed new antiship ballistic missiles, developed the new ships and submarines described in this chapter, and would employ cyber and space attacks.

The Pentagon's response to China in the Pacific is designed to ensure that despite any sea denial or sea control measures by the PLA, U.S. forces are able to operate throughout the region. The Center for Strategic and Budgetary Assessments, a Washington think tank, articulated "AirSea Battle"[89] as a response to what it characterized as an "unprovoked challenge" to U.S. forces in the western Pacific, where the proponents of the strategy describe China as trying to create "no-go zones."[90]

In a publication titled *Joint Operational Access Concept*, the Joint Chiefs of Staff explained that "the intent of Air-Sea Battle is to improve integration of air, naval, space, and cyberspace forces to provide combatant commanders the capabilities needed to deter and, if necessary, defeat an adversary employing sophisticated antiaccess/area-denial capabilities."[91] The fact that the strategy is largely aimed at China and its military capabilities is not lost on PLA strategists. Two Chinese military strategists traced the lineage of Air-Sea Battle to NATO's "AirLand Battle," the Cold War strategy to confront the Soviet Union in Europe. The Chinese commentators believe the United States conceives relations with China in a Cold War context and that the American approach runs counter to "the trend of peace and development."[92]

The Air-Sea Battle strategy envisions a U.S. military reduced in scale, with primarily the Navy and the Air Force operating together but partnered with other allies and states in the region. The basic idea is to bring together countries with a common interest in preventing one country, such as China, from preventing others from using the global commons in the western Pacific. Their common mantra is that building new partnerships and military capabilities "are not aimed at any particular country in the region," but the reality is that China's actions and military growth are driving the effort.[93]

Over the next decade China will likely react to this U.S. strategy as it evolves, creating a dynamic security situation in the Pacific where nations that have strong trade and political links will still "hedge" against each other in the security realm. The PLA will probably see U.S. actions as an attempt to "contain" China, while China's neighbors and the U.S. military will paint the approach as a logical response to what appears to be a growing capacity of the PLA to deny other nations the ability to move freely around the western Pacific.

4 The PLA Air Force and China's Approaches to Aerospace

China has a long history of naval operations and maritime power. However, the same is not true of its activities in military aviation and aerospace. These are newer domains of war, of course, but the People's Republic of China and, by extension, the PLA Air Force got off to a slow start. Before the end of the civil war between the Communists and the Nationalists, the PLA's air inventory consisted of a few transports and some combat aircraft captured from Japan and the Nationalists.[1] The PLAAF was formally established in November 1949.[2]

When the Chinese People's Volunteers flowed into the Democratic People's Republic of Korea (North Korea), the PLA received help from the Soviet Air Force. The troops were supported from inside China by their own Fourth PLA Air Force division for the first half of 1951, and by October 1951 four other PLAAF divisions had joined the conflict. Seven more PLAAF divisions were introduced into the theater during the remainder of the war. By the end of 1953, the PLAAF had three thousand fighters and bombers.[3] It was the third-largest air force in the world, with some of the most advanced fighter and bomber aircraft available.[4] Most of these were provided by the Soviet Union. By the time of the July 1953 armistice, the PLAAF had ten fighter divisions and two bomber divisions.[5] Although based in China, the PLAAF operated in Korea. China had eight hundred pilots and 59,700 ground personnel by the end of the war.[6]

In 1954 and 1955, in the Yijiangshan Islands campaign against Nationalist forces, PLAAF aircraft flew "strike, reconnaissance, fighter escort, and air defense" missions.[7] Operations were conducted in the area off the Chinese coast near Taiwan. The PLAAF also attacked Nationalist ships, conducted bombing missions, and supported an amphibious operation.[8] In a series of operations similar to those in the Korean War, "the PLAAF and naval aviation massed aircraft from several units to conduct the campaign," which some analysts say was characterized by a lack of coordination among the ground, air, and naval elements of the PLA.[9]

The PLAAF also was active in the 1958 Taiwan Strait Crisis, where the PLAAF fought thirteen air battles, according to PLA records. U.S. and Chinese records on aircraft losses differ. The PLA says it only lost five aircraft, while the Nationalist forces of the Republic of China lost fourteen aircraft; U.S. records say the PLAAF lost thirty-two aircraft and the Nationalists only lost three.[10]

After the crisis, the PLA received SA-2 surface-to-air missiles (SAMs) from the Soviet Union. The surface-to-air missile batteries were merged into the PLAAF, giving the PLA aircraft along with logistics units, airborne forces, SAMs, antiaircraft artillery, radar and communications units.[11] By 2012 the PLAAF had added electronic warfare and electronic countermeasures units, space attack forces, airborne early-warning aircraft, helicopters, and aerial refueling units to its arsenal.[12]

Still, over the years, the PLA has been hesitant to use its air forces when it engaged in combat. There was no air involvement in the 1962 Sino-Indian War and none when the PLA confronted Soviet forces in 1969 at Zhenbao (Damansky) Island. During the U.S. involvement in Vietnam, the PLA sent air defense, engineer, and other units into Vietnam and Laos. However, the PLAAF (and PLA Navy aviation assets) conducted no significant air combat outside China's own borders.[13] The PLAAF engaged in air combat on a few occasions when U.S. aircraft or drones entered China's airspace, but it was ground forces, engineers, and air defense forces that came to North Vietnam's direct assistance.

Although a lot of PLAAF aircraft, SAM, and antiaircraft artillery units were activated and moved close to the Vietnamese and Soviet borders during the 1979 Sino-Vietnamese War, there was no air action.[14] The PLAAF moved aircraft around China in the event the war widened, to reinforce the capacity to control borders, and to be prepared in the event of an air attack on China. And it moved forward command-and-control elements from its headquarters in Beijing to the areas of combat in the event operations widened. But it seems clear that the Central Military Commission in Beijing and the General Staff Department had made decisions to keep the conflicts confined to the ground and to air defense.

The most likely explanation for the lack of PLAAF aircraft commitment to combat or to combat support operations was a political decision to limit the scope of the conflicts. In the Korean War, in particular, the CMC was careful to ensure that the scope and geographic area of combat did not escalate.[15] In the more recent conflicts, it is most likely that the CMC and the Politburo Standing Committee decided that, as a "war control" measure, it was better to limit the focus of conflict to ground operations and to avoid actions that might lead to escalation.[16] At the same time, however, the PLAAF made serious efforts to modernize its force.

Force modernization for China's air force was a dispersed effort that drew from defense industries in China and around the world. Perhaps the biggest contributor to PLAAF modernization was the Soviet Union and then Russia. However, there also were American, Israeli, and European contributions. Russia initially equipped the PLAAF, but the United States seemed to look the other way when Israel provided what appears to be assistance and designs for the Lavi, a fighter modeled on the American F-16. One explanation for this is that this occurred in the 1980s, when China and the United States were cooperating to oppose the Soviets' domination of Asia in the wake of their invasion of Afghanistan.

The United Kingdom had a long-standing cooperative program with China on jet engine production, although even after two decades the Rolls-Royce Spey project with Chinese defense industries failed to produce a viable jet engine for civilian or military aircraft.[17] From 1986 to 1989, the United States worked with the PLAAF to upgrade fighter and air-defense aircraft with an all-weather look-down/shoot-down radar capability. The Tiananmen Square massacre, however, brought an end to this program.[18] European nations picked up some of this business, with Spain, France, and Italy providing avionics and electronics systems to the PLAAF.[19] By and large, however, the Soviet Union, and then Russia, have been the largest contributors to the PLAAF.

The Modern Chinese Air Force

The PLA Air Force is the third largest air force in the world. Only those of the United States and Russia are larger.[20] The PLAAF is composed of units of fighters, bombers, transport aircraft, helicopters, and various surveillance and electronic warfare aircraft. The chart below describes the inventories of these aviation forces. However, in addition to aviation forces and units, the PLAAF also includes its own SAM, engineer, antiaircraft artillery, communications, radar, electronic monitoring (or "technical reconnaissance"), electronic countermeasures, radar, and chemical defense units.[21]

Table 4.1   PLA Air Force Major Aircraft

Fighters	Bombers*	Fighter/Attack	Transport	EW/AEW/ISR**	Helicopters
890	82	535	320	124	104

* Includes ten H-6 bombers configured as tankers.
** Electronic warfare; airborne early-warning; intelligence, surveillance, and reconnaissance aircraft. Includes eight airborne early-warning and control aircraft and ninety-six fighter aircraft equipped for electronic warfare.

Source: International Institute for Strategic Studies, *The Military Balance 2012* (London: Routledge, 2012).

Although there are a lot of aircraft and personnel in the PLAAF (300,000 to 330,000 people), it remains a force that is in a "conversion from a force for limited territorial defense to a more flexible and agile force able to operate off-shore in both offensive and defensive roles."[22] PLA publications that discuss PLAAF modernization want it to be able to accomplish six core missions:

- Deterrence, or the capacity to discourage other countries from conducting air and other military operations against China or to convince any adversary to abandon its own military operations;
- Offense, or the ability to carry out effective air strikes as part of a larger campaign, or to prosecute offensive air campaigns designed to identify PLAAF targets and to destroy them;
- Defense, or the capacity to integrate traditional missions of protecting the government and its ability to rule, protect military and key civilian installations, intercept enemy air and space forces (air defense), and conduct counterattacks on enemy forces;
- Airlift, or the ability to conduct logistical operations, move forces and equipment for power projection, and the capacity to be part of disaster relief or other military operations other than war;
- Blockade support, or the capacity to establish no-fly zones or assist the PLA Navy in its own counterintervention or antiaccess/area-denial missions beyond China's periphery; and
- Airborne operations. The PLAAF has its own airborne forces, a full group army (comparable to a U.S. Army corps) that can conduct forced insertion and power projection missions in large or small numbers, inside or outside of China.[23]

Making the transition to a force able to accomplish these missions requires the PLAAF to modernize its forces, add new weapons, electronics, and sensor packages, and change its operational concepts. The Chinese defense white paper of 2008 explained that "the Air Force is working to accelerate its transition from territorial air defense to both offensive and defensive operations, and increase its capabilities for carrying out reconnaissance and early warning, air strikes, air and missile defense, and strategic projection, in an effort to build itself into a modernized air force."[24] The PLAAF, therefore, distributes its aircraft around China, with concentrations of bases and aircraft in areas where it perceives the likelihood of a threat to be highest.

Map 4.1 PLA Air Force Bases and Major Forces

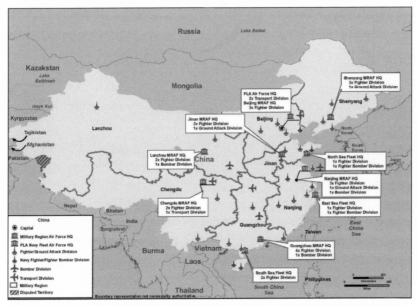

Source: Office of the Secretary of Defense, *Annual Report to Congress: Military and Security Developments Involving the People's Republic of China, 2011* (Washington, DC: Department of Defense, 2011), 77.

Transforming itself from a force focused on territorial defense to one that can project aerospace power around the world and support other military operations means that the PLAAF must make some serious changes. It must transition from a force that could not refuel its own aircraft while in flight, to one that has "longer legs" and can operate at extended distances. It must transition from a force that was unable to communicate between aircraft and with the ground except by radio, to a force that can use digital data links to exchange information rapidly. And it needs new, smart weapons designed to defeat a range of enemy electronic and thermal countermeasures. The PLAAF must reduce its dependence on foreign suppliers and systems integrators. This means that China must develop its indigenous aircraft production capacity, weapons industry, and electronics industry so that it can reduce, if not eliminate, its dependence on foreign assistance and purchases. Most seriously, the PLAAF must integrate the capacity to operate as an air force with the growing capacity to conduct reconnaissance and even offensive and defensive operations in space.

One part of making such a major transition was to develop strategic concepts of how to employ the PLAAF. Early in its development, the PLA treated the Air

Force as a means for air defense but also used it as a form of artillery and support for ground forces. Observing U.S. and coalition or allied operations in Iraq in 1991 and in the Balkans when Yugoslavia split up made the PLA far more aware of the need to change Air Force strategy and doctrine.[25] Gradually airpower specialists began to articulate the need for "improving warfighting capabilities," requirements for "new technologies to enable new capabilities," and a need for "high technology aircraft, missiles, and different air platforms such as tankers, transport aircraft, fighters, and bombers."[26]

These demands for a different type of air force with a new strategy and modern weapons and aircraft have been reflected in Chinese military publications.[27] The strategic discussion of China's future has included concepts about how to include space warfare, and even cyberwarfare, in aerospace operations, leading to a qualitatively and quantitatively different form of airpower for the PLA.[28]

Still, China's defense and aircraft industries are not yet up to the task of developing and producing what is needed and must rely on foreign help.[29] Thus the PLAAF remains a hybrid force, combining imported foreign (almost all Russian) aircraft, aircraft produced under foreign license, indigenous aircraft, and the same mix of aviation electronics and weapons. In terms of fighter aircraft, virtually all in China's inventory—from the MiG-15 procured in 1950 to the Su-27 procured in 1992—have come from Russia.[30] The MiG-23, which China bought from Egypt in 1978, is also a Russian aircraft. The same is true of the PLAAF's bomber force. With a few exceptions like the J-10, derived from the Lavi, and the prototype J-20 and J-31 stealth fighters under development, its aircraft was either imported from the USSR or Russia, or derived from Soviet or Russian designs.[31]

The case is almost the same for the air-to-air missiles in the PLAAF inventory. Almost all the missiles came from Russia (or the Soviet Union). The Matra 550 came from France and was designated the PL-7, but it never entered service, and the Chinese Navy HQ-7 also was developed from the French Crotale NG.[32] Even Israel has made a modest contribution to PLAAF air-to-air missile development, with the Rafael Python III, which China produces as the PL-8 (Pelei-8).[33]

In a nutshell, the PLAAF has aircraft from a range of generations, as outlined in the following chart. This means it faces the challenges of integrating generations of aircraft and a range of items that are bought, produced under license, or reverse-engineered, modified, and produced in China; putting useful electronics and weapons on this range of platforms; and operating them effectively. The result is an air force that is at the same time developing new weapon systems, "hanging" very modern weapons and sensors on old-generation aircraft, importing new platforms, and testing the latest in domestically produced stealth fighters.[34] The J-20, China's first advanced fighter with stealth features, first tested on January 11, 2011, while Secretary of Defense Robert Gates was visiting China, continued flight testing, and a second stealth fighter, the J-31, is under development.[35]

PLA air warfare and operations strategists conceive of operations as multidimensional (air, space, and informational or cyber) and a mix of offensive and defensive measures.[36] China's strategists are convinced that the air and space domains of war will merge so that war in aerospace, supported by cyber and information attacks, will be integral parts of other military operations.[37] Moreover, whether

Table 4.2. PLA Air Force Generations

FIGHTER AIRCRAFT GENERATIONS

Jet engine combat fighters are usually categorized by "generations." International norms generally use five or six categories, loosely based upon the prevalent set of capabilities at the time of the aircraft's development:[*]

- **First generation** (c. 1945–1955): This generation includes the original jet fighters powered by turbojet engines.

- **Second generation** (c. 1955–1960): These fighters generally had a higher top speed and were outfitted with radar and guided air-to-air missiles.

- **Third generation** (c. 1960–1970): In addition to having increased overall capabilities, these fighters also were the first to be capable of both air defense and ground-attack missions.

- **Fourth generation** (c. 1970–1990): These multirole fighters were equipped with increasingly sophisticated avionics and weapon systems. A key area of emphasis was maneuverability rather than speed.

- **Fourth+ (or 4.5) generation** (c. 1990–2000): A concept that not everyone agrees exists, it implies some combination of advanced capabilities and upgrades to a normal fourth generation airframe.

- **Fifth generation**: These have a combination of stealth, high-altitude capability, maneuverability, advanced radar, high-capacity data links, "plug and play" avionics, and supercruise capabilities low radar cross-section ("stealthy").[†]

[*] Chinese categories for fighter aircraft generations differ from accepted international norms. Normal conventions identify fighters based upon the decades of the fighter's inception and its relevant capabilities. China, however, identifies its aircraft according to when they are inducted into the air force. Because of this difference, Chinese analysts regard China's new fighter projects as "third generation" aircraft, while U.S. analysts use international norms, calling these same planes "fourth generation." In order to avoid confusion, this book follows the international naming norm. Office of Naval Intelligence, *China's Navy 2007* (Suitland, MD: Department of the Navy), 47–48.

[†] John Woo, "Fighter Generations," Aerospaceweb.org (June 27, 2004), http://www.aerospaceweb.org/question /history/q0182.shtml.

Source: *2010 Report to Congress of the U.S. China Economic and Security Review Commission* (Washington, DC: Government Printing Office, November 2010), 77–78.

Table 4.3   PLA Air Force Diversity of Aircraft Generations in Service

Aircraft	Generation	Features	Comparison	Number
Y-5	Second	Propeller-driven light transport and for airborne operations	Russian An-2	170
Y-8	Third	Turbo-prop transport; EW/AWACS	Russian An-12	13
H-6	Third	Jet-powered, bomber	Russian Tu-16	82 (+10 tankers)
J-7	Second	Jet fighter/ ground-attack/ISR	Russian MiG-21	609
J-8	Fourth	Jet fighter/ISR	Russian MiG-23	216
J-10	Fourth	Jet fighter/ ground-attack	Russian MiG-29 & Su-27, Israeli Lavi	200
J-11	Fourth	Fighter/ground-attack	Russian Su-27	134
Su-27/ J-11	Fourth	Fighter/ground-attack	Purchased or licensed from Russia	75
Q-5/A-5	Second/ Third	Ground-attack/ light bomber	Russian MiG-19	120
J-20	Fifth	Stealth fighter	U.S. F-117	1-3

Source: International Institute for Strategic Studies, *The Military Balance 2012* (London: Routledge, 2012).

attacks come from space or from the air, so long as they are directed against surface targets, China's strategists see the PLAAF as heavily involved in future military operations.[38]

The problem for the PLAAF, however, is that it is not a uniformly high-technology force. That is, neither the PLAAF, nor the rest of the PLA, can field and operate a fully digitized force that can take advantage of an integrated picture of the battlefield and apply weapons in a fully coordinated manner.[39] China's own major air strategists expect the PLAAF to lag behind the more modern air forces of stronger powers, such as the United States, Russia, and Japan, "for some time to come."[40]

If one looks at potential air combat in a crisis over Taiwan, for example, the PLAAF has some distinct advantages. It has in its inventory an overpowering number of fourth-generation fighter aircraft, some roughly equal to those in the ROC Air Force and some with better radar, avionics, and data-exchange capabilities. Taiwan is somewhat overmatched. Given its strategic depth, the PLAAF also can mobilize its second- and third-generation fighters for use across the Taiwan Strait, a short distance. The ROC Air Force would probably be simply overwhelmed in such a scenario. The sort of airpower-generation capacity China has with respect to Taiwan is similar if one looks at a potential conflict on the Korean Peninsula, where the distances are also close.

Transfer the area of conflict to the littoral areas of South China Sea, and Vietnam as well as the Philippines face a strong challenge, but one less daunting than Taiwan's. Those older Chinese aircraft simply would not be able to get to the area of conflict. This kind of scenario would force the PLAAF to use some of its light bombers (since they have more range), but China still lacks adequate refueling aircraft to sustain large-scale air combat at long distances from its shores.

If China were to be in conflict with Japan, however, the older aircraft in the Chinese inventory would not be of much help because of the distances involved. Moreover, Japan has a modern air force with ten squadrons of fourth-generation fighter/attack aircraft (some 275).[41] Also, Japan would probably not be the aggressor in such a situation, which means that the PLAAF, and the PLAN aviation force, would need more refueling aircraft than are available in the Chinese inventory to sustain a conflict. This is one reason that China wants to purchase from Russia thirty-six Il-76 heavy-transport aircraft and four Il-78 air-refueling aircraft.[42] The PLAAF is aware of its own limitations and is methodically improving its capacity for projecting power. Its planners believe that joint operations—integrating all the military services and conducted across the domains of war (air, space, land, sea, and in the electromagnetic spectrum—are key to future defense policy.[43]

In the traditional sense, PLAAF strategists have always believed that airpower could be concentrated and used on the battlefield or at sea to support ground or surface naval operations and to augment artillery, missiles, and rockets.[44] Probably as a result of studying U.S. and coalition operations in campaigns such as in Kosovo in the 1990s and Libya in 2011, PLAAF strategists seem to think that they must be able to execute independent air campaigns and to use airpower for strategic coercion.[45] Still, other "new missions" are envisioned for the PLAAF. Chinese air power planners and strategists discuss the concept of conducting "deterrence and intimidation operations" by taking steps and moving forces to suggest that combat is imminent in order to deter or dissuade a potential adversary from taking a course of action.[46] Other PLAAF strategists suggest that in future combat, the PLAAF must be prepared to conduct precision first-strike operations designed to paralyze an enemy at the start of a conflict.[47] Thinking about how to employ the PLAAF in the future is not limited to the air domain of war. Aerospace warfare strategists also are exploring how they might integrate information attacks into the precision strikes they advocate, and they are exploring space "warning attacks" that might destroy an enemy's most critical space systems.[48]

Organization

The PLAAF organizes to accomplish all of its missions out of a service headquarters in Beijing. This headquarters is responsible for overseeing PLAAF assets in each of China's seven military regions, as well as for training and testing bases around China. Inside the MRs, the MR commander is responsible for all integrated military operations, and the MR Air Force commander is a deputy MR commander. Then, within the MR Air Force, there are operations command posts that take control of and coordinate activities for Air Force units subordinated to them for training, exercises, or operations. In a major Rand Corporation study of the PLAAF, the authors said that "operational units within an MR [Air Force] may report to a command post, be directly controlled by the MR headquarters, or be directly controlled by the PLAAF headquarters" in Beijing.[49] In wartime or in crisis operations, when an MR converts to a theater of war, these command-and-control relationships remain the same, with the MR Air Force commander remaining subordinate to the commander of the theater of war.

Inside the military regions, the units are structured in relatively standard military formations.[50] Each MR has a couple of fighter divisions or more and a ground-attack aircraft division. Some have bomber divisions (Lanzhou MR, Nanjing MR, and Guangzhou MR). The Chengdu, Guangzhou, and Beijing MRs have their own air transport divisions. The divisions contain a mixture of fighter, attack, and transport regiments, depending on the mission or geographic area. Some of the MRs also have an electronic warfare regiment, but these units can be shifted around the country as required. Also, other specialized organizations are distributed around the PLAAF. In the Guangzhou, Nanjing, Jinan, and Shenyang MRs, there are intelligence, surveillance, and reconnaissance regiments. The Shenyang MR has its own independent electronic warfare regiment, and the Nanjing MR, opposite Taiwan, has the Twenty-Sixth Special Mission Division, with all of China's airborne early-warning and control aircraft, a coastal search-and-surveillance regiment, and the ISR regiment mentioned above.

Exercises and Deployments

The PLA exercises its forces regularly, practicing scenarios that require rapid deployment. In Exercise Airborne Maneuver (Kongjiang Jidong) in 2009, thirteen thousand airborne troops and huge amounts of equipment were moved, all inside

China. That same year, the PLA conducted major exercises in mountainous regions and in coastal areas. In Kuayue (Stride) 2009, a month-long exercise, the PLA employed fifty thousand troops and sixty thousand vehicles, as well as a variety of arms and support services. The exercise was conducted across four different regional training areas around China. In addition to these operational wartime exercises, the PLA was involved in other exercises devoted to humanitarian operations and air-sea rescue.[51]

In 2010 several large-scale exercises emphasized "large joint combat formations." One in the Lanzhou Military Region in 2011 converted it into a theater of war with the MR commander in charge. A noteworthy part of this exercise was that the PLA ground forces, the PLAAF, and forces from the Second Artillery Corps all formed the theater joint command in an integrated battle scenario. A subsequent exercise in the same area explored support capabilities of the logistics units needed to sustain a large deployed force.[52]

Perhaps the most noteworthy exercise for the PLAAF, however, was the deployment to Turkey in 2010 to participate in Anatolian Eagle.[53] Although this was a small-scale operation, it involved a number of coordination requirements and new initiatives for the PLAAF. The flight of the four Su-27 fighter aircraft that were sent from China exceeded the 3,500-mile range of the aircraft, requiring the pilots to refuel in Iran and again in Turkey. From a military coordination and diplomatic standpoint, this meant that the PLAAF had to secure overflight rights and permission to land and refuel during the flight to Turkey. That is exactly the same sort of coordination that would be required in a real-world deployment.

These exercises are steps toward a PLAAF with greater reach, an air force that can operate as part of a broad, integrated joint task force or operate independently across long distances. The most realistic experience in developing a "global reach," however, probably came from actual deployments. For the Navy, the continued deployment of the antipiracy task force in the Gulf of Aden provided this realistic experience. For the PLAAF, however, the evacuation of Chinese nationals from Libya in February 2011 provided real-life experience.[54]

For the Libya operation, the Chinese government employed chartered Chinese airliners and ships, a PLAN frigate from the Gulf of Aden, and four PLAAF Il-76 transport aircraft to evacuate thirty-five thousand diplomats, tourists, businessmen, workers for Chinese-run projects, and students. The PLAAF flew "nearly continuous evacuation flights from Urumqi, Xinjiang, flying over Pakistan, Oman, Saudi Arabia, Sudan, and Libya."[55] The aircraft refueled in Sudan and Pakistan during their missions. This is the sort of joint-service, civil-military coordination that the PLAAF will need to be capable of to achieve the kind of global reach called for in its own strategic literature.

Airborne Forces

The PLA Air Force has an entire airborne corps under its command, the Fifteenth Airborne Army, with headquarters in Xiaogan, Hubei Province.[56] This force is neither a fully integrated group army, such as exists in the ground forces, nor an exact equivalent of the U.S. Army's Eighteenth Airborne Corps. Still, the PLA airborne forces are large and can be employed as ground forces, as part of the Air Force, or in reconnaissance elements. There are three airborne divisions: the Forty-Third Division, in Kaifeng, Henan Province; the Forty-fourth in Guangshui, Hubei Province; and the Forty-Fifth in Wuhan, Hubei Province. They are supported by a dedicated Air Force air transport division.

In addition to the airborne divisions, the Fifteenth Airborne Army also has a special operations regiment and a separate reconnaissance regiment (*dadui*). It also has its own integral airborne logistics support group and a signals group for command and control. It supported by some lighter towed artillery (122mm guns), towed multiple rocket launchers, and the normal infantry complement of mortars and antitank weapons.

China has not employed these airborne forces in combat, but they have been used in crises, including as initial reconnaissance forces in the area struck by the 2008 Sichuan earthquake.[57] The PLAAF deployed four thousand troops—perhaps two regiments—to the area by aircraft in forty-eight hours. In 1989 the author made a parachute jump in Kaifeng with the Forty-Third Airborne Division while serving as a military attaché in China and was told that PLA airborne troops make about six times the number of jumps in airborne training that American airborne trainees make. And the PLA airborne troops all are taught to repack their own parachutes after landing, while U.S. troops get fully packed parachutes from parachute riggers assigned to their units. The operational impact of this difference is that the PLA troops can be dropped in one place, complete a mission, consolidate, repack without the support of riggers or the resupply of new parachutes, and be employed again in a reasonably short time.

In doctrine, there are similarities between how the United States and China would employ airborne forces. The PLA envisions airborne operations to be highly mobile, fast means to concentrate forces quickly.[58] Because of their speed and the inherent surprise and shock value of their employment, airborne forces are intended for use to seize "political military and economic centers, and other strategically important ground."[59] Such objectives may include ports, airfields, critical parts of an enemy's infrastructure, and critical nodes on lines of communication. Airborne forces also can be employed in smaller elements for such missions as raids and destroying command-and-control centers.

PLA manuals note, however, that airborne operations require a great deal of intelligence and preparation.[60] They also must be executed precisely and supported by other ground or air operations. A large airborne operation requires a number of air corridors and multiple drop zones, all of which must be thoroughly reconnoitered beforehand.[61] Thus they are complicated operations.

During the Tiananmen Square massacre, the author observed elements of one division of airborne forces land by aircraft at a PLA airfield south of Beijing. They did not make a parachute jump. When they were sent into Beijing to the area of Tiananmen Square, the airborne forces got vehicle and armored support from another PLA ground unit. And the mission of the airborne forces did not differ from that of other PLA units.

Campaign doctrine talks about mass tactical jumps by airborne forces and discusses the number of approach lanes and drop zones for a division.[62] In exercises, however, airborne forces have made parachute jumps primarily in battalion-size units, probably enough to secure an airfield or major terrain feature. In riots in Tibet in 1988, the PLAAF airlifted about ten thousand airborne troops (equivalent to a division) to the area by transport aircraft in less than forty-eight hours. In 1996 in a PLA exercise simulating an invasion of Taiwan conducted on Dongshan Island, off Guangdong Province, a battalion of airborne forces supported an amphibious landing by a brigade of PLA marines.

In a major exercise in 2009, fifty thousand PLA personnel, thirteen thousand PLAAF airborne personnel, fifteen hundred vehicles, and seven thousand pieces of equipment were involved. But all moved to the exercise area by rail, and then some of the troops were airdropped following the rail movement.[63] Still, this was the largest and most complex exercise of airborne personnel in China since 1996.[64]

The thirty-five thousand or so PLAAF airborne troops are highly trained, well exercised, and motivated. Even with direct support from an air transport division, however, it is unlikely that the PLA can deliver more than a regiment in one mass drop; there are only fourteen Il-76 aircraft in the inventory of the unit trained and equipped to support the airborne troops.[65] It will take some time before the PLA is able to undertake the sort of operations France conducted when, with U.S. assistance, foreign legionnaire cavalry and paratroopers were airlifted to Mali in 2013, or the brigade-sized airborne assault the U.S. conducted in Iraq. That said, for crises along China's borders, natural disasters, or internal instability, the PLA's Fifteenth Airborne Army can be mobilized rapidly and move where needed. PLA airborne units also have conducted exercises with Army helicopter regiments and with the regiment of transport helicopters in the PLAAF. To date, however, these exercises have been in China and forces have not deployed outside the country.

Air Defense: Antiaircraft Artillery and Surface-to-Air Missile Units

The PLAAF's historical emphasis on air defense relied on very strict ground control and followed Soviet tactical air doctrine.[66] The aircraft employed in air defenses were controlled from the ground, and all coordination with air defense artillery (ADA) forces was at ground headquarters. As the PLAAF began to make use of beyond-visual-range radars in aircraft and AWACS aircraft, its fighters could be freed from strict ground direction and control. However, the PLAAF still has extensive ground-based air defense forces.[67]

Under PLAAF control there are three surface-to-air missile divisions, two divisions of combined SAM and ADA units, nine SAM brigades, two mixed SAM/ADA brigades, two ADA brigades, the equivalent of ten independent SAM regiments, and an independent ADA brigade.[68] In all, the PLAAF has over nine hundred SAMs and sixteen thousand air defense artillery guns. But that is not all the PLA has in terms of air defenses. In the PLA reserves there are seventeen air defense divisions, eight air defense brigades, and eight more air defense regiments around China, employing another 290 surface-to-air missiles and over 7,700 air defense guns.[69] The PLA Army, the ground forces, have another twenty-two or so air defense brigades. There is a lot of coast and border to protect, plus strategic areas and infrastructure around the country, and the PLAAF is not alone in providing a formidable air defense.

Space as a Component of Aerospace Operations

Chapter 7 deals specifically with space warfare programs in the PLA. An examination of a number of writings by PLA military theorists, however, makes it clear that the air and space domains of war are seen as integrated. Airpower deployments depend on space-based surveillance and communications, as well as geospatial navigation and timing systems (e.g., GPS). PLAAF major general Cai Fengzhen believes that "control of portions of outer space is a natural extension of other forms of territorial control," such as air control.[70] In the book *The Aerospace Battlefield and China's Air Force* (*Kongtian Zhanchang yu Zhongguo Kongjun*), Cai and his coauthor

Tian Anping do not distinguish between air raids or surprise attacks on surface targets (on the ground or at sea) from aircraft or, when space-based ground-attack systems evolve, from space. All are just "surface attacks."[71] Further, PLA authors argue that "it is in space that information age warfare will come to its more intensive points. Future war must combine information, firepower, and mobility."[72]

PLAAF Shortfalls, the United States, and the Asia-Pacific Region

The deployment of Su-27 fighter aircraft to Turkey in 2010 and the use of civil and military transports for the evacuation of Chinese citizens from Libya in 2011 show that the PLAAF is starting to "go global." One must keep in mind that in evaluating its response to the 2008 Sichuan earthquake. The commander of the Guangzhou Military Region air force, who was responsible for moving a lot of the initial forces deployed then, said that airpower projection is still the weakest part of China's strategic power–projection capacity and needs improvement.[73] The large number of fighter aircraft in China's inventory, China's air defenses, and the ability to mass even older generations or aircraft armed with multiple air-to-air missiles, however, can still present quite a challenge to air forces in the Asia-Pacific region. Map 2.2 in chapter 2, showing PLA air defenses and missile ranges, helps to illustrate the challenge facing the United States, Taiwan, and other countries in the region.

There are a number of areas where the PLAAF falls short and needs to improve if it is to manage a global posture. Among these is the capacity of Chinese industry to manufacture military aircraft without depending on foreign suppliers for engines. One authoritative study noted that as civil aircraft production—especially engine manufacturing—improves in China, military aircraft production will likely follow.[74] The PLAAF is still heavily dependent on foreign assistance for its aircraft engines. That may not affect the number of aircraft available at the start of any conflict but would be a major limitation on the PLAAF in a sustained conflict. It also is a factor in engine replacement and repair for aircraft deployed outside the country. Another shortfall is in air-to-air refueling. The PLAAF needs more tankers with greater range.

Across the Taiwan Strait against the ROC Air Force, the PLAAF has a clear advantage in numbers of aircraft, air-to-air missiles, and in fourth-generation fighters. However, on a regional basis, the PLAAF cannot match either the United States or Japan, although certainly it can put more aircraft into the air. Also, as the distances away from the Chinese mainland increase, the PLA cannot sustain air combat, patrol, or reconnaissance without more tankers for air-to-air refueling.

When Chinese leaders travel internationally, they sometimes use military aircraft. This means that some pilots are familiar with the international norms of moving through another nation's airspace and landing for refueling or maintenance. In terms of force projection and sustainment, although the PLA managed participation in Anatolian Eagle with refueling across Iran and Pakistan into Turkey, the PLAAF still has not really deployed significant airpower at a distance for a sustained period of time. The Defense Department's annual report to Congress on China in 2011 noted the limitations in extended operational reach for the PLAAF.[75] Many of the milestones increasing PLAAF operational reach already have been discussed in this chapter. However, the DOD also noted that PLAAF B-6 bombers had conducted long-range bombing missions in Kazakhstan as part of a regional exercise.

In space the PLA already has global reach. It has the capacity to down satellites, jam satellites, and interfere with global command and control as well as surveillance. However, the PLAAF has a way to go before it is able to achieve the global posture some of its military strategists would like to see.

The PLA Navy was the priority service for strategic development and investment for about a decade, along with the Second Artillery. Over the next decade, it is likely that the PLA Air Force will get a higher priority and more funds.

5 Modernized Ground Forces, Doctrine, and Missions

When the PLA was founded in 1927, it consisted solely of ground forces and had no armor and very limited artillery. Thirty thousand Communists and disaffected, Communist-led elements of the Republic of China's Nationalist Army began an insurrection to take over the Nanchang Arsenal.[1] That insurrection and subsequent uprisings failed, but the PLA established itself in a revolutionary base area in Jiangxi until about 1934. At that time, in the strategic withdrawal and relocation known as the Long March, the PLA moved its forces through southern and western China to a new base area in Yan'an, Shaanxi Province, arriving there in 1935.[2]

By 1937, Japanese troops were firmly in control of Manchuria. On July 7, Japanese troops conducting night maneuvers south of Beijing clashed with Nationalist Army forces. This precipitated a Japanese reaction. From 1937 to 1940, Japanese forces went on the offensive and consolidated their hold on China, attacking both Communist and Nationalist forces, while the Nationalists withdrew to the area around Chongqing and to southwestern China. In August 1940, PLA forces launched a major effort, the Hundred Regiments Campaign, in central China against the Japanese as a way to relieve Japanese pressure on the Nationalists.[3] However, disagreements about areas of responsibility between Communist and Nationalist forces led to a major clash in January 1941, with Nationalist forces killing approximately three thousand PLA troops.[4] Throughout the war against Japan (1937–1945), the PLA operated out of its Yan'an base area with units distributed around China, primarily as guerrilla forces.[5]

After the defeat of Japan, the PLA began to build strength and had made the transition from a dispersed force into major land forces able to conduct maneuver warfare with combined arms and services. What the PLA lacked in armor, artillery, engineering equipment, and transport during World War II, it supplemented by capturing large amounts of weapons and equipment. In 1946 and 1947, in the Sungari River and Siping Offensive campaigns, the PLA started by relying on its more traditional guerrilla tactics and mobile warfare to secure parts of northeastern China. When at the end of each of these campaigns Nationalist forces were captured or surrendered, along with them came a great deal of arms and matériel.

After the PLA secured the cities of Siping and Changchun, they controlled the major road and rail corridors in central Manchuria. To secure the rest of Manchuria, the PLA Central Military Commission decided to kick off the strategic offensive of the Liaoning-Shenyang (Liao-Shen) Campaign of September 12 through November 2, 1948. In fact, by the end of the second phase of the campaign, Communist forces had captured over thirty-eight thousand prisoners, one hundred and fifty artillery pieces, twenty-two tanks, six thousand horses, and six hundred vehicles.[6]

The next objective was to bring under Communist control the entire geographic corridor of northeastern China from the point where Hebei Province meets the Bohai Gulf (on the Yellow Sea at the eastern end of the Great Wall) northward. This would effectively give the Communists control of the heartland of the heavy industries of China and petroleum production in an area adjacent to their ally, the Soviet Union.

After securing the area around Beijing and Tianjin, the PLA shifted its weight south to destroy Nationalist forces in the Yangtze River area (called the Changjiang in Chinese). The PLA carried out the Huai-Hai Campaign between November 6, 1948, and January 10, 1949, securing the area around Shanghai, Nanjing, and Xuzhou. Nationalist forces from that point on were on the defensive and ultimately withdrew from mainland China to Taiwan.

On October 1, 1949, the People's Republic of China was established, with a capital in Beijing. PLA forces still were actively consolidating control over outlying areas. Between October 18 and 19, 1950, however, PLA forces moved at night as Chinese People's Volunteers across the Yalu River, in reaction to the successes of U.S. and United Nations forces in the Korean War. In Korea the PLA conducted a series of five major campaigns between 1950 and 1952, with bitter fighting taking place. On June 4, 1953, the Chinese and North Koreans agreed to UN truce proposals, and fighting on the peninsula ended.[7]

The 1962 border war with India was a major victory for the PLA and also showed that the Army could deploy forces rapidly around China.[8] The PLA also demonstrated its focus on defending China's sovereignty in the border clash with the Soviet Union in 1969, risking potential escalation and nuclear conflict when it challenged Soviet forces over border disputes.[9] Despite all the assistance China gave to North Vietnam during its war with the south and the United States, on February 17, 1979, the PLA conducted a punitive attack on Vietnam.[10]

The PLA used between five hundred thousand and six hundred thousand troops in the attack on Vietnam, depending on which figures you accept. The Vietnamese claim to have lost around twenty thousand men in the fighting, and the PLA, according to Vietnamese estimates, suffered twenty-five thousand killed in action and another seventy-five thousand casualties.[11] Chinese claims are that the Vietnamese forces had fifty thousand total casualties, while the PLA only suffered twenty thousand.[12] Regardless of the discrepancies, the PLA came out of the conflict bloodied and with problems that needed to be addressed. PLA leaders reduced the number of units in the PLA, streamlined their organization, and improved command and control.[13] The PLA also changed its exercise and training programs, and made significant improvements to its logistics system.[14]

PLA Ground Forces and the "PLA Army"

The term "People's Liberation Army" refers collectively to all the military forces in China, active and reserve. Traditionally, to make special reference to land or "army" forces, one mentioned "PLA ground forces." In its recent white papers on national defense, however, China's State Council Information Office has called the ground forces "the PLA Army," or PLAA.[15]

The PLAA is composed of a numbers of branches or arms and support units. These include:

- Infantry (motorized, mechanized, mountain, and amphibious)
- Armor
- Artillery
- Air defense (antiaircraft missiles as well as artillery)
- Engineer and bridging units
- Aviation forces (mostly helicopter)
- Chemical defense units
- Communications units
- Electronic warfare and electronic countermeasures units
- Logistics organizations that handle food, fuel, medical support, supplies, transportation, and repairs
- Armaments units that handle equipment storage, ammunition storage, and large-scale repairs[16]

At the time that the PLAA conducted its thirty-day invasion of Vietnam in 1979, it had thirty-six "armies," or corps-size maneuver elements. During the 1980s the structure of the PLAA evolved, and the number of large maneuver elements was reduced. These PLAA units are structured in group armies (*jituan jun*), which control various divisions, brigades, regiments, and smaller military organizations. A group army is roughly analogous to a U.S. Army corps (between twenty-five thousand and forty thousand people). It is an organization that generally combines some elements of the arms, support units, and services described above: infantry, armor, artillery, air defense, aviation, engineering, chemical defense, and communications.[17] With its headquarters, it can be expanded by attaching other forces, or a GA can detach elements to augment other organizations.

There are other specialized units in the PLAA as well, including technical reconnaissance (signals intelligence and electronic warfare), electronic countermeasures, reconnaissance, and mapping units. These specialized organizations are generally subordinate to a military region or are directly subordinate to the General Staff Department.

The PLAA had eighteen group armies in 2012. They are the direct descendants of the numbered army corps system that the PLA maintained from 1955 to 1985.[18] As discussed above, some of the lessons taken from the 1979 experience with Vietnam led the PLA to reduce its size and change its structure. For decades the PLA ground forces were made up of "armies," still about corps-size units, but a restructuring and reduction in size in 1988 resulted in the creation of twenty-four GAs. Further reduction and reorganization brought the number down to eighteen (plus the Fifteenth Airborne Army, a PLAAF organization).

To review the structure of a group army, introduced in chapter 1, each GA has two to three infantry divisions or brigades along with armored, artillery, and antiaircraft artillery divisions or brigades. GAs also contain an engineer regiment, and combat support units such as communications, chemical, and reconnaissance forces. Some military regions also have independent divisions, brigades, or regiment-size units. GAs have twenty-five thousand to forty thousand personnel.[19]

Regiments and brigades generally have "integrated elements from more than one arm, such as infantry, armor, antiaircraft artillery, engineer, chemical defense and logistics," forming one large unit. A regiment may have a thousand to twenty-five hundred personnel, depending on the type of unit. For example, engineer, artillery, or armor brigades may have fewer personnel because they have a higher level of mechanization. Brigades are larger than regiments and may contain regiments or smaller, battalion-size units. A brigade generally has between two thousand and six thousand personnel.[20]

Below the regimental or brigade level, PLA ground forces are formed into battalions of two hundred to seven hundred officers and men. Each battalion has three to five companies, each with one hundred to one hundred and fifty personnel. Company commanders, usually a captain (and political commissar), exercise their command through platoons of roughly forty personnel. Platoons are led by a lieutenant who is responsible for their readiness, training, and equipment maintenance. Each platoon has several squads of ten to twelve personnel, depending on the type of unit. An armored platoon, for example, generally has three or four tanks, and the tank crews are the squads.[21]

The exact size and composition of a group army varies around China, depending on the primary mission that it is expected to accomplish and the geographic orientation of the MR to which it is assigned. All GAs, however, and the entire PLA, have the basic mission of suppressing any domestic unrest, maintaining domestic security, and keeping the Chinese Communist Party in power.

The three group armies in the Shenyang Military Region in Manchuria, along the border with Russia and North Korea—the Sixteenth, the Thirty-Ninth, and the Fortieth—all have an armored division and mechanized infantry and/or motorized infantry forces. The artillery also tends to emphasize self-propelled artillery units. The Thirty-Ninth GA has its own aviation regiment. This terrain is highly suitable for armor operations and has an extensive network of rail and road communication.

The Beijing Military Region, to the south and southwest, has similar terrain and communications features. In the Beijing MR, the Twenty-Seventh, Thirty-Eighth, and Sixty-Fifth GAs also have armored brigades or divisions and mechanized infantry brigades or divisions. Both the Thirty-Eighth and Sixty-Fifth GAs

Table 5.1   Approximate Size of PLA Army Ground Force Units

Unit Type	Division	Brigade	Regiment	Battalion
Infantry	10,000–12,000	5,000–6,000	2,800	700
Armor	10,000	2,000	1,200	175
Artillery	5,000–6,000	2,200	1,100	275
AAA	5,000	2,000	1,100	250
Airborne (PLAAF)	8,000–9,000	5,000–6,000	2,300	700

Sources: Defense Intelligence Agency, *Handbook of the Chinese People's Liberation Army* (Washington, DC: Defense Intelligence Agency, 1984), and Dennis J. Blasko, *The Chinese Army Today: Tradition and Transformation in the 21st Century* (New York: Routledge, 2006).

have aviation regiments. This is a politically sensitive area, however, because going back to the 1960s the Thirty-Eighth has also acted as a "protector" of the capital from civil unrest. Also, because Beijing and Tianjin are large, separate municipalities, each city has its own garrison command roughly the size of a GA.

Moving further south and east, the Jinan MR has the Twentieth, Twenty-Sixth, and Fifty-Fourth GAs. Jinan is a strategically important region that can rapidly reinforce northward to the Shenyang MR, westward to the Beijing MR, or southward to the Nanjing MR. The Twentieth and Fifty-Fourth GAs each have an armored division, but the Fifty-Fourth has two mechanized infantry divisions and is considered a rapid reaction unit, while the Twenty-Sixth has three motorized infantry brigades. In addition to their artillery and aid defense organizations, the Twenty-Sixth and Fifty-Fourth GAs have aviation regiments. The Twentieth GA, a lighter, smaller organization, has an armored brigade, a mechanized infantry brigade, and a motorized infantry brigade.

The Lanzhou Military Region covers all of northwestern China out to Xinjiang Province and the borders with Kazakhstan, Pakistan, and Afghanistan. The Twenty-

Map 5.1   Group Army Locations and Military Regions

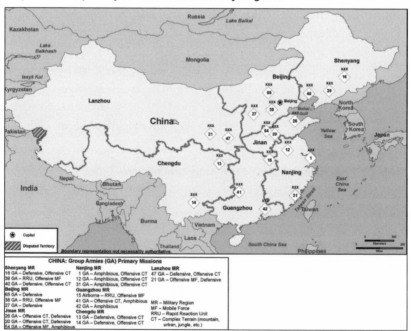

Source: Office of the Secretary of Defense, *Annual Report to Congress: Military and Security Developments Involving the People's Republic of China, 2011* (Washington, DC: Department of Defense, 2011), 73.

First GA and the Forty-Seventh GA are the major maneuver units. The Twenty-First has an armored division, a motorized infantry division, and artillery and air defense brigades, plus a regiment of engineers. In the Xinjiang Military district, in consideration of its mountainous and desert terrain and the long distances, there is an additional high-altitude-trained mechanized infantry division, two independent mechanized infantry brigades, three high-altitude motorized infantry divisions, an aviation regiment, and the normal complement of air defense and engineers.

The Nanjing Military Region, on the coast opposite Taiwan, is a particularly sensitive and critical area. Some of its units are trained and equipped for amphibious warfare. Also, it has the short-range, surface-to-surface ballistic missile systems targeted against Taiwan. The First Group Army has an amphibious mechanized infantry division and an artillery division, an armored brigade, a motorized infantry brigade, an air defense brigade, and aviation and engineer regiments. It is designed to get across the Taiwan Strait. The Twelfth GA has an armored division, three motorized infantry divisions, artillery and air defense brigades, and an engineer regiment. The Thirty-First GA, like the First GA, is configured for warfare against Taiwan. It has an amphibious armored brigade, two motorized infantry divisions, a motorized infantry brigade, an artillery brigade, an air defense brigade, and its own aviation regiment. Subordinate to the MR headquarters, there is a special operations unit and a brigade of missiles from the Second Artillery.

The Guangzhou Military Region, in China's southeast, also has responsibility for Taiwan and the Taiwan Strait. In addition, its area of responsibility includes the border with Vietnam; the South China Sea and Gulf of Tonkin, with all of China's territorial claims; Hainan Island; Macao; and Hong Kong. Like the Nanjing MR, the Guangzhou MR has a number of amphibious forces. The Forty-First GA has an armored brigade, a mechanized infantry division, a motorized infantry division, artillery and air defense brigades, and an engineer regiment. The Forty-Second GA has an amphibious mechanized infantry division, an armored brigade, a motorized infantry division, an artillery division, an air defense brigade, and an aviation brigade. There are more specialized units directly subordinate to the MR headquarters: a special forces unit, a motorized infantry brigade, a composite motorized infantry brigade stationed in Hong Kong, an air defense brigade, an electronic warfare brigade, and a missile brigade.

The Chengdu Military Region is responsible for southwestern China, including Tibet and the Indian border, as well as part of the border with Vietnam. The Thirteenth GA is tailored for high-altitude operations with an armored brigade, a mechanized infantry division trained to operate at high altitudes, a motorized infantry division, artillery and air defense brigades, and both engineer and aviation regiments. The Fourteenth GA is tailored for jungle operations; it has an armored brigade, a motorized infantry division trained for jungle operations, another motorized infantry division, and artillery and air defense brigades. Subordinate to the MR headquarters are a special forces unit, a mechanized infantry brigade trained for high-altitude operations, two mountain infantry brigades, and an electronic warfare regiment.

Regardless of size, organization, and structure, however, during its entire history the PLA was often configured by the Communist Party leadership and military authorities to meet specific national security needs. It was and is the military instrument of foreign and domestic policy. The operational concepts it follows also are set by the Central Military Commission and the senior party leadership. These operational concepts have adjusted over time and inform the operations of all of the PLA, not just the Army.[22]

PLAA Operational Concepts

Based on combat experience in the campaigns against Japan and Nationalist forces, Mao Zedong wrote in detail about the conduct of "wars of annihilation" against opposing forces. The Nationalists tried on successive occasions to encircle and destroy Communist forces before the war against Japan. Then during the war with Japan, Mao had to wrestle with ways to get dispersed guerrilla forces to concentrate at the right time and place. Mao's view was that a war (or battle) of annihilation (*jianmie zhan*) was the proper tactic for the PLA, and this is the doctrine that the PLAA follows. This war of annihilation "entails the concentration of superior forces and the adoption of encircling or outflanking tactics" to destroy enemy forces at a specific and critical point on the battlefield.[23] He believed that battles and campaigns of annihilation were decisive and had a greater impact than simply "routing the enemy" and letting him retreat. As an example of why this is so, Mao said "injuring all of a man's ten fingers is not as effective as chopping off one, and routing ten enemy divisions [which could fight again elsewhere] was not as effective as annihilating one of them." This thinking still informs PLAA doctrine and therefore is worth noting.

Taking this philosophy and putting it into doctrine to be followed across the PLA, Mao set out the broad operational principles for the decisive phase of combat he envisioned after 1948 with the following ten principles of operations:

1. Attack dispersed isolated enemy forces first; attack concentrated, strong enemy forces later.[24]

2. Take small and medium cities and extensive rural areas first; take big cities later.

3. Make wiping out the enemy's effective strength our main objective; do not make holding or seizing a city or place our main objective. Holding or seizing a city or place is the outcome of wiping out the enemy's effective strength, and often a city or place can be held or seized for good only after it has changed hands a number of times.

4. In every battle, concentrate an absolutely superior force (even five or six times the enemy's strength); encircle the enemy forces completely, strive to wipe them out thoroughly and do not let any escape from the net. In special circumstances use the method of dealing crushing blows to the enemy, that is, concentrate all our strength to make a frontal attack and also attack one or both flanks, with the aim of wiping out one part and routing another so that our army can swiftly move its troops and smash other enemy forces. Strive to avoid battles of attrition in which we lose more than we gain or only break even. In this way, although we are inferior as a whole (in terms of numbers) we are absolutely superior in every part and every specific campaign. . . . As time goes on, we shall become superior as a whole and eventually wipe out all the enemy.

5. Fight no battle unprepared, fight no battle you are not sure of winning; make every effort to be well prepared for each battle, make every effort to ensure victory in the given set of conditions as between the enemy and ourselves.

6. Give full play to our style of fighting—courage in battle, no fear of sacrifice, no fear of fatigue, and continuous fighting (that is fighting successive battles in a short time without rest).

7. Strive to wipe out the enemy through mobile warfare. At the same time, pay attention to the tactics of positional attack and capture enemy fortified points and cities.

8. With regard to attacking cities, resolutely seize all enemy fortified points and cities which are weakly defended. Seize at opportune moments all enemy fortified points and cities defended with moderate strength, provided circumstances permit. As for strongly defended enemy fortified points and cities, wait till conditions are ripe and then take them.

9. Replenish our strength with all the arms and most of the personnel cap-

tured from the enemy. Our army's main sources of manpower and matériel are at the front.

10. Make good use of the intervals between campaigns to rest, train and consolidate our troops. Periods of rest, training and consolidation should in general not be very long; permit the enemy no breathing space.[25]

These general principles served the PLA well and have informed the way that the ground forces approached combat for decades. And they are based to some extent on China's ancient strategies of war. The table below compares Mao's operational principles to concepts in Sunzi's *The Art of War*.[26]

Table 5.2   Mao Zedong and Sunzi Compared

Modern military writing and strategy in China echoes many basic concepts from the ancient Chinese classics. From the time he began to think and write on military matters, Mao Zedong studied classical Chinese military history, theory, and even the classical novels of military action in China. In his own works, Mao often cited the lessons of the classics. To highlight the influence of classical concepts on modern Chinese strategy and the continuity in Chinese military thought, the ten operational principles Mao used to guide the Huai-Hai campaign are compared below to the relevant passages in Sunzi's *The Art of War.*

Mao Zedong: Operational Principles	Sunzi: The Art of War
1. Attack dispersed isolated enemy forces first; attack concentrated, strong enemy forces later.	I, 21. When he concentrates, prepare against him; where he is strong, avoid him.
	III, 12. When ten to the enemy's one, surround him;
	III, 13. When five times his strength, attack him.
	III, 14. If double his strength, divide him.
	VI, 15. For if he prepares to the front, his rear will be weak; and if to the rear, his front will be fragile . . . and when he prepares everywhere he will be weak everywhere.
2. Take small and medium cities and extensive rural areas first; take big cities later.	III, 7. The worst policy is to attack cities. Attack cities only when there is no alternative.
	VIII, 7. There are some roads not to follow; some troops not to strike; some cities not to assault; and some ground which should not be contested.

(continued)

Mao Zedong: Operational Principles	Sunzi: The Art of War
3. Make wiping out the enemy's effective strength our main objective; do not make holding or seizing a city or place our main objective. Holding or seizing a city or place is the outcome of wiping out the enemy's effective strength, and often a city or place can be held or seized for good only after it has changed hands a number of times.	II, 3. Victory is the main object in war. If this is long delayed, weapons are blunted and morale depressed. When troops attack cities their strength will be exhausted. III, 7. The worst policy is to attack cities. Attack cities only when there is no alternative.
4. In every battle, concentrate an absolutely superior force (. . . even five or six times the enemy's strength); encircle the enemy forces completely, strive to wipe them out thoroughly and do not let any escape from the net. In special circumstances use the method of dealing crushing blows to the enemy, that is, concentrate all our strength to make a frontal attack and also attack one or both flanks, with the aim of wiping out one part and routing another so that our army can swiftly move its troops and smash other enemy forces. Strive to avoid battles of attrition in which we lose more than we gain or only break even. In this way, although we are inferior as a whole (in terms of numbers) we are absolutely superior in every part and every specific campaign. . . . As time goes on, we shall become superior as a whole and eventually wipe out all the enemy.	VI, 13. If I am able to determine the enemy's dispositions while at the same time I can conceal my own, then I can concentrate and he must divide. And if I concentrate when he divides, I can use my entire strength to attack a fraction of his. Therefore, I will be numerically superior. III, 12. When ten to the enemy's one, surround him. III, 13. When five times his strength, attack him. III, 14. If double his strength, divide him. V, 13. When torrential water tosses boulders, it is because of its momentum. V, 14. When the strike of a hawk breaks the body of its prey, it is because of timing. V, 15. Thus the momentum of one skilled in war is overwhelming and his attack is precisely regulated. V, 16. His potential is that of a fully drawn crossbow; his timing, the release of the trigger. VI, 7. To be certain to take what you attack is to attack a place the enemy does not protect.
5. Fight no battle unprepared, fight no battle you are not sure of winning; make every effort to be well prepared for each battle, make every effort to ensure victory in the given set of conditions as between the enemy and ourselves.	X, 26. Know the enemy, know yourself; your victory will never be endangered. Know the ground, know the weather; your victory will then be total.

(continued)

Mao Zedong: Operational Principles	Sunzi: The Art of War
6. Give full play to our style of fighting—courage in battle, no fear of sacrifice, no fear of fatigue, and continuous fighting (that is fighting successive battles in a short time without rest).	I, 17. All warfare is based on deception. I, 18. Therefore, when capable, feign incapacity; when active, inactivity. I, 21. When he concentrates, prepare against him; where he is strong, avoid him. I, 24. Keep him under a strain and wear him down. I, 25. When he is united, divide him. I, 26. Attack where he is unprepared, sally out when he does not expect you.
7. Strive to wipe out the enemy through mobile warfare. At the same time, pay attention to the tactics of positional attack and capture enemy fortified points and cities.	II, 3. Victory is the main object in war. If this is long delayed, weapons are blunted and morale depressed. II, 4. When the army engages in protracted campaigns the resources of the state will not suffice. V, 14. When the strike of a hawk breaks the body of its prey, it is because of timing. V, 15. Thus the momentum of one skilled in war is overwhelming and his attack is precisely regulated.
8. With regard to attacking cities, resolutely seize all enemy fortified points and cities which are weakly defended. Seize at opportune moments all enemy fortified points and cities defended with moderate strength, provided circumstances permit. As for strongly defended enemy fortified points and cities, wait till conditions are ripe and then take them.	III, 7. The worst policy is to attack cities. Attack cities only when there is no alternative. VIII, 7. There are some roads not to follow; some troops not to strike; some cities not to assault; and some ground which should not be contested. XI, 57. Concentrate your forces against the enemy and from a distance of a thousand *li* you can kill his general. . . . VI, 13. If I am able to determine the enemy's dispositions while at the same time I can conceal my own, then I can concentrate and he must divide. And if I concentrate while he divides, I can use my entire strength to attack a fraction of his. Therefore, I will be numerically superior. Then, if I am able to use many to strike few at the selected point, those I deal with will be in dire straits.

(continued)

Mao Zedong: Operational Principles	Sunzi: The Art of War
9. Replenish our strength with all the arms and most of the personnel captured from the enemy. Our army's main sources of manpower and matériel are at the front.	XI, 32. Pay heed to nourishing the troops; do not unnecessarily fatigue them. Unite them in spirit, conserve their strength.
	II, 15. Hence the wise general sees to it that his troops feed on the enemy, for one bushel of the enemy's provisions is the equivalent to twenty of his; one hundredweight of enemy fodder to twenty hundredweight of his.
	II, 19. Treat the captives well and care for them.
	III, 2. To capture the enemy's army is better than to destroy it; to take intact a company, battalion or squad is better than to destroy them.
10. Make good use of the intervals between campaigns to rest, train and consolidate our troops. Periods of rest, training and consolidation should in general not be very long; permit the enemy no breathing space	VII, 13. When campaigning, be swift as the wind; in leisurely march, majestic as the forest; in raiding and plundering, like fire; in standing, firm as the mountains.
	VII, 15. He wearies them [the enemy] by keeping them constantly occupied, and makes them rush about by offering them ostensible advantages.

Note: The Roman numerals in the Sunzi translation refer to the chapters in the Griffith translation; the Arabic numerals indicate the passage in the Griffith translation.

Sources: Mao Tse-tung, "The Present Situation and Our Tasks," *Selected Works of Mao Tse-tung*, vol. 5 (Peking: Foreign Languages Press, 1975), and Samuel B. Griffith III, trans., *Sun Tzu: The Art of War* (London: Oxford University Press, 1963).

Ancient Chinese Strategy, Mao's Principles, and Modern PLA Doctrine

The PLA approaches military operations through a formalized, unified body of operational concepts that are approved by the Central Military Commission of the Chinese Communist Party.[27] These operational concepts have roots in classical Chinese military thinking from strategists such as Sunzi and Sun Bin, and they also draw on descriptions of ancient battles and tactics in historical novels.[28] Layered over the ancient traditional thought are lessons the PLA learned from its own history, its own major wars, and from observing other armies at war.

Among the key principles taken from ancient Chinese thought are the use of deception, the importance of surprise in war, and the use of a combination of military, economic, and political means to achieve victory.[29] Certain principles of war may be immutable, but the PLA places special emphasis on discipline, deception, surprise, mass (of fires and forces), flexibility, offense, and maneuver.[30]

One can find a similar blend of ancient military thought and twentieth-century military strategy in an essay by Mao on "Problems of Strategy in Guerilla War against Japan."[31] In that 1938 essay, he discusses how to use district guerrilla forces and Communist Army main forces against a coordinated attack by the Japanese. Mao advises relieving the pressure on the main force's interior lines of communications by using small detachments of guerrilla forces to attack the enemy's exterior lines of communication. Mao refers to this as "relieving the state of Zhao by besieging the state of Wei (*wei wei jiu zhao*),"[32] a classic strategy taken from Sun Bin, referring to "a classic move in Chinese literature and military strategy" of marching on the enemy's capital (or base area) to force the opponent to disengage from an attack.[33] In this reference, Mao Zedong takes an example from the 353 B.C. siege of Hantan, the capital of what was then the state of Zhao, a story that comes from the *Records of the Historian* (*Shi Ji*).[34]

Today the PLAA's doctrine and strategies, operational art, and tactics are captured in a series of volumes published by the main academies of military higher education in China, the Academy of Military Science and the PLA National Defense University.

These publications guide the PLAA, but are equally applicable across the other arms and services of the PLA. In *The Science of Military Strategy* (*Zhan Lue Xue*), *The Science of Military Campaigns* (*Zhanyi Xue*), and *The Science of Military Tactics* (*Zhan Shu Xue*), Chinese military thinkers set out their operational principles, from the highest levels of warfare down to the way that small units should operate on the battlefield.[35] These doctrinal publications blend what has been passed down in ancient texts and stories with what the PLA learned in its own operational experience and what it observed in contemporary foreign military operations.

Summary of Contemporary PLAA Operational Concepts[36]

For the twenty-first century, the PLAA has updated its operational concepts to incorporate joint operations, the application of airpower and missiles along with ground forces, and lessons learned from contemporary conflicts. Such concepts as "shock and awe," employed in Iraq and the Balkans conflict, as well as the rapid maneuver warfare employed against Iraq in Operation Desert Storm in 1991, have informed contemporary Chinese operational concepts, summarized as follows:

- *Avoid Direct Confrontation*: If faced with a superior adversary, such as the United States, develop operational doctrine and combat capabilities that allow the PLA to exploit the adversary's vulnerabilities. This is often called "asymmetrical warfare."
- *Seize the Initiative Early:* Do not allow an enemy to deliver a first, decisive blow. Use an "active defense" (offensive action). This argues for the importance of acting first and capturing an enemy by surprise. The concept is particularly important to cyber and electronic warfare, space operations, and China's antiaccess/area-denial strategy.
- *Use Surprise*: Strike at an unexpected time in an unexpected place to seize the initiative in a conflict. Disguise one's intent. Use camouflage, deception, feint, or stratagem, or take advantage of bad weather.
- *Emphasize Preemptive Strikes*: Aggressive actions buy battlespace and time; preemptive strikes (*xianji zhidi* or *xian fa zhi ren*) may help prevent the absorption of heavy damage early in a conflict. Preemptive action also reduces political costs in a conflict. Strike as the enemy masses his forces or before the enemy can launch a devastating strike. Judge the most effective time and place to initiate action. This concept applies especially to naval, air, cyber, and space warfare.
- *Wait for the Enemy to Strike First*: This clearly conflicts with the concept of preemptive strikes. Classical military theory in China emphasizes "striking only after the enemy has struck" (*hou fa zhi ren*), and that concept is formally China's nuclear doctrine. The PLA has been creative in interpreting this operational concept. Often China's military actions are couched as "self-defensive counterattacks," which justifies preemptive action by making it appear to be defensive.
- *Use Soft and Hard Strikes*: Combine information warfare (including cyber operations and electronic warfare, as well as psychological and information operations) with concentrated firepower strikes. This concept meshes well with the approach to integrated network electronic warfare (INEW) described in chapter 8.
- *Emphasize Asymmetrical Strikes*: Avoid symmetrical conflict with a strong power. Take advantage of an opponent's weaknesses.
- *Strike the Enemy's Center of Gravity*: The most critical center of gravity is the support system for an enemy's forces, especially if the enemy is fighting from extended, exterior lines. Strike an enemy's support bases, fuel dumps, ammunition depots, repair facilities, and embarkation areas.

Disrupt highways, railways, bridges, military-industrial complexes, energy centers, power installations, and communications. Putting this operational concept into action means that the PLA must strike into its enemy's critical infrastructure and logistics planning systems.

- *Use Trump Card Weapons*: In a beyond-the-horizon attack, use weapons and asymmetrical operations that attack the enemy's greatest weaknesses. These may be supersonic cruise missiles, submarines, ballistic missiles, antisatellite systems, China's newly developed antiship ballistic missile with its maneuvering warhead, or computer network attacks.

- *Focused Attacks*: Mass forces and fires (i.e., concentrate a high degree of accuracy and lethality) against the main direction of attack. Achieve strategic objectives in the shortest possible time. Another term for this concept is "concentrated strikes." This concept is as applicable to the PLA Army as it is for naval forces or air forces, which can "swarm" large number of small ships or combat aircraft against targets and focus many air-to-air or antiship missiles or torpedoes against critical targets.

- *Sustain the Fight*: Have an integrated support system. Ensure that the military can be kept in active battle across long distances and for lengthy periods.

- *Achieve Information Superiority*: Maintain one's own ability to communicate command and control while cutting off the enemy's ability to use information to influence the battlefield. Exercise this capability at the critical time.

- *Combine the Offense and the Defense to Seize the Initiative*: Active offensive operations must seize and maintain the initiative. At the same time, defensive actions protect one's own strategic points and areas.

- *Integrate Operations*: Fight a joint (multiarm and -service), integrated (all arms and services working in an integral system) campaign. Integrate operations across the domains of war (land, maritime, air, space, and electromagnetic, including cyberspace); use reserves and militia.

- *Key Point Strikes (Attacks)*: Paralyze the enemy first, then annihilate the enemy with crippling, degrading key point attacks (*zhong dian da ji*). Use the top troops and most effective weapons to establish superiority over an opponent. Emphasize firepower, mobility, and lethality or destructiveness.

- *Raise the Cost of Conflict for the Adversary*: Establish information control and combine negotiation and combat to compel a superior enemy to pull out of a conflict. Inflict sufficient casualties and costs on the enemy to cause the enemy's populace to question the conflict.[37]

Undoubtedly, these operational concepts will continue to be refined. They are exercised in China on a regular basis and in a variety of conditions, including under simulated cyber and electronic attacks. They are aggressive military concepts that apply to all arms and services of the PLA, even if the leadership of China's military remains heavily army-dominated. They are war-fighting concepts, however, that depend on the ability to reach out and actively engage an enemy over long distances—even in the enemy's homeland.

The PLAA and Force Projection

Inside China and on its periphery, the PLAA is an effective, lethal force that can be mobilized quickly, reinforced with local forces and reserves, and rapidly deployed in large numbers. However, it is also the service that has been the slowest to modernize, and it has exhibited the slowest speed of adopting information-age electronics systems. Because the PLAA is most likely to face armies on its periphery, the speed with which it can mobilize, its ability to mass forces, and the sheer number of forces available mean that the PLAA is the predominant land force in the region.

In terms of training, the PLAA is now conducting regular force-on-force training that is less scripted than in the past. This sort of training improves the capacity of leaders to think independently and to react quickly to changing battlefield situations. The PLAA has exercised with Russian forces in the Shenyang and Lanzhou Military Regions, affording senior commanders and unit leaders a chance to see how other forces conduct operations and approach combat.

As for mobilization and movement inside China the PLAA does well. Even in 1979, in about a thirty-day period, the PLA moved twenty divisions to the Vietnamese border with two air divisions and six to eight divisions to the Russian border with one air division. During the buildup around Beijing before the Tiananmen Square massacre, the PLAA mobilized twelve divisions and moved them into assembly areas around the capital in about three weeks.

The PLAA has the capacity to take control of and use for its support civil rail, aircraft, road systems, and transport for national security reasons during mobilization.[38] It did so in response to the disastrous flooding around China in 1998 and the 2008 Sichuan earthquake, and it does that today during major exercises. Moreover, when the PLAA moves large forces by rail, air, or road, it often diverts all civilian traffic. All of this can move military forces rapidly inside China and is important for disaster mitigation, dealing with incidents of civil unrest, and positioning mass forces against an enemy on China's immediate periphery. This capacity would threaten Taiwan should China decide to use force there. However, for the United States, unless there is another war on the Korean Peninsula, it is not very likely that American and Chinese ground forces will be in a fight in the near future.

The PLAA's weakness is still its capacity to project decisive force over long distances away from its borders. PLA planners and strategists may envy what the British did in the Falkland Islands, but Chinese forces lack the required airlift, amphibious ship and landing craft capacity, and logistics support to conduct an operation on that scale. If the PLAA continues to develop at its current pace, it still will be some time—perhaps a decade—before it can conduct forced insertions in the face of hostile forces at distances away from China on the scale of France, Great Britain, Australia, or even Russia. Its infantry forces are mechanized, they are supported by strong firepower, and they are highly mobile inside China and along its periphery. If China is to extend its reach beyond its borders with ground forces in the next ten years or so, it is the countries on China's borders that have the most to be concerned about. In the contested islands and archipelagos in the South and East China Seas, the PLA has the capacity to reinforce those claims with its amphibious army forces, with marines, and with special forces units. If a contingency develops in Korea, the PLAA response could be massive.

6 Strategic Rocket Forces, Nuclear Doctrine, and Deterrence

China has maintained some form of nuclear deterrent since it demonstrated its nuclear capability in 1964. Over the decades since, China's nuclear forces have evolved from depending on gravity bombs to a sophisticated arsenal of ballistic missiles of various ranges. The newest missiles are road-mobile or rail-mobile, making it harder for any adversary to target China's relatively small nuclear force, and they have solid-fuel engines, making them faster and easier to launch (and harder to detect) than the older, cumbersome liquid-fueled missiles. And the current systems are more accurate, with satellite guidance. China's nuclear force now has missiles with multiple warheads and penetration aids to circumvent any adversary's missile defenses.[1]

Yet, despite the modernization and improvement of China's nuclear forces, they remain relatively small in comparison to the arsenals of Russia and the United States. In that sense, Chinese leaders have been content with maintaining a "minimal deterrent capability": they want enough missiles to ensure that they can make a retaliatory "second strike" at any adversary that attacks them first.

Still, there is some controversy over the size of China's nuclear force. The U.S. Defense Department maintains that China has approximately fifty-five to sixty-five intercontinental ballistic missiles (ICBMs) and about two hundred nuclear warheads, while estimates from Taiwan and the International Institute of Strategic Studies are as much as two times higher.[2] The former chief of staff of Russia's strategic missile forces Col. Gen. Viktor Esin estimates that China may have as many as sixteen hundred to eighteen hundred warheads and bombs, about half of which are active and the other half held in reserve.[3] The differences in the estimates of the size of China's arsenal are significant because they affect U.S. deterrent policy, decisions on ballistic missile defense, and arms control discussions, especially with Russia.

For decades very limited information has been available on China's strategic deterrent. Today China's academic community, its scientific researchers, think tanks, and military thinkers are publishing a wealth of information about the People's Liberation Army's Second Artillery Force, their strategic missile force.[4] According to the 2010 white paper on China's National Defense, "The PLA Second Artillery Force (PLASAF)[5] strives to push forward its modernization and improves its capabilities in rapid reaction, penetration, precision strike, damage infliction, protection, and survivability. . . . Through the years, the PLASAF has grown into a strategic force equipped with both nuclear and conventional missiles."[6]

Table 6.1   PLA Ballistic Missile Forces

The International Institute for Strategic Studies and U.S. Department of Defense at times use the abbreviations in parentheses for these missiles: DF-4 (CSS-3), DF-31 (CSS-9), DF-31A (CSS-9 Mod 2), DF-41 (CSS-X-10), JL-2 (CSS-NX-4), DF-3A (CSS-2), DF-21 series (CSS-5), DF-15 (CSS-6), DF-11 (CSS-7). The ballistic missile range map used in this chapter is from the U.S. Department of Defense and uses the CSS designations.

Class of Missile	Range (Kilometers)	Number
Intercontinental Ballistic		
Dongfeng-4 (transportable)	5,400	10–15
Dongfeng-5A (silo)	13,000	20
Dongfeng-31 (road-mobile)	7,200	15+
Dongfeng-31A (road-mobile)	11,200	24+
Dongfeng-41 (road or rail)	14,000	Under development, MIRV
JL-2 (submarine-launched)	7,200	Under development
Intermediate-Range Ballistic		
Dongfeng-3A	2,800	5–10
Medium-Range Ballistic		
Dongfeng-21/21A	ca. 1,700	80
Dongfeng-21C	ca. 1,700	36
Dongfeng-21D (Anti-ship)	ca. 1,800	6
Short-Range Ballistic		
Dongfeng-15	450–550	100+ launchers
Dongfeng-11	185–370	100+ launchers
Land-Attack Cruise		
Donghai-10	2,000–4,000	50–250 (various estimates)

Sources: International Institute for Strategic Studies, *The Military Balance 2012* (London: Routledge, 2012); Office of the Secretary of Defense, *Annual Report to Congress: Military and Security Developments Involving the People's Republic of China, 2011* (Washington, DC: Department of Defense, 2011); and Kim Noedskov, *The Return of China: The Long March to Power* (Copenhagen: Royal Danish Defence College, 2009).

A number of doctrinal publications by the PLA provide insights into why China's leaders and military thinkers see the United States as the most serious potential threat.[7] Compared to China's nuclear forces, the U.S. has more nuclear warheads and delivery systems, better developed missile defenses, and has used nuclear weapons in war. Xue Xinglin's *A Guide to the Study of Campaign Theory* (*Zhanyi Lilun Xuexi Zhinan*), a doctrinal text for PLA institutions of higher military education, is very informative on the Second Artillery.[8] This book is an unclassified "study guide" for PLA officers on how to understand and apply in warfare the campaign doctrine presented in the PLA book *The Science of Campaigns* (*Zhanyi Xue*).[9] These materials also discuss the relationships they see between conventional missile units and nuclear ballistic missile units in war-fighting doctrine. The materials have explicit discussions of how to use missiles to attack deployed United States naval forces. There are also important discussions of how the control of space relates to China's nuclear deterrence (see chapter 7 for more on this topic). In addition, there is information about frontal and national-level command and control of missile units. Moreover, the materials provide insights into the evolving debate in China between civilian strategic thinkers and military leaders on the viability of China's official policy that it will not initiate a nuclear attack, but will only retaliate if first attacked with nuclear weapons (*hou fa zhi ren*).

China's no-first-use policy means that it will only use nuclear weapons if struck first. Among China's academic community, younger PLA authors and strategists, and the older generation of PLA leaders, there is a simmering debate about whether such a policy is viable in an age of precision mass-effects conventional weapons.[10] In *The Science of Second Artillery Campaigns*, however, the policy is more ambiguous; this book says that "under our predetermined nuclear guidelines, in general cases (*tongchang shi*) China would retaliate only after being hit first."[11] But the reader is not given any hint as to what special cases may lead China to decide on a first strike. This chapter explores way that the PLA's concept of "active defense" and the concepts of operations in chapter 5 relate to nuclear doctrine.

The United States as the Greatest Potential Threat

One of the key insights from these documents is that China identifies the United States as its main potential enemy, even if in some materials the references to the United States are indirect. This is an important change in China's strategic literature because in the past Russia (the Soviet Union) was also identified as a major threat to China. Now the United States stands alone. One reason for this change is that senior PLA leaders and military strategists consider it to have the most advanced military force on which to base their own military development. They also see the United States as the most advanced and likely potential enemy against which they may need to employ ballistic and cruise missiles or counter advanced command, control communications, computers, intelligence, surveillance, and reconnaissance (C⁴ISR) technologies.

According to the monthly Hong Kong magazine *Contend* (*Cheng Ming*), after a large-scale Second Artillery exercise, vice chairman of the Central Military Commission Gen. Guo Boxiong addressed the exercise participants to discuss what posture the PLA should maintain toward the United States. General Guo told them that "China must strive to increase the capabilities of its strategic nuclear weapons if it wants to stand firm against the United States, which routinely treats China as an enemy in its strategic planning."[12] Even if such explicit language from a senior official has not been used more recently, other Chinese strategists make it clear that the United States is seen as China's most likely enemy. Yan Xuetong, dean of modern intenational relations at Beijing's Qinghua University, noted in a *New York Times* opinion piece that China and the United States do not trust each other and remain cautious because of a fear of nuclear war.[13] Yan, who spent decades working for China's Ministry of State Security, sees the United States as "a typical hegemon . . . presenting norms as the principle for dealing with friends, but power politics as the principle for dealing with its enemies."[14]

As discussed earlier, many in the PLA think that given the relative military power of the United States, it could use that power to coerce or dominate China. Also, believing that few other countries have the ability to threaten China's pursuit of its own vital interests makes PLA officers wary of the United States. In addition, PLA strategists' belief that the United States is likely to come to Taiwan's assistance in the event of Chinese aggression in the Taiwan Strait magnifies the threat that PLA officers perceive. As noted in chapter 3, furthermore, as U.S. diplomats have reminded China and other claimants to the disputed Senkaku Islands, the United States sees any use of force against Japan over the Senkakus as falling under article 5 of the U.S.-Japan mutual defense treaty. This perceived threat drives the PLA to be prepared to counter American forces.

Over the past two decades, authors at the PLA National Defense University have singled out the United States as the world's greatest political, military, and economic power, and the only such power that can act on a global scale. An assessment of the U.S. nuclear posture in the post–Cold War period said: "The goal of America's new military strategy after the collapse of the Soviet Union is to maintain the U.S. position as a world superpower and maintain America's position as a world leader. The maintenance of a strong nuclear deterrent . . . is an important tool for the U.S."[15] Maj. Gen. Wang Baocun of the Academy of Military Science summarized the view of the United States this way:

> The new military transformation has led to the rise of a United States possessed of overwhelmingly dominant military might. The United States is also an arrogant country with strong ambitions for hegemonism. The United States will take advantage of its absolute superiority in supreme military might in order to pursue power politics and hegemonism, seek to maintain its position as the world's only superpower, and slow down the process of mulitpolarization for the world's strategic structure.[16]

Gen. Zhang Wannian has argued that "modern limited warfare under high technology conditions is conducted under a shadow of becoming a nuclear war [*he sheng hua yinying*] and this shadow of nuclear war will limit the scope of warfare."[17] Zhang suggests that the "forces of hegemony in the world"—a common Chinese reference to the United States—"will use nuclear weapons to dominate other nations," thus China must have nuclear capabilities. Zhang also suggests that China's nuclear weapons can be used to "deter moves to split the sovereign state," a reference to Taiwan. Finally, Zhang notes that the conduct of "bloody actual combat" (during conventional war) is, in itself, a deterrent measure because when a nation engages in destructive combat it increases the likelihood of effective deterrence.[18]

The view that the United States has greater potential than other nations to threaten China is also a central thesis in the book *Thinking about Military Strategy* (*Junshi Zhanlue Siwei*), by one of the most respected PLA strategists and leaders, Lt. Gen. Li Jijun.[19] Li concludes that the major problem facing China is "large countries" that create "threat theories, including the countries that espouse the 'China threat theory.'"[20] Li says "like England in the Napoleonic age, the U.S. is the world's strongest power; the United States has the greatest number of international interests and 'colonial' relationships; U.S. military power is dispersed widely throughout the world; the wide range of interests and military deployments mean that U.S. forces are over-committed and stretched thin; and there is a great need to work with allies and coalition partners to achieve security goals."[21]

China's white paper on national defense of December 29, 2006, also warns "the United States is accelerating its realignment of military deployment to enhance its military capability in the Asia-Pacific region." It further expresses concern that "the United States and Japan are strengthening their military alliance in pursuit of operational integration," while Japan's military posture is "becoming more external-oriented."[22] The 2010 white paper on national defense, published in March 2011, expresses concern that "international competition remains fierce," Asia-Pacific security is "intricate and volatile," and the United States is "reinforcing its regional military alliances, and increasing its involvement in regional security affairs."[23]

Guided Missiles in Conventional War Campaigns

New doctrine for the employment of missiles in warfare emphasizes the value of strategic missiles as a form of offset attack, particularly in China's military strategy of the active defense. This concept holds that warfare is a "holistic entity that includes offensive as well as defensive action."[24] Formal discussions of active defense in party publications emphasize that the "first principle is to gain the advantage by striking only after the enemy has struck."[25] This active defense strategy was reinforced at the 2012 Party Congress, and party strategists see it as a major tool for countering threats to China.[26] However, some Chinese military officers and civilian strategists argue that, practically speaking, if an enemy force appears to be preparing for imminent military action, the concept of active defense permits preemptive attacks.[27]

The doctrine in *A Guide to the Study of Campaign Theory* gives specific guidance for the conduct of conventional guided-missile campaigns.[28] According to this text, conventional Second Artillery Force units in a theater of war are subordinate to the headquarters of the "conventional guided missile campaign army group" (*di er paobing changgui daodan zhanyijijtuan*).[29] The army group must be "continuously prepared for a rapid response," which indicates a series of prepared war plans are maintained within the conventional force. The doctrine for conventional guided-missile forces calls for the use of a "small amount of force as a deterrent against attack.[30]

The targets suggested for conventional guided-missile campaigns are designed to achieve battlefield effects that will destroy an enemy's ability to wage war effectively. These targets would disrupt the enemy's economy and reconstitution and resupply capabilities:

- Major enemy military bases and depots
- Enemy command centers
- Enemy communications and transportation networks
- Major troop concentrations[31]

The Second Artillery Conventional Guided Missile Campaign Army Group, like its nuclear counterpart, operates under the direct leadership of the Central Military Commission. However, conventional battlefield missiles are assigned to military regions or theaters of war and operate under the control of the MR or theater commander.[32] At some Second Artillery Force bases, conventional missile brigades are co-located with nuclear missile brigades; and, in some cases, missile units are equipped with both nuclear and conventional warheads.[33] What is left unclear in the doctrinal explanations on conventional missile forces is the level of freedom of action given to theater commanders. The doctrine clearly indicates that an officer from the PLASAF is assigned to the MR or theater command post; however, it does not list whether the MR or theater commander can incorporate conventional missile strikes in his war plans on his own initiative or whether he must go back to the CMC or the PLASAF commander and obtain permission to use the missiles.

Moreover, the doctrine concerning conventional guided missile campaigns is not clear whether if war plan annexes approved by the General Staff Department include conventional missile strikes, the theater commander can launch the missiles without checking again with higher headquarters. Further, the doctrinal publications do not tell us whether a theater of war commander may initiate the use of conventional ballistic missiles on targets outside of China's borders. Exercises to date have given the commander the authority to use the missiles on exercises inside China. But one can envision a contingency, such as on the Sino-Indian border, where the theater commander may want to augment artillery fire with conventional ballistic missiles.[34] Doing so could seriously increase the possibility of escalation. Thus the CMC might insist on being questioned before such use.

There are regular references to the need to "mass fires" (*jijong huoli*) using these missiles against critical targets. This is consistent with twenty-first century PLA operational principles. Gen. Zhang Wannian reminds the PLA in one text "from the standpoint of firepower, air bombardment, artillery, and guided missiles must be massed for the greatest long range destructive and killing effect."[35] Xin Qin makes the same point several times in his book *Information Age Warfare*. He emphasizes that "to ensure a decisive attack against a target, guided missiles [ballistic or cruise missiles] must be massed against their objective."[36] He asserts that if used effectively, conventional ballistic missiles can "win a war without employing one's own troops in direct combat if their offensive fires are concentrated effectively."[37]

Illustrating how these lessons affect military thought today, Xin argues in *Information Age Warfare* that Iraqi missile forces failed by not gathering the necessary intelligence of American and allied assembly areas, and they compounded that failure by not taking the initiative to attack them.[38] He believes that if Iraq had massed its "guided missile strength against the weaker coalition forces before they left training and assembly areas, they could have destroyed them before they moved into combat formations and attack positions."[39]

This doctrine on the employment of concentrated ballistic missile fires clearly informs the PLA's strategy against Taiwan. The PLA has deployed approximately fourteen hundred DF-11 and DF-15 missiles against the island.[40] The PLA also has developed new classes of land-attack cruise missiles for use against Taiwan.[41]

Massing fires to gain the maximum effect from conventional missiles has been the consistent view in the PLA for over a decade. In *Guided Missile Combat in High Technology Wars*, the authors point out that "the combat power of missiles is very high, but they must be used on enemy troop concentrations, important bases or facilities, or other command and control nerve centers in a *sudden attack by concentrated fires* [author's emphasis]."[42] They note that "Iraq fired 81 *Scud* missiles but failed to produce serious casualties or to affect battlefield operations in a significant war. Therefore, Iraq failed to take advantage of either the killing power of missiles or their psychological effect on operations." The authors summarized their study with the lesson that "missiles must be massed on critical targets, must be accurate" to be effective in war.[43]

With respect to Japan, PLA planners think that because of U.S. bases and forces there, and because Japan has maritime and air self-defense forces of its own, Chinese missile force planners must maintain enough of an arsenal, with missiles of adequate range, to hold those bases and forces at risk. To do this, the PLA has fielded a series of road-mobile, solid-fuel missiles with a range of about seventeen hundred kilometers, the DF-21.[44] If Beijing's military planners hold true to their own doctrine, the United States and Japan will probably see an expansion of the numbers of DF-21s that can target Japan, especially as missile defenses develop. China is developing a DF-25 medium-range ballistic missile (MRBM) with multiple warheads, may be developing a DF-16 MRBM to supplement its shorter-range missiles, and apparently has extended the range of the DF-21.[45]

Attacking Deployed Carrier Battle Groups

The PLA is close to achieving a goal of being able to attack a deployed U.S. Navy aircraft carrier battle group with ballistic missiles. Gen. Chen Bingde, PLA chief of the General Staff, in 2011 confirmed that the Dongfeng-21D antiship ballistic missile "is still undergoing experimental testing" but that the PLA still needs advanced technologies and personnel to fully develop the system."[46] Once deployed, Chen said, the missile will have a range of twenty-seven kilometers. It is not clear, however, if the intent is to use conventional warheads on the missile or to conduct a nuclear attack. Nor is it clear whether, in the event of a nuclear attack, the carrier battle group would be targeted directly or if a high-altitude burst would be used to ensure that only electromagnetic pulse effects are felt, destroying command, control, and sensor systems, and clearing the way for a conventional attack.

With respect to cyber- and electronic warfare, one Academy of Military Science researcher expressed the view that to engage in modern war, the PLA must be able to "attack the enemy's knowledge systems [*renshi tixi*] and such high value targets as communications, carrier battle groups, and aviation warfare units."[47] According to an officer from the Navy Command Academy who addressed a PLA-wide conference on missile warfare, "the Second Artillery is the major factor in successfully attacking an enemy naval battle group."[48] To accomplish such an attack, this officer said that "the PLA must use all of its electronic warfare and reconnaissance assets properly, must neutralize enemy anti-missile systems and missile sensor systems, and should use electronic jamming on the enemy fleet. The PLA can then attack the enemy fleet or naval bases with a combination of explosive, anti-radiation and fake warheads to deceive enemy radar and sensor systems and defeat a deployed battle group or one in port."[49]

In 2011, Adm. Robert F. Willard, who then commanded all U.S. forces in the Pacific, said that China probably has what the United States would call an "initial operational capability" for the DF-21D but that it would probably be several years before the missile was fully operational.[50] For a military force such as the PLA, without a naval air arm with a long reach, with a very limited aerial refueling capability, and with older air platforms, using ballistic missiles for this purpose makes sense. Three PLA officers from the Second Artillery Command Academy have advanced the idea that "guided missile forces are the trump card [*sa shou jian*] in achieving victory in limited high technology war."[51] The keys to achieving such capabilities, in the argument of other PLA officers, lie in three areas: the use of countermeasures, the ability to achieve precision targeting, and the use of space platforms to support the effort.[52] One thing is certain: the United States already modified some of its operational concepts to account for the DF-21D's capabilities, as noted in chapter 3.

China's missile force has changed significantly in the past decade, adding new missiles and modifying designs. Designations for the missiles can be confusing, as

China has published more about its own missile force; reference volumes now use China's designations (Dongfeng, or DF) for the CSS designations that Western countries once used for Chinese missiles. Map 6.1, originally published by the U.S. Department of Defense, adds to the confusion by mixing the designators. To explain the missiles on the map: The CSS-4, or DF-5, is an intercontinental ballistic missile (ICBM) that carries a three-megaton nuclear warhead. The JL-2 (CSS-NX-4) is a submarine-launched, intercontinental ballistic missile that can carry a single or multiple conventional or nuclear warheads. The missile is based on the DF-31 design. The DF-31 (CSS-9) and DF-31A (CSS-9 Mod) also are ICBMs; the DF-31 can carry a one-megaton nuclear warhead and the modified DF-31A can carry three nuclear warheads in independent reentry vehicles (MIRV) of between twenty kilotons and one hundred fifty kilotons. The CSS-3 (DF-4) is an intermediate range ballistic missile (IRBM) that carries a three-megaton nuclear warhead. The CSS-2 is the medium range DF-3A ballistic missile and can carry a conventional or nuclear warhead. The CSS-5 is the DF-21, medium range missile and can carry a nuclear or conventional warhead.[53]

Map 6.1   Strategic Ballistic Missile Ranges

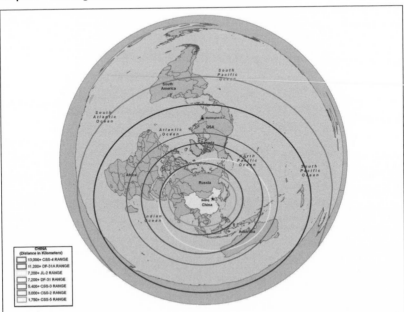

Source: Office of the Secretary of Defense, *Annual Report to Congress: Military and Security Developments Involving the People's Republic of China, 2011* (Washington, DC: Department of Defense, 2011).

Nuclear Counterattack Campaigns

Long-standing published military doctrine, statements by senior leaders, and force preservation measures undertaken by the PLA all support the conclusion that the Second Artillery's strategic mission is principally to be a deterrent and retaliatory force. The accounts in military press and journals of tunneling by the Second Artillery's engineers, as well as its command-and-control measures, all reinforce this conclusion.[54]

There are still several large and unanswered questions, however, about whether China would adhere to its declared doctrine. First, would the PLA execute a preemptive nuclear counterattack if it believed an adversary were about to attack China? One part of the PLA doctrine says: "Advance warning may come to the Second Artillery before an attack if there is notice that the enemy may use nuclear weapons on any scale."[55] This implies that the PLA might order a launch to preempt an enemy surprise attack.[56] Such a preemptive attack is consistent with the concept of the active defense, which permits sudden, surprise attacks on enemy territory and self-defensive counterattacks.[57] Moreover, as China achieves improved levels of sophistication in space surveillance, tracking, and relay, will judgments about the propriety of "preemptive nuclear counterattack" change?

Taken together, these considerations undermine the strength of China's no-first-use guarantees. Even the language in the 2006 national defense white paper is somewhat ambiguous. It declares "China remains firmly committed to the policy of no first use of nuclear weapons at any time and under any circumstances." However, the next sentence tells the reader "it unconditionally undertakes a pledge not to use or threaten to use nuclear weapons against non-nuclear weapon states or nuclear-weapon-free zones. . . ." One does not need to be an international lawyer or grammarian to understand that being "firmly committed to a policy" is not as strong a position as "unconditionally undertaking a pledge." And as discussed earlier in this chapter, *The Science of Second Artillery Campaigns* further qualifies this declaration by saying that "in general cases" China adheres to a no-first-use policy (see note 11).

The Second Artillery has three main missions: deterrence, support of conventional war with ballistic missile attacks, and nuclear counterattack.[58] With regard to strategic systems, the PLA focus is "executing nuclear counterattack campaigns."[59] The PLA's plans for nuclear counterattack campaigns are to "deter and prevent the enemy from using nuclear weapons against China" or to "execute a counterattack with nuclear and precision conventional weapons."[60] The PLA's published doctrine, as well as statements by members of the leadership, emphasize that

China intends to maintain a survivable nuclear force that can ride out any nuclear attack wait underground or in tunnels, and then emerge, deploy, and inflict a nuclear counterattack on the enemy.[61]

At the strategic level, Xue's *A Guide to the Study of Campaign Theory* lays out the characteristics of a nuclear counterattack campaign. The Second Artillery would use long-range nuclear weapons to destroy strategic targets several thousands of kilometers away. Campaign planners envision carrying out a nuclear attack "only after the enemy carries out a nuclear surprise attack" requiring a force that can absorb and survive an enemy nuclear attack.[62] The existing nuclear counterattack campaign plans involve missile units of the Second Artillery, supplemented by forces of the PLA Navy and/or PLA Air Force. Moreover, now that the PLA has developed longer-range, nuclear-capable cruise missiles, these campaign plans call for the Navy to use submarine-launched ballistic or cruise missiles.[63] The PLAAF could attack with nuclear cruise missiles or bombs.

In planning nuclear counterattack campaigns, the PLA gives primacy to the Second Artillery. According to Xue, PLA doctrine says that "if it is a joint or combined nuclear counterattack campaign plan, the Second Artillery will be the main component combined with naval nuclear submarines and air bombardment with nuclear weapons."[64]

China's nuclear retaliatory plans require that the Second Artillery maintain a force sufficient to "threaten the opponent by striking his cities" and employ a strike force of "moderate intensity" that is "sufficient and effective" to cause the enemy to incur "a certain extent of unbearable destruction."[65] Thus the size and composition of any nuclear counterattack is a function of a nuclear net assessment by Chinese political and military leaders. It is a function of what they assess as the level of damage the American public, and its leaders, would find unbearable.

The objectives for nuclear campaign planning are also ambiguous enough to leave open the question of preemptive action by the PLA. A major objective of a nuclear counterattack campaign is to "alter enemy intentions by causing the enemy's will [to engage in war] to waver."[66] Preemption, therefore, would be a viable action that is consistent with the PLA's history of "self-defensive counterattacks."[67]

The prioritized objectives of nuclear counterattack campaigns are as follows:

Cause the will of the enemy (and the populace) to waver;
Destroy the enemy's command-and-control system;[68]
Delay the enemy's war (or combat) operations;

Reduce the enemy's force-generation and war-making potential;
Degrade the enemy's ability to win a nuclear war.[69]

To do this, the PLA intends to target and destroy enemy political and economic centers, especially important urban areas, with a goal of creating great shock in the enemy population's spirit and destroying their will to wage war; the critical infrastructure of the enemy to weaken the enemy's capacity for war (for example petroleum refining, storage and shipping links; electric power generation and transmission lines, major heavy industry, and transportation networks); major military targets such as air force and navy staging areas and bases to degrade the ability of these services to wage war; and major deployed military forces.[70]

The PLA has outlined far more than a minimal or limited counterstrike. Instead, if these descriptions of Chinese strategy are accurate, it would escalate any nuclear exchange.

Survive a Nuclear Attack—Then Retaliate

The guiding motto for the Second Artillery is "strictly protect counterattack capability and concentrate [nuclear] fires to inflict the most damage in the counterattack" (*yanmi fanghu, zhongdian fanji*).[71] Guidelines for readiness of missile forces emphasize that the Second Artillery's strategic warning system is closely tied to the General Staff Department and that the Second Artillery must continually keep up an estimate of whether the enemy will use other forms of weapons of mass destruction.[72]

According to members of a Chinese delegation at a 2005 strategic dialogue organized by the U.S. Defense Threat Reduction Agency, the goals of China's nuclear policy are to maintain a retaliatory force of minimum deterrent value and to hold enemy populations at risk.[73] China seeks to ensure that it has a reliable force with adequate delivery systems that can survive a foreign attack and maintains a "counter-value force" that requires modernization.[74]

Moreover, the force is under strict central control by the Central Military Commission.[75] Second Artillery command orders are centralized, encoded, and protected, and require human authentication, ensuring tight control by political leaders.[76] PLA military writers completely eschew automated command-and-control systems. There is a very strong emphasis on the need for a "man in the loop" even in modern, information age warfare. One writer specializing in command-and-control issues makes the point that "no matter how advanced a computer is used in a command-and-control system, it will never substitute for the strength and utility of the human brain."[77]

To maintain the force at high levels of readiness, strategic missile force commanders gather intelligence, maintain a system for indications and warning of attack, and focus on force survivability.

Classes of Readiness for the Second Artillery

According to *A Guide to the Study of Campaign Theory,* the Second Artillery must "continually focus on discovering the enemy's attempts at attack, its times of attack, and must always conduct defensive exercises and preparations."[78] PLA doctrine requires that the Second Artillery "operate and coordinate with air, ground and other defensive organizations under the direction of the CMC to implement a nuclear counterattack campaign."[79]

The Second Artillery has a system of three classes of readiness to which its units must adhere. Under normal conditions, the firing units are at "third class" status. In this status, forces train, conduct exercises, and conduct normal maintenance. If the CMC receives some warning that the enemy may use nuclear weapons, it directs units to raise their readiness levels to "second class" readiness status. At this status, units must prepare to move to firing positions or may actually deploy to firing positions, many of which can be in tunnels or prepared, protected underground positions. The highest readiness status is "first class warning." Here missile forces are fully ready to fire and are either deployed or in combat positions and with their support elements, warheads, and fuel, waiting for a launch order.[80]

When firing units actually move to firing positions, the individual unit commanders are responsible for the security of their own prime movers and must conduct a check of the firing status of each missile and the warheads. They must report this status to the headquarters.[81] After firing their missiles, they would disperse and get the results of a postfiring reconnaissance and new intelligence.[82]

Combat orders must come through special command department channels of the Second Artillery or General Staff Department, but only the CMC can send a launch order.[83] The combat order would give the current friendly and enemy situation, the status of the war and a determination on the use of nuclear force, the combat objectives for an attack, and the limits of an attack. The actual firing order would contain the time limits for each unit to fire and instructions for postfiring movement and disposition.[84]

Support for Survivability and Retaliatory Strike

The concept of a "guaranteed survivability and strike" is fundamental to PLA Second Artillery doctrine. This means that strategic rocket forces must be able to ride out a nuclear attack and emerge later to conduct their counterstrike. To accomplish this, the Second Artillery maintains its own support infrastructure, including maintenance, supply and food services, engineers, and road and rail transport.

In a 2005 Second Artillery nuclear war simulation exercise reported by China's *Xinhua* news service, China stayed with its no-first-use policy and absorbed a nuclear strike. After the strike, the exercise scenario required that the Second Artillery Force stay in protected underground areas for as long as several days before emerging to conduct a retaliatory "nuclear counterattack."[85] Survivability seems to be the focus of most of the capital investment in Second Artillery infrastructure. Col. Gen. Viktor Esin reports the "construction of an elaborate series of underground tunnels by military builders . . . that may contain mobile missile launchers . . . as well as nuclear munitions storage facilities."[86]

An article in *Rocket Soldiers Daily* (*Huojianbing Bao*), the Second Artillery's newspaper, provides insight into the tactic of absorbing a strike, waiting a fixed period of time, and then emerging for a "nuclear counterstrike." According to two Second Artillery authors, a 2004 nuclear counterattack exercise had to be stopped in its third day because the troops involved developed vomiting and diarrhea from a spoiled food supply.[87] The Second Artillery's logistics department improved the safety of the food supply in future exercises and allowed soldiers to conduct the exercises under "sealed" conditions, ensuring food supply was refrigerated and shielded from contamination. This assured that the Second Artillery could remain underground long enough to emerge safely and conduct a retaliatory strike.

In addition to the PLA Second Artillery Force's engineering and construction units for tunneling and construction of roads, a transportation support infrastructure is integral to the organization. Colonel General Esin, in a meeting in Virginia in 2012, suggested that some of the specialized rail construction to support the Second Artillery may also be designed to be the rail system for a whole new class of mobile ballistic missiles that can carry ten warheads.[88] This may mean that what many U.S. newspapers have reported as the road-mobile Dongfeng-41 (DF-41) ICBM may be rail-transportable.[89] A 2005 article in the Second Artillery newspaper *Rocket Soldiers Daily* discussed the Second Artillery rail transport system. A mobile system moved what was termed a "national treasure" by a "rail transportation battalion of a special transportation regiment."[90] Another article in the same paper documented the importance of mobile missiles and mobility training. Rapid mobility, it said, is a way to "improve survivability and nuclear counter-deterrence."[91] There also is a continuous program to upgrade and improve missile position design inside the Second Artillery. The objectives of this program are to ensure that missile positions are positioned is a way to avoid foreign reconnaissance, take advantage of the geography and environment, and have the maximum possible protection against foreign attack.[92] And the Second Artillery exercises this capability with opposing forces, requiring its troops to contend with attacks by simulated enemy aggressor forces conducting bombing runs, artillery raids, and ambushes on the missile trains.[93]

The objectives of these integrated support systems are to meet the Second Artillery's "guiding principles for nuclear counterattack campaign strategy." To restate these principles, the guiding motto for the Second Artillery is "strictly protect counterattack capability and concentrate [nuclear] fires to inflict the most damage in the counterattack." To protect and preserve the force, the Second Artillery is to defend against the enemy's precision-weapons attack, defend against enemy air raids, defend against enemy special operations forces attacking China's nuclear forces, organize to respond to sudden surprise attacks, and organize to restore China's nuclear war-fighting capability rapidly.[94]

To meet the requirement to "guarantee or safeguard the survivability of the nuclear response system to counterattack," Second Artillery doctrine requires its forces to protect its nuclear campaign plan and to prepare in advance for the campaign, ensure reliability of weapons (that is, making sure they will operate), be prepared to respond quickly, and ensure its counterattack force can survive.[95]

In order to maintain that level of communication throughout the force, command and control for missile forces is highly centralized, redundant, and networked.[96] According to the 2008 China national defense white paper, "the Second Artillery Force is a strategic force under the direct command and control of the CMC, and the core force of China for strategic deterrence."[97]

Two PLA officers writing in the book *Ballistic Missile Combat in High Technology Wars* (*Gao Jishu Zhanzheng Zhong de Daodan Zhan*) describe Second Artillery command and control this way: "The nodes in a ballistic missile command-and-control network are 1) the commander in chief [*tongshuaibu*], 2) the command organizations of the military departments, 3) the missile bases, and 4) the firing units."[98] Furthermore, they say, "especially where it concerns strategic missiles, the ability of the supreme command authority [*tongshuaibu*] to control firing orders must be executed quickly, and firing orders must be encrypted [encoded]."[99] It seems clear that that the chain of command only passes through the GSD, while control resides in the Central Military Commission of the Communist Party and the Politburo Standing Committee as the supreme command authority.[100]

The term *tongshuaibu* can be confusing. In some cases, it is used to designate the commander in chief of a particular force or theater of war. In the case of strategic missile forces, however, the CMC is invariably the *tongshuaibu,* or supreme command authority.

Conclusions

The PLA has evolved from a force that was able to use missiles and nuclear weapons to threaten only nations on China's periphery, such as Russia, India, Taiwan, Japan, and South Korea, to a global force. In the 1980s, the United States was threatened by a handful (four to ten) of China's ICBMs. Today, the U.S. Department of Defense believes the PLA's arsenal has fifty-five to sixty-five ICBMs, and Russian estimates are higher, making the PLA a global nuclear force.[101] A critical factor in the Sino-U.S. nuclear threat equation is the Central Military Commission's calculation that China would be able to absorb nuclear strikes with less catastrophic effects than the United States. This judgment is a function of China's historical military culture, geography, and an intentional state-directed policy of civil defense and risk distribution.[102] For the United States, this means that Chinese leaders may miscalculate American will and mistakenly take risky actions.

Beijing's decision to put nuclear and conventional warheads on the same classes of ballistic missiles and colocate them near each other in firing units of the Second Artillery also increases the risk of accidental nuclear conflict. If a country with good surveillance systems, such as the United States, detects a missile being launched, it has serious choices to make when weapons have been colocated. It can absorb a first strike, see whether it is hit with a nuclear weapon or a conventional one, and retaliate in kind, or it can decide to launch a major strike on warning. If the nation under attack has ballistic missile defenses, it might be able to stop an incoming missile and seek other ways to reduce tensions and avoid a wider war.

Any American decision on the intensity and timing of a nuclear threat would rest on the capabilities of American space-based sensor systems. Accurate sensors may be able to determine whether China has launched a conventional or nuclear-tipped missile, and such a determination could prevent immediate escalation of a crisis or conflict.

However, as chapter 7 on space systems and space control will discuss, some PLA officers advocate the capability for China to ensure that foreign space surveillance assets cannot observe China from space, particularly in times of tension or conflict. Indeed, the PLA has taken actions to demonstrate that it has moved from theoretical research and simulations of space warfare to demonstrating the capability to blind or destroy satellites over China.

The discussion of the need to mass missile fire and use missiles decisively, with surprise, in a theater war also undermines the likelihood that China would adhere to its own declared no-first-use policy in a conflict. These considerations reinforce the need for the United States to have effective ballistic missile defenses.

Perhaps the most serious questions raised in this chapter are about the PLA's concentrated efforts to attack a deployed, moving aircraft carrier battle group. The PLA is coming closer to achieving that capability. The ambiguity over what form any ballistic (or cruise) missile attack might take creates a volatile situation in case of any crisis over Taiwan or between China and Japan. But some PLA officers believe that in any conflict involving Taiwan or contested areas of the South or East China Sea, the United States most likely would intervene, which would result in an attack on U.S. naval forces.[103]

The debate inside China over the viability of its no-first-use policy is real. Older veterans and senior officers of the Foreign Ministry and the PLA insist that the policy stay unchanged. However, younger scholars, soldiers, and diplomats will keep up the pressure to pull back from this policy, which requires continued attention and strategic dialogue with China's policy community.

China is only at the initial stages of developing a real-time global space surveillance capability. Such a capability requires a system of relay satellites, which China may have just achieved.[104] Thus, as China's space surveillance improves over the next decade, its nuclear doctrine will probably evolve.

These are serious matters for the American armed forces. China's nuclear forces are evolving, and the way they are used is under debate. It is also possible that China has between two and three times the number of nuclear missiles and warheads than the United States estimates.[105] The way that the PLA handles its commitment to dominating space and its commitment to being capable of attacking American C[4]ISR systems affects strategic warning, missile defenses, and command and control. For the U.S. military, with the responsibility to defend the United States against missile attack, it means that watching the evolution of this debate in China is critical to success.

7 Space Warfare, Systems, and Space Control

Military operations today depend on access to outer space. Routine military activities such as communication, the exchange of supply data, personnel movements, navigation, the timing of operations, and targeting weapons rely on satellites and routinely pass through satellites. The United States and Russia may be the two earliest space powers, but China caught up quickly.[1] The People's Liberation Army now has an active space program, with a deployed range of communications, positioning, and earth observation satellites, and a strong antisatellite warfare (ASAT) capability.[2]

The Department of Defense, in 2011, commented that "China's space activities and capabilities, including ASAT programs, have significant implications for anti-access/areas denial efforts in Taiwan Strait contingencies and beyond."[3] The Defense Department characterizes space as "congested, contested and competitive."[4] The U.S. government believes that in future conflict, adversaries may attempt to "deny, degrade, deceive, disrupt, or destroy space assets."[5] Many of these concerns focus on China, which has its own active counterspace program.[6] Likewise in China, military thinkers recognize that space warfare must be an integral part of battle planning by the People's Liberation Army in any future conflict. Thus in future military conflict or periods of tension, we must anticipate operations in space.[7] In testimony before the Senate Armed Services Committee, the director of the Defense Intelligence Agency, Lt. Gen. Ronald L. Burgess Jr., said that the "space program, including ostensible civil projects, supports China's growing ability to deny or degrade the space assets of potential adversaries and enhances China's conventional military capabilities."[8]

During the Cold War, the Soviet Union and the United States reached a tacit agreement that in the interest of strategic stability, neither side would interfere with the other's space assets, which were critical to detecting ballistic missile launches and maintaining nuclear stability. However, no such understanding exists with China, a factor that could lead to an unintentional nuclear exchange if one side, particularly the United States with its better space surveillance capabilities, were to perceive that any Chinese action blinding the U.S. capacity to detect nuclear missile launches was a prelude to an attack.

In China one of the major proponents of space power for the PLA, Maj. Gen. Cai Fengzhen, believes that "control of portions of outer space is a natural extension of other forms of territorial control" such as sea or air control.[9] More seriously, because of American superiority in space, China's military theorists treat the United States as the most likely opponent in that domain of war.

Once Chinese leaders made the decision to move into the realm of military space, they moved quickly. By 2010 China had demonstrated the capabilities to kill satellites with kinetic attack by rockets launched from the ground, to "dazzle" observation satellites with laser beams, to jam satellites, and to launch small constellations of microsatellites that could disrupt or degrade enemies' satellites.[10] Two officers from the Academy of Military Sciences made this point in *China Military Science*, emphasizing that offensive and defensive capabilities in space depend on both soft and hard attacks on enemy space systems. Soft attacks include attacks on the information chain supporting the satellites, as well as jamming and deception, and hard attacks mean the destruction of satellites and ground stations.[11]

The Genesis of China's Space Warfare Doctrine

Developing a space warfare doctrine for the People's Liberation Army is not some sui generis phenomenon. Rather, the PLA carefully absorbed and reacted to what the U.S. armed forces have published on space warfare and counterspace operations.[12] The PLA also has studied Soviet-era and contemporary Russian thinking on space operations, using these studies to guide its own evolving doctrine.[13]

China's neighbors are also developing the sort of space warfare capabilities that the United States and the Soviet Union worked on decades ago, providing impetus for the PLA's programs. Former Indian Air Force air chief marshal S. P. Tyagi recently advocated establishing a jointly manned "aerospace command" so that the Indian armed forces could effectively use its missile, satellite, and communications capabilities.[14] Japan has developed reconnaissance satellites, and South Korea is working on its own satellite launch program.

One of the most senior and widely published authors in the Chinese military on aerospace doctrine, Major General Cai, takes most of his terminology and concepts from U.S. military doctrine. He credits the late U.S. Air Force lieutenant general Daniel O. Graham and his book *High Frontier: A New National Strategy* with developing the original concept for conducting military campaigns in outer space, and he traces the idea of expanding one's borders directly into space to Graham and his "high frontier" theory.[15] Cai argues that space control is a natural extension of other forms of territorial control, such as control of territorial waters and the control of a nation's airspace.[16]

High Frontier sought to break away from the nuclear doctrine of Mutually Assured Destruction (MAD) by developing effective space-based missile defenses. Some security literature in China, however, sees missile defenses in space as a way of extending national sovereignty and territorial airspace control into outer space. An article on weapons in space by Huang Zhicheng of the Beijing Systems Engineering College expresses the view that "the United States is trying to build a 'strategic external border' in space" with its ballistic missile defense plans. In Huang's view, "whoever controls the cosmos can control the earth [*shei neng kongzhi yuzhou, shei jiu neng kongzhi diqiu*]," reflecting China's deep uneasiness about U.S. intentions.[17] Liu Jixian, a major general at the Academy of Military Science, had similar views: "Whoever controls the cosmos, controls our world, whoever controls space, controls initiative in war."[18] The idea that control of outer space was key to superiority in military competition is not new. In addressing the situation with the Soviet Union in 1957, then Senate majority leader Lyndon Johnson said, "Control of space means control of the world."[19]

A good deal of the strategic literature coming out of China is a PLA reaction to what its officers observed about U.S. and allied military operations in the Gulf War, the Balkans, Afghanistan, and the Iraq War.[20] In all these cases, joint operations and the control forces were more effective because they relied on U.S. space assets.

The Falklands, or Malvinas, conflict taught the PLA the importance of command and control, the timing of operations, and the importance of power-projection employing coordinated forces.[21] Perhaps the biggest lesson, however, and one that China is applying to its own strategies to deny U.S. forces the ability to approach waters around Taiwan in the event of conflict, is that coordinated naval operations supported by aircraft and submarines are critical to mission success.

Observations from the coalition attacks in Kosovo left the PLA with conflicting lessons. The air campaign showed Chinese military planners the importance of precision bombing and network-centered warfare. Allied operations depended for targeting on GPS satellites and timing, as well as clear imagery.[22] But the PLA also saw that camouflage, smoke, deception, and concealment worked to obscure targets from air and space observation.

America's two wars against Iraq reinforced for the PLA the importance of integrated, networked, high-technology operations coordinated across the military services.[23] PLA strategists took from these conflicts the need to move the PLA into the information age and just how interconnected space was with military operations.

Space Warfare and Other Forms of Military Operations

Military operations in space are now critical components of PLA information age warfare (see chapter 8).[24] Doctrinal publications from the PLA make it clear that any future conflict will include space operations.[25] Because China's military thinkers realize that "future enemy military forces will depend heavily on information systems in military operations," they believe China must develop effective countermeasures to other nations' space systems and operations.[26] Two specialists writing in *China Military Science* argue that "it is in space that information age warfare will come to its more intensive points. . . . Future war must combine information, firepower, and mobility."[27] Another common view in the PLA is that future military threats will primarily come in aerospace and that the dividing line between outer space and the airspace inside the earth's atmosphere will be blurred.[28] In 2009, Gen. Xu Qiliang, PLA Air Force commander, told China's *Xinhua News Agency* that the PLA Air Force would develop integrated capabilities for offensive and defensive operations in space and in the air.[29]

China's strategists suggest that in future wars, space will be used to "carry out war between space platforms and to attack strategic surface and air targets."[30] For this reason, the PLA is especially watchful of American programs such as the X-37B space plane, which one PLA author believes has "combat applications." China's military observers argue that the X-37B has the capability to serve as a reconnaissance platform that can maneuver away from antispace weapons, capture or destroy enemy satellites, or act as a command platform in space.[31] Long before the United States began testing the space plane, however, theorists in the PLA advocated work on laser weapons, particle beam weapons, and other forms of directed energy and electromagnetic systems as elements of a space warfare system.[32] Other PLA organizations are conducting basic and applied research into space-to-ground kinetic weapon systems.[33]

Senior Col. Zhang Zhiwei and Lt. Col. Feng Zhuanjiang of the Nanjing Army Command Academy express the view that "space supremacy" must be an integral part of other forms of supremacy over the battlefield.[34] They see this as a necessary and logical extension of other forms of military conflict, where space is an integrated part of other military operations, and offensive and defensive actions blend together.[35]

Justifying Military Operations in Space

There are significant differences in approach to access and activities in the global commons between China and the United States. As mentioned earlier, by this term we refer to the high seas, international airspace, and outer space. Chapter 9, which deals with information warfare and what the PLA calls the "three warfares," addresses this issue in more detail. For the PLA, "legal warfare" is one of the "three warfares" that fall under the purview of the General Political Department. Chinese legal scholars have taken strong positions on what they think countries may not do in space.

PLA strategists think about the implications of warfare in space, while international law specialists in China are examining ways to establish positions in domestic and international law as a legal basis for military action in space or to limit the freedom of action of other nations there.[36] The U.S. position on activities in space is clear and has been consistent for some time. Deputy Assistant Secretary of State Frank Rose, the head of the Department of State's Bureau of Arms Control, Verification, and Compliance, explained it this way: "A long-standing principle of U.S. national space policy is that all nations have the right to explore and use space for peaceful purposes, and for the benefit of all humanity, in accordance with international law."[37] In the PLA's General Political Department, officers are setting out positions China could use to justify attacks on space bodies, while other scholars and military thinkers deal with the nuances, and limits, of national sovereignty.[38]

Outer space is essentially treated as a "global commons," like the high seas in international law. Therefore, many of the arguments used to justify military action on the seas are applied to potential military action in space. And some of the concerns that Chinese security thinkers apply to military reconnaissance activities in the exclusive economic zone around China or in waters near China are applied to military reconnaissance in space (see chapters 3, 4, and 9).[39]

The PLA is convinced that it is important to set forth legal justifications for military actions in advance of military operations or any potential conflict.[40] While military planners and strategists in the PLA explore future military operations, the General Political Department, in parallel, is developing ways to justify potential military actions in domestic and international law. Such activities are designed to affect both law and international opinion.[41]

Arguments by scholars in China on national sovereignty, sovereignty over the EEZ, and sovereignty in space have a common theme. The foremost concern for China's security thinkers is "sovereignty control," or the ability to define and protect national sovereignty, which for them directly applies to the need for "space control" in modern war. Should any conflict come about in space, in the PLA's view, the concepts and legal arguments set out today by China will provide the outlines of any justification for military action.

Antiaccess Strategies and "Sovereignty Control" in Space

Chapter 1 discussed China's sensitivity about its nineteenth-century history of foreign invasion and the establishment of extraterritorial zones by foreign powers. This is the basis for the PLA's strong national security concerns about sovereignty.[42] As noted earlier, PLA military and legal thinkers see the control of outer space as a natural extension of a nation's control of its territory. PLA officers believe that "space control today is the way to guarantee the control of airspace . . . and is an absolute necessity for conducting modern 'informationalized' warfare."[43]

When satellite images of China's new *Jin*-class submarine appeared on Google Earth in 2007,[44] the revelation sent shock waves through the PLA, although the military had already been thinking about the implications of the open availability of space imaging before this.[45] One PLAAF engineer commented that the threat to China's equipment and installations from high-resolution reconnaissance satellites was more severe than that of Google Earth, and the PLA needed to focus on better camouflage, paints, and screening to avoid detection.[46] The engineer, a member of the PLAAF Logistics Department, noted that "China's traditional 'security vaults' are evolving and remote areas of the country are less secure." He suggested defensive responses to these threats, saying that "the PLA needs better camouflage and concealment to counter imaging from space, and better computer network security to keep secrets."[47] Other Chinese researchers have suggested various means of space-based alarms to warn of imaging, decoys on the ground to confuse imaging satellites, and multispectrum stealth camouflage systems to mask China's activities.[48] Thus a range of defensive measures to respond to imaging and intelligence collection from space are under consideration in China.

Other PLA officers have suggested active, offensive measures to counter foreign surveillance from space. A debate in China focuses on concerns about the freedom of other nations to undertake military activities in, or over, sovereign

Chinese territory.[49] In addition, elements of this debate broaden the interpretation of sovereignty from that normally accepted in international law and practice.[50]

Military thinkers in China also are debating how matters of sovereignty affect warfare in space. One legal scholar, Ren Xiaofeng, summarizes Beijing's sensitivity to reconnaissance and military activities in its EEZ and adjacent airspace this way: "Freedom of navigation and overflight does not include the freedom to conduct military and reconnaissance activities. These things [military reconnaissance activities] amount to forms of military deterrence and intelligence gathering as battlefield preparation." Such reconnaissance activities, according to Ren, connote the preparation to use force against a coastal state, and his concerns in reference to "adjacent airspace" includes outer space and space reconnaissance.[51] Two scholars from the Wuhan Military Engineering College believe that "one advantage of warfare in space is that once in space a nation is free from the restrictions imposed on military operations by international borders; therefore there are no restrictions on operations because of territorial airspace."[52] The national space policy statement promulgated by President George W. Bush on August 31, 2006, takes a different view: "The United States rejects any claims to sovereignty by any nation over outer space or celestial bodies, or any portion thereof, and rejects any limitations on the fundamental right of the United States to operate in and acquire data from outer space."[53]

One study on the legal limits of sovereignty in space notes that "before the Soviet Union launched its *Sputnik* satellite in 1957, Soviet authors insisted that state sovereignty extended to unlimited height," but after *Sputnik* orbited the earth Soviet writings took the position that in orbit in space, *Sputnik* did not violate the airspace of any country.[54] U.S. policy generally favored space as being open. In 1956, Secretary of State John Foster Dulles said that the United States should have the right to send observation balloons at certain altitudes all around the world.[55] President Dwight Eisenhower held the view that communications or reconnaissance satellites were nonaggressive and therefore peaceful uses of space.[56] By the time the United States began launching satellites, however, the Department of Defense and the Air Force were reluctant to take a position on the vertical limits of sovereignty.[57] Because of their own space programs and satellites, both the Soviet Union and the United States avoided defining the upward extent of airspace and each avoided differentiating airspace from outer space.[58] However, some commentators suggested that the end of the atmosphere, about a hundred kilometers, ought to be the ceiling of sovereignty.[59]

Military theorists in China realize that outer space is critical for military operations, including command of the sea.[60] International legal theorists argue that satellites, even those in geosynchronous orbits over another nation's territory, are operating in the global commons and not subject to state sovereignty.[61] The dominant argument in China agrees with this view but reasons that even though outer space is undivided and "the common domain of all mankind, space security is a necessary part of a nation's security and it is necessary to develop defensive mechanisms" over one's territory.[62] Maj. Gen. Cai Fengzhen and his coauthors make the argument in the most detail: "The area above ground, airspace and outer space are inseparable and integrated. They are the 'strategic commanding height of modern informationalized warfare.' . . . The airspace over territorial waters and territorial land are protected, but there is no clear standard in international law as to the altitude to which territorial airspace extends."[63] Cai asks the rhetorical question, "Does sovereignty extend into outer space?" He acknowledges that a debate exists and discusses various interpretations of whether sovereignty extends only to a hundred kilometers above the earth's surface or whether a nation can defend its sovereign airspace overhead up to an altitude of thousands of miles.[64] His bottom line, however, is that a nation can defend itself and seek to control space out as far as its weapons can reach.[65]

There are also strong differences in the positions set forth by Chinese and American strategists and legal scholars on the conduct of reconnaissance. The U.S. position, according to Jerome Morneff writing in *World Peace through Space Law*, is that reconnaissance is a peaceful activity designed to provide some element of self-defense and assess another country's military potential.[66] The concept of reconnaissance as a peacetime activity that is neither aggressive nor threatening is explained regularly to senior Chinese military officials by U.S. diplomats and visiting American military leaders. but the Chinese side routinely dismisses these explanations, arguing that such activity is aggressive.[67]

For some time, the Soviet Union and the United States mutually recognized that the ability to conduct reconnaissance from space provided strategic stability in the Cold War. Their 1972 Anti-Ballistic Missile Treaty provided that "each Party undertakes not to interfere with the national technical means of verification of the other Party operating in" a manner consistent with generally recognized principles of international law.[68]

In Chinese texts, questions of sovereignty in space are treated as analogous to the extension of national sovereignty into the EEZ and are viewed as an inherent right of a nation, like the control of its territorial airspace. Nevertheless, the advocates for "sovereignty control" recognize that they cannot continuously control the passage of space bodies through what they see as their territory. They seek a more limited and temporal ability to control space.[69] In their text on integrated aerospace operations, Cai Fengzhen and his coauthors give perhaps the most complete explanation of how space control relates to the PLA's military theory on outer space operations: "Space control is the capability of one belligerent in a state of war, in a specified period of time, in a defined area of space, to carry out its own operations with freedom while hindering or preventing an enemy from carrying out its own operations or using space."[70]

The most senior PLA Air Force officer who has written authoritatively on the matter of space and China's national security interests is Gen. Zheng Shenxia, then commandant of the Academy of Military Science. Zheng and his political commissar at the time, Lt. Gen. Liu Yuan, accuse the United States of maintaining a "policy of containment" toward China (*meiguo dui hua 'e- zhi' zhanlue*).[71] The two PLA officers argue that to meet this challenge, Beijing must be capable of controlling the electromagnetic spectrum, as well as maintain traditional sovereignty over land territory, the maritime domain, airspace, and space.[72]

The Laws of War and Space

Cai and his colleagues also examine the "legal environment" surrounding the application of the laws of war in space. They believe that many of the concepts surrounding the conduct of war in the airspace above the "common seas" apply in space. They note that just as belligerents have the right to conduct warfare at sea beyond their territorial waters, they should have the right to attack the space bodies (craft or satellites) of belligerents.[73]

In their 2004 book they see no restrictions on defending one's nation in space or protecting the space bodies of allies.[74] They note in their 2006 book that, on common seas, acts of war by belligerents should not interfere with normal commerce for noncombatants, but that a belligerent can make war on commercial ships engaged in supporting the war effort.[75] Therefore, they decide, it is reasonable to apply similar rules in outer space. Two other Chinese scholars argue that in time of conflict, space bodies are vital for the conduct of war; therefore, space bodies of a belligerent nation are valid targets for attack anywhere in the common skies, just as ships of a belligerent can be attacked on the common seas.[76] Furthering these analogies, one scholar has argued that in the event of a conflict, the satellites of third nations can be attacked if they are carrying the military data streams of a belligerent nation.[77]

The Chinese interpretation of the laws of war as they may apply in space is generally consistent with American and other Western legal views.[78] There are serious implications for commerce and international communications here. Should Beijing decide to attack commercial spacecraft because they are carrying military data streams, it would severely affect international commerce, as well as China's own use of space.

Reconnaissance or "Battlefield Preparation"?

As noted earlier, China and the United States deeply disagree about the nature of, and intent behind, the conduct of reconnaissance and surveillance.[79] Objections to aerial and maritime reconnaissance in common seas and airspace by Chinese military leaders are not new.[80] Indeed, the 2001 collision between the U.S. reconnaissance aircraft and pursuing Chinese fighter raised new objections from Beijing over military reconnaissance in the EEZ. Reading these recent legal articles that equate reconnaissance with battlefield preparation puts that incident into perspective. Chinese commentators are extending this thinking into considerations about space reconnaissance.

In an international law journal, one Chinese writer acknowledged the disagreement between the United States and China on the matter, noting that the U.S. position on outer space treats "peaceful use" to mean "nonaggressive," whereas the Chinese interpretation is that to be peaceful use, it must be "nonmilitary."[81] One analyst in China argues that "battlefield situational awareness is the core of information age warfare . . . which means that one must be able to destroy or jam the systems that are fundamental to that situational awareness."[82] Other PLA authors believe that the "intelligence war [*qingbao zhan*]" has to be fought before the start of armed conflict, which includes various means of reconnaissance and information gathering (military, diplomatic, economic, and electronic).[83]

These differences between the United States and other countries on the nature of space are not new. The Soviet Union's students of space law have generally interpreted "peaceful" to mean "nonmilitary." Both Soviet and Chinese scholars have argued that the use of surveillance satellites constitutes an aggressive use of outer space, while the U.S. position remains that such surveillance is a "nonaggressive use" of outer space.[84] Thus we can expect that any future dialogue between the United States and China on these strategic issues will debate the question of the nature of reconnaissance activities. Now that China has a number of its own reconnaissance satellites in continuous orbit, China's position on this matter may evolve.[85]

The PLA Considers Tools of Space Warfare

The PLA is exploring in theoretical research, basic research, and applied research a variety of forms of space weapons.[86] These counterspace programs include:

- Satellite-jamming technology
- Collisions between space bodies
- Kinetic energy weapons
- Space-to-ground attack weapons
- Space planes that can transit and fight "up or down" in the upper atmosphere or space
- High-power laser weapons
- High-power microwave weapon systems
- Particle beam weapons
- Electromagnetic pulse[87]

PLA authors credit the United States with having the most advanced capabilities in the areas of kinetic energy weapons, particle beam weapons, and directed energy in general. However, the PLA excels at various forms of jamming and has done a lot of work on the concept of colliding space bodies.

PLA theorists think that internal lines of communication are most favorable for successful military operations.[88] Thus they see their regional position in Asia as superior to that of the United States because if the United States has to fight there, communications and resupply along extended exterior lines would be difficult, while China would enjoy interior lines of communication within the range of its own aircraft, missiles, and submarine fleet. This means that in a conflict, they probably would use their jamming and antisatellite systems to disrupt American lines of communication, command and control, situational awareness, and efforts at coordination at the extended ranges of military conflict.

Also, the PLA believes that the United States is more dependent than it is on satellite systems. However, as the PLA modernizes its own C⁴ISR systems and becomes dependent on space and information systems, its positions will likely evolve. Therefore, the contest could well be over which force can most effectively disrupt the other's military operations. Space warfare would become an integral part of traditional conflict.

Implications of Attacks on Reconnaissance Satellites

One unresolved question is the extent to which inside the PLA, the Politburo Standing Committee, and the Central Military Commission there is serious discussion of the implications of exercising the counterspace capabilities China is developing. When researchers in China consider a form of space warfare or develop capabilities in space weapons, are there also PLA officers in the policy or war-planning sphere thinking through the implications of employing that capability? If not, an incident could quickly escalate and get out of control, leading to an exchange of weapons or a deeper crisis.[89]

For example, in 2001 four officers from the PLA's Second Artillery Command College published an analysis of how to jam or destroy space-based ballistic missile warning systems of the United States.[90] The officers note "a space borne missile early warning system will play a pivotal role in future space wars."[91] They set out the capabilities and parameters of the U.S. Defense Support Program (DSP) early-warning satellites, which are intended to monitor foreign ballistic missile launches. The authors document the geosynchronous orbits of the satellite sets, their axis of look angle on the earth, the infrared bands they cover, and their shortcoming, and discuss how to destroy the DSP satellites with other satellites, ground-based lasers, or direct-ascent weapons.[92] They also have a discussion of how to jam the satellites, disrupt their satellite-to-ground transmissions, and camouflage the infrared radiation emitted by a missile to make it more difficult for the warning satellite to detect an attack.[93]

In their conclusion, the authors argue that by maintaining a strategic ballistic missile capability, China has a powerful deterrent to prevent the United States from launching a large-scale military attack or intervention aimed at China's own military operations on its southeastern coast (that is, to intervene in Chinese military operations against Taiwan).[94] Their view is that "destroying and jamming" an adversary's ballistic missile warning systems "not only can paralyze such anti-missile systems, but also will help us win the war in space."[95] Astonishingly, PLA officers do not seem to be discussing how the United States might react to blinding or attacking the DSP system. Such an action could precipitate a preemptive strike against Chinese ballistic missile bases in response to China's attacking the DSP system. Such thinking in the Second Artillery without considering the reaction that such an attack might bring can lead to serious nuclear instability.

Such attacks on spacecraft or the disruption of its missile early-warning systems may cause the United States to think it is coming under immediate attack and launch its own strike against China's strategic missile forces. Another reasonable, albeit equally escalatory, response by U.S. forces might be to strike the source of the Chinese attack, particularly if it were to come from a ground-based laser or direct ascent launch. Even if such a reaction used conventional weapons, the PLA may find it has created a deeper crisis that led to an American strike on Chinese soil. Unfortunately, there seems to be no open discussion in China of the ramifications of all this space warfare theory, and the PLA has avoided direct discussions with the

U.S. military on these issues. There is some hope, however, that in the future these important topics can be discussed. On December 24, 2012, the Second Artillery Force established a strategic research institute, which may mean the PLA is finally prepared to discuss nuclear stability and space warfare with foreign militaries.[96]

PLA Views on "Space Deterrence"

Space power theorists in China argue for the ability to control parts of space for limited periods of time. Huang Zhicheng advocates a regime of "space deterrence" to counter American "space superiority."[97] For him, this shift toward "space deterrence" mirrors a trend in U.S. space theory.[98] Huang calls for "the use of strong aerospace power to create or demonstrate a threat to an opponent's space power to deter that opponent in a practical way."[99] The goal of this concept of deterrence is to increase the PLA's power in weapon systems, information gathering, and command and control to improve national warning systems in China, create fear in an adversary, and degrade the adversary's power.[100]

The key to achieving this level of deterrence, according to Huang, is to employ China's economic, military, and science/technology power to "ruin an opponent's economy and ability to function in space."[101] The PLA's intentions in a December 2006 dazzling and temporary blinding of a U.S. satellite by a Chinese laser, and the January 2007 destruction of a Chinese weather satellite by the PLA's own direct-ascent kinetic-kill vehicle have been widely debated in the United States.[102] However, when viewed through Huang's reasoning, these acts are means to demonstrate "space deterrence." As Huang concedes, for a deterrent to be credible, it must be demonstrated.

The importance of demonstrating one's military capacity requires that one "display one's own power to the enemy," according to officers of the Second Artillery Command Academy. The enemy must "perceive the deterrent force and realize this force is capable of creating losses or consequences that it is difficult for them to accept."[103]

We have seen the PLA demonstrate various forms of jamming. Also, China's orbital spacecraft, the Shenzhou series, have launched clusters of microsatellites that could be used to collide with or jam foreign satellites.

Civil Space Systems and the PLA

China has announced intentions to put a man on the moon and to put its own space station into orbit. The spacecraft intended as China's own space station is projected to be built in three modules, which are slated to launch in 2020, 2021, and 2022.[104] China also projects lunar exploration, with the landing of a rover on the moon in 2012, and another landing projected for 2015 to 2020 designed to collect samples and return them to earth.[105] Some of these steps to move out into civil space are for prestige, and some of it is a case of "sour grapes." After the PLA destroyed China's own weather satellite, some members of Congress acted aggressively to ensure that China would not work with the United States in civil space programs.[106] Congressman Frank Wolf put forward legislation that bars the National Aeronautics and Space Administration (NASA) from spending any money on programs with China.[107]

There are also political reasons for Beijing to have its own space station and put a man on the moon. Such activities increase China's international prestige and present alternative power centers for countries that are barred from working with the United States or would prefer not to do so for political reasons.

The Rand Corporation has concluded that China's "strongest and most marketable space capability probably remains its space launch capability."[108] With more than seventy satellites in orbit, and its satellite capacity growing, China is an attractive and inexpensive launch service for other countries. Many of the satellites China has in orbit nominally may be civilian, but they have military applications.[109] Using its military reconnaissance satellites, the PLA can identify the "locations, numbers and types of enemy forces and . . . detect the massing of forces."[110] But civil weather satellites have direct military application for forecasting and planning operations and for calculating the entry points for missile warheads. Earth-observation satellites, with their multisensor payloads, can assist military operations also. And some of China's earth-resource and remote-sensing satellites resemble the satellites of the U.S. Navy's Naval Ocean Surveillance System, providing the capability to detect deployed ships.[111]

Implications for the United States

It is clear that the PLA is serious about space programs and also counterspace programs, which makes it more likely that in any future conflict, space will be a domain of war. This is an area where the PLA excels at what it is doing, and arguably it is an area where actions give the PLA the ability to affect military operations and commerce around the globe.

Based on the policy positions advocated by senior PLA officers involved in China's national security decision making, it is likely that Beijing will develop capabilities to control or act in space up to the limits of its technical capabilities. However, the succinct suggestion by two of the PLA's leading experts on space warfare, Cai Fengzhen and Tian Anping, that such control be exercised only in a defined area and period of time will probably prevail. Beijing probably will exercise sovereignty control in space only in times of serious crisis or war. However, China's substantial civil and military satellite programs support a range of military operations.

To summarize the major findings and judgments in this chapter: In the event of conflict with the PLA, we can expect to see military operations carried out across all the domains of war, ground, sea, air, space, and the electromagnetic spectrum, and they will include information warfare. Further, it is likely that military operations in space will be part of a more coordinated cyber attack on an enemy's knowledge and command systems.

In the event of a conflict or crisis, there would probably be strategic warning from China, even if there is operational or tactical surprise. That is, the PLA and the CMC would likely justify any of its actions in advance in the international and diplomatic realm by conducting what it calls "legal warfare." In a crisis or conflict, however, the PLA would seek to exercise "space control" in a limited area.

Finally, in peacetime, the PLA would probably observe the internationally accepted definitions of "commons" in space (more than a hundred kilometers) in peacetime and periods of tension. If conflict were to break out, however, altitude limits on space control are off, and any systems carrying adversary military traffic or signals would probably be fair game for the PLA.

American defense officials continue to express concerns over Chinese intentions and the ultimate goals of China's space programs and military modernization.[112] A number of China's activities and policy positions make it hard to interpret Chinese intent. Among these are China's expansive territorial claims, combined with periodic incidents of the use of armed force to reinforce these claims[113]; the justifications by China's legal scholars for extending the territorial claims of China into the reaches of outer space; and the shaping of the "space battlefield" with legal arguments that would justify China's actions to prevent space observation over its territory.

Whether one is a proponent of arms control agreements or not, the dialogue between the United States and the Soviet Union over arms control and treaties produced a body of mutual understanding that holds up today. Both countries seemed to realize that it is potentially destabilizing to define the upper limits of sovereignty. Thus neither country interfered with the other's free passage in space. Also, both countries agreed that the ability to conduct strategic verification from space stabilized the nuclear balance.

No such dialogue has taken place with China, although it would improve strategic stability and U.S. confidence. Indeed, the PLA has either ignored or rebuffed American efforts to engage it on these issues.

We can at least infer China's intentions from its actions. The laser-dazzling of a U.S. satellite and the destruction of its own weather satellite demonstrate a capability to wage war in space. We can also infer Beijing's intentions from judicious reviews of its military literature. By observing the military capabilities China is acquiring and by reading its military literature, we know that China's leaders are preparing as though they may have to fight the United States.

8   Information Age Warfare and INEW

This chapter explores concepts of information age warfare in the PLA, how the Chinese military envisions adapting those concepts to its own organization and doctrine, and the way that the PLA has adopted its traditional tactics and blended in concepts from the Soviet military, adapting them to the computer age. The chapters that deal with command, control, communications, computers, intelligence, surveillance, and reconnaissance (C⁴ISR); the PLA Second Artillery Force and China's nuclear doctrine; and space warfare discuss PLA programs that depend on incorporating information technology and networked information operations in the Chinese military. Many of the concepts used in signals intelligence or electronic warfare apply to forms of cyberwarfare, and the PLA routinely employs such military actions. Chapter 9 explores another aspect of information age warfare: the PLA's combination of psychological warfare; the manipulation of public opinion, or media warfare; and the manipulation of legal arguments to strengthen China's diplomatic and security position, or what China calls "legal warfare."

In modern military operations, it is becoming impossible to find forms of military activity that are not in some way dependent on information technology. Navigation and positioning is no longer done with compasses or sextants, maps or charts. Today it is done with satellite broadcasts. Physical reconnaissance is complemented by electronic means and a range of sensors employed on land or in the air, sea, and space. Information systems support logistics activities such as resupply and refueling, and the systems facilitate personnel and casualty management. Information technology and data exchange today are the basis for a shared awareness of the battle area (battlefield or battlespace). And in most military organizations, including those in China and the United States, units that were engaged in signals intelligence collection and electronic warfare also have taken on the mission of cyber warfare and cyber penetration.

During World War II and into the Cold War, opposing forces used electronic warfare techniques such as jamming, imitative communications deception, and meaconing (the intercept, alteration, and rebroadcast of navigation signals) to disrupt an adversary's communication system and radar or to alter electromagnetic signals. In the information age, similar actions are possible, and cyber exploitation or attacks can supplement electronic warfare. This matters because operational concepts such as cooperative target engagement—where different combat platforms in the air, on the sea, on land, or on submarine share data on a target and fire at it simultaneously from various directions with different weapons—is based on information systems being linked.

For the PLA, information warfare is directed at "the enemy's information detection sources, information channels, and information processing and decision making systems."[1] The goals are information superiority, disruption of the enemy information control capabilities, and maintaining one's own information systems and capabilities.

We are in an age of information operations, and the militaries that embrace information systems have begun to think about information dominance, or the ability to identify a range of threats against one's own forces, to counter them, and to attack the enemy's information systems.[2] The PLA is working to create an information-based "system of systems operations capability that forms an all-inclusive master network."[3] This effort builds on, and depends on, the redundant, national command-and-control architecture that the PLA began to develop in the 1990s. In July 1997, at an exhibition in the PLA Military History Museum in Beijing, the author observed an overlay for a national and theater-level automated command-and-control system.

The PLA's national command-and-control system is a redundant, military-region or theater of war networked system linking the General Staff Department headquarters and the PLA's arms and services with regional combat headquarters and their subordinate major organizations. An Indian defense researcher described this *Qu Dian* system as using fiber-optic cable, high-frequency and very-high-frequency communications, microwave systems, and multiple satellites to enable the CMC, the General Staff Department, and commanders to communicate with forces in their theater of war on a real-time or near-real-time basis.[4] The system also permits data transfer among the headquarters and all the units under its joint command. More on this system and its operation can be found in chapter 2, on C[4]ISR.

The PLA observed the transformation taking place in American and other Western military forces and worked hard to understand them. And the Chinese military is moving steadily to take advantage of information technologies.[5] In a New Year's Day 2006 editorial, the *PLA Daily* reminded the armed forces to transform from a force that operates under mechanized conditions to one that operates under "informatized conditions."[6] Less than a month before this reminder, in a testimonial to Hu Jintao's speech on the historic missions of the PLA, *PLA Daily* made it clear that the military had to "improve integrated combat operations capabilities under informatized conditions."[7] A range of military activities depends on how information technologies make military units and systems "interconnected." But the PLA still is not fully able to connect various command posts at different levels of the military to the national level and to each other. Nor are all the arms and services of the PLA as yet fully interconnected. The PLA's goal is to create a "system of systems in operations" (*ti xi zuozhan*) that can coordinate activities across the military inside and between military regions, arms, and services.[8] One objective of the effort is designed to develop a networked command-and-control system inside the PLA at the tactical, operational, and strategic levels, ultimately from the national command level to the soldier.[9] It is clear, however, that China's military ultimately envisions an information system or complex that can ensure that reconnaissance, electronic warfare, cyber systems, and combat strikes are integrated.[10]

In their book *The Science of Military Strategy*, Peng Guangqian and Yao Yunzhu highlight the effectiveness of precision-guided weapons and information age technologies. They note that in a war that depended a great deal on information systems, the Gulf War, "precision-guided weapons made up only 7 percent of all weapons used by the U.S. military, but they destroyed 80 percent of important targets."[11] Further, in what is probably one of the most authoritative books in Chinese military publishing, Peng and Yao argue that "under high tech conditions, the outcome of war not only depends on the amount of resources, manpower and technology devoted to the battlefield," but also depends on the control of information on the battlefield." Battle effectiveness, they maintain, is a function of the acquisition, transmission, and management of information.[12]

The PLA however, moved into the information age from a less advantageous position than did the United States. For decades, military culture in China emphasized the importance of people, not equipment, in warfare and employed massed forces or weapons—the strengths China brought to bear in the Korean War, the Sino-Indian War, and the Sino-Vietnam War.[13] And although the PLA had electronic systems, it did not modernize a force with the intent to use and even depend on these systems. The educational base of the average soldier in the PLA is probably lower than that of American or European soldiers, and the same is true of PLA officers.

At all levels of the PLA, however, attitudes about the relative importance of technology in warfare are changing, especially information technology. As China's military moves into the second decade of the twenty-first century, it is embracing the information age. The PLA is updating twentieth-century mechanized and joint operations, and combining them with electronic warfare, cyberwarfare, what the PLA calls "firepower warfare," and precision strike. In a book published by the PLA Academy of Military Science, Ye Zheng describes information age operations as "a new type of operations that are derived from the basis of mechanized operations moving from 'platform-based operations' to systematic operations and network-centric operations."[14]

Even though some PLA theorists argue that "the next 20 years are a period for China's 'peaceful rise,' meaning that China should not threaten others," this does not mean that China cannot be prepared to defend itself from aggression.[15] Further, information age warfare involves the Global Information Grid, a term the U.S. National Security Agency uses to describe an "interconnected, end-to-end set of information capabilities for collecting, processing, storing, disseminating and managing" information for warfighters and policymakers.[16] For the PLA this means connecting global command-and-control systems and global positioning satellites to provide data for strategic operations and theaters of war.[17] Ultimately, however, PLA theorists acknowledge that warfare is about killing and destruction, "just as mechanization in war made war more destructive, information age warfare will allow fires to be more destructive."[18]

First "Informatize," Then Network

Setting the tone for wider implementation of the PLA's "informatization," the Communications Department of the General Staff Department explains that the process will be both long and dynamic.[19] The PLA must embrace information age operations in support of all forms of military operations: in creating space-, ground-, and service-based system networks, by integrating electronic systems in military regions, and by establishing effective command organizations and structures that will "possess powerful capabilities with regard to mobile suppression of the enemy [*jidong zhi di*], long-range strikes [*yuancheng daji*], precision support [*jingque baozhang*], and three-dimensional defense [*quanwei fanghu*]."[20]

Space-based information networks are described as the "backbone" of any informatization effort for the PLA; surface-based systems are the key elements of the effort, supported by air and sea platforms; and the "integrated ground air and space elements must be compatible with the various services and their surrounding regions."[21] The PLA also is concerned about such matters as bandwidth, which is the basis for the ability to support a high volume of transmissions, system survivability, and the capacity to confront enemy information systems.[22]

An article in *PLA Daily* emphasized that today we are all living on a "smart planet" that is interconnected, with economic, political, and cultural activities all available to see on information systems, allowing military forces to take advantage of this transparency on the battlefield.[23] PLA strategists argue that "battle-space awareness is the core of information age warfare," which means that one's forces must be able to destroy or jam the adversary's systems that are fundamental to situational awareness. Given this, PLA experts believe that "information age warfare will take place in a range of strategic battle-space: land, maritime, air, space, and 'knowledge areas.'"[24]

Using the same formula for decision making in the information age relied on by the U.S. armed forces, Ye Zheng tells his PLA audience that the interaction of systems, platforms, communications, and decisions shortens the "OODA loop" (observe, orient, decide, and act, or *faxian, juece, jihua, xingdong*), allowing a military to take action in real time.[25] Moreover, as he explains, in information operations the traditional concepts of air, land, and sea battlespace expand to include the electromagnetic spectrum, cyberspace, and space, becoming "virtual battle space" (*xu kong jian*).[26] The PLA defines this as "the space created by technology, computers and the 'web' [Internet], that is subject to human control and reflects human will." Its components are cyberspace (*saibo kongjian*), information space (*xinsi kongjian*), and digital space (*shuxue kongjian*).[27]

The truly distinguishing characteristic of operations in the information age in PLA doctrine, however, is that "information power and various types of firepower are merged" so that mobility and precision fires are integrated to increase their operational effects.[28] Ultimately, the PLA must execute integrated operations combining computer network warfare, networked firepower warfare, electronic warfare, and sensor systems.

Part of the dilemma for the PLA, however, is to develop new cyberwarfare doctrine appropriate for the PLA's level of modernization while at the same time taking advantage of the Chinese armed forces' existing strengths in electronic warfare, electronic information gathering, precision attack, and massed firepower.[29] The PLA also lacks a deep reservoir of personnel who can manage or operate such systems. Chinese military leaders, however, recognize this weakness and intend to develop a talent pool of people who can conduct or plan joint military operations, manage information systems and cyber technology, and use or maintain advanced weapon systems.[30] The PLA's goal is to have these personnel by 2020.

However, the degree to which individual units or combat platforms are truly integrated into a data-sharing and command system varies in the PLA by service, branch, and arm. In major ground formations (infantry, armor, artillery), few units are networked below the regimental level. In the PLA Navy, the majority of surface combatants and submarines have the communications and data-sharing capabilities to be networked, as do PLA Air Force combat and support aircraft and Second Artillery Corps missile-firing battalions. By comparison, in the U.S. military the networked C⁴ISR system extends to every major combat platform and organization— often down to the rifle squad or individual combat vehicle. All aircraft and ships are in the networked system.

Looking back at the article by the GSD Communications Department, we see that it calls for establishing five major networked systems in the PLA:

- Theater-level, joint operational command communications and liaison subsystems that will synchronize broadband, multimedia information transmission.
- Integrated processing subsystems for the operational command services such as message processing, mapping, simulations, and automated decision making for peacetime, exercises, and wartime.
- Fixed and mobile or portable theater reconnaissance and detection systems to improve intelligence, reconnaissance, detection, information processing, and the rapid relay of such information to other defense posts, ports, stations, and substations. These should be able to cover four levels of units: military regions, group army-level organizations, divisions or brigades, and regiments. And they should include such arms as air defense and missile units.
- Electronic countermeasures and intelligence database systems that can integrate and share electromagnetic intelligence among headquarters, service arms in a theater of war, command posts at different levels, and reconnaissance stations.
- Theater subsystems for political work operations, logistics, equipment monitoring, managing information systems, and managing theater-level intelligence-integrated processing systems.[31]

The Communications Department article highlights two issues: First, as discussed earlier, the PLA cannot include units at lower echelons in its communication and data exchange information networks. For the ground forces, in 2004 when the article was published, the information network only extended to the regimental level. In the PLA, the term adopted for this effort is "integrated network electronic warfare," or INEW, which is discussed in the next section.[32]

In *An Introduction to Informationalized Operations*, Ye Zheng explains that the PLA concept of informationalized operations means "networked firepower warfare employed across the domains of war."[33] The Chinese military realizes that integrated network electronic warfare attacks must be combined with integrated firepower warfare. This use of precision fires, as conceived in Chinese doctrine, includes beyond-visual-range fires.[34]

A good deal of this discussion is similar to the concept of radio-electronic combat (REC) in Soviet military doctrine.[35] China's military, however, has added another dimension to this older concept. Taking a cue from U.S. operations in Iraq and the Balkans, China has moved beyond the tactical and theater realm of operations to take integrated network electronic warfare to the strategic level of war. Also, the PLA has added cyberattacks and attacks on satellites to its offensive operations. As Dai Qingmin envisions future combat operations, they will focus on "the destruction and control of the enemy's information infrastructure and strategic life blood, selecting key enemy targets, and launching effective network-electronic attacks."[36] In doing so, the PLA expects to weaken and paralyze an enemy's decision making and also to weaken and paralyze the political, economic, and military aspects of his entire war potential. This suggests that INEW operations would take place within a theater of war but would also extend to an enemy's homeland, including the civil infrastructure and the economy.[37]

The concepts applied by the PLA are derivatives of both Soviet and American doctrine, as discussed earlier. A major contribution from U.S. doctrine resulted from the PLA's research into the U.S. Navy's writings about networkcentric warfare.[38] This dependence on American concepts is discussed in more detail in chapter 2.

One American researcher characterizes the PLA's efforts at informatized warfare as "a focused transformation of the nation's mode of thinking" to integrate traditional and mechanized military operations into a "systems-oriented environment characterized by rapidly changing time-space relationships."[39] Just as REC theory seems to have evolved from Chinese research on Soviet military doctrine, the PLA's ideas on information operations were based on observations by China's military thinkers of U.S. and allied actions in operations in Iraq and Kosovo.[40]

This mode of thinking involved maintaining information superiority over an adversary, integrating air, ground, and naval warfare, and taking "command and control of forces as a major part of military science."[41] In essence, as the PLA envisioned this form of operations, the information and communication networks of engaged forces became the focal point for the conduct of military operations, as well as for finding and engaging enemy forces. Wang Zhengde conceived it as "merging weapons, equipment, resources, operational structure, and information resources to enable operational troops to truly form a grand system that fully exploits overall effectiveness."[42]

If we take Wang's embrace of informatized warfare concepts as a barometer of how the PLA approached the concept, by 2007 the threads of integrated network electronic warfare begin to emerge. In the book *On Informationalized Confrontation*, he explores warfare (or military confrontation) in the electronic realm (*dianzi lingyu duikang*). Wang argues that "both sides in any conflict want control of the electromagnetic spectrum," making jamming and electronic countermeasures critical parts of military operations.[43] Further, as the PLA and other militaries evolve in the information age and come to depend on networks, informatized confrontation evolves into "network confrontation operations," where each side in a conflict is seeking to immobilize the other's communications, data, command and sensor networks.[44]

INEW, Computer Network Warfare, and Strike

One way to understand what the PLA is doing to expand and modernize what they learned is to think of Soviet REC on Chinese steroids. That is, by combining electronic warfare and precision strikes, and adding cyberwarfare (including attacks on space systems), the PLA believes it can improve operational success on the modern battlefield.[45]

China's military strategists expand the Soviet concept further. Whereas the Soviet military applied REC to tactical situations in a limited battlespace or within a theater of operations such as Europe, PLA military theorists introduce strategic attacks on an adversary's homeland sustainment and supply systems. This new doctrine, as China's armed forces envision it, extends across all levels of warfare, from the tactical battlefield to the theater of operations and to the strategic level of war. And none of these effects can be achieved without the PLA achieving its objectives in integrated, or networked, informatized operations.[46]

China's military researchers are aware of the Soviet REC doctrine and acknowledge the goals that the Soviet military set for radio-electronic combat.[47]

In developing the REC concept during the Cold War, the Soviets expected their forces would inflict 60 percent casualties or combat damage on enemy forces through a combination of traditional electronic warfare and combat strikes by aircraft, helicopters, missiles, rockets, and artillery in the opening moves of any conflict.[48] The Soviet military goal was to destroy "thirty percent by jamming and thirty percent by destructive fires."[49] The U.S. Army described REC as "the total integration of EW [electronic warfare] and physical destruction resources to deny us the use of our electronic systems."[50] Chinese researchers imply that in the information age, by adding in cyberwarfare and attacks on space systems, the PLA can improve on the Soviet casualty ratios, even if they do not give specific numbers.[51]

Soviet REC was part of a broader operational campaign. Soviet forces intended to employ radio-direction finding, signals and radar intercept, and artillery radars to attack U.S. troop formations and headquarters, in addition to electronic systems to support strikes by artillery, combat aircraft, helicopters, and rockets or missiles. Among some of the measures included in Soviet REC operations were suppressive fires, jamming an adversary's communications assets, deceptively entering an adversary's radio nets, and interfering with the normal flow of an adversary's communications.[52]

Starting in the 1970s the American response to Soviet doctrine, in the event of war in Europe, was AirLand Battle, an integrated attack plan using airpower, special operations forces, artillery, armor, and electronic warfare.[53] The United States also employed AirLand Battle doctrine in the Gulf War during the campaign to drive Iraqi forces out of Kuwait, a campaign the Chinese military establishment studied with intense interest.[54]

Ultimately the PLA rolled all these concepts into what it now terms "integrated network electronic warfare." On the information systems side of China's INEW planning, Ye Zheng discusses network electronic attack (*wangdian yiti xinxi gongji*) as integrating electronic warfare and computer warfare to destroy the enemy's information systems and to preserve one's own.[55] Other PLA operations experts, however, expand the concept to include attacking and destroying enemy equipment and personnel, bringing the PLA's doctrine in line with the way that the Soviet Union conceived REC doctrine.

Chinese military thinkers built on the American concept of networkcentric warfare to introduce concepts such as precision weapon strikes and the use of space-based and battlefield sensors with the goal of moving away from what one Chinese strategist called "obsolete and rigid conceptual thinking."[56] Unlike the Soviet publications on REC, Chinese publications do not give explicit estimates of battle casualties. As explained by Maj. Gen. Dai Qingmin, then director of the PLA General Staff Department's Electronic Warfare and Electronic Countermeasures Department (Dianzi Duikang/Leida Bu, aka the Fourth Department), the operational concepts are similar. However, the PLA expands on and modernizes REC doctrine by including "the integrated use of electronic warfare and computer network warfare . . . to paralyze an opponent's information systems."[57] These concepts are incorporated into military exercises, including "force-on-force" confrontation, where a "red" unit, representing the PLA, is in confrontation with a "blue" unit, representing the enemy, an advanced military force capable of operating at the highest levels of information age warfare.[58]

INEW is a "systems versus systems" form of military confrontation on the twenty-first-century battlefield, dependent on space, cyber, and various information technologies.[59] One objective is to destroy the enemy's C[4]ISR, to blind the enemy and prevent enemy forces and commanders from communicating. But the PLA also wants to inflict battlefield casualties on an enemy force and to disrupt logistics, resupply, and personnel systems in the enemy's homeland so that combat losses cannot be restored and the deployed force cannot sustain battle. As Dai Qingmin states, "after the information attack succeeds in suppressing the enemy, the enemy's plight of temporary 'blindness, deafness, and even paralysis' can be exploited for the quick organization of an 'information/firepower' assault."[60] Dai advocates integrating "soft and hard attacks," employing information suppression, information warfare, and the firepower of missiles."[61]

Other cyberwarfare strategists, such as Xu Rongsheng, the chief scientist for cyber security at the Chinese Academy of Sciences, writes that in wartime, cyberwarfare should be targeted to "disrupt and damage the networks of infrastructure facilities, such as power systems, telecommunications systems, and educational systems."[62] This approach is not something new in the PLA; the two PLA senior colonels who wrote the book *Unrestricted Warfare* introduced these concepts in 1999.[63] However, it took people like Dai Qingmin to formalize these ideas as military doctrine. As for those Western-based specialists on China and journalists who dismissed *Unrestricted Warfare* when it was published because it was written by two PLA political commissars, it should be noted that by 2011, one of them (Qiao Liang) was a major general at the PLA Air Force Command College.

Cyberwarfare

PLA military thinkers include cyberwarfare as part of information age warfare. Cyberwarfare takes place in the electromagnetic spectrum, thus there is a good deal of conceptual and operational overlap with traditional electronic warfare. These operations are designed to penetrate, exploit, and perhaps damage or sabotage thru electronic means an adversary's "information systems and networks, computers and communications systems, and supporting infrastructures."[64] And, as outlined above, cyber operations are a component of INEW. Cyber operations also are closely linked to operations in space and to traditional forms of espionage or information-gathering. Indeed, most thinking about cyberwarfare in China is "an extension of its traditional strategic thinking."[65]

China, like other states, is heavily involved in computer network operations. They are conducted primarily for five reasons:

- to strengthen political and economic control in China;
- to complement other forms of intelligence collection and gather economic, military, or technology intelligence and information;
- to reconnoiter, map, and gather targeting information in foreign military, government, civil infrastructure, or corporate networks for later exploitation or attack;
- to conduct the exploitation or attacks using the collected information; and
- to develop defenses or conduct defensive operations in the PLA's (and China's) own cyber systems. [66]

With respect to strengthening political and economic control in China, skilled computer operators exploit computer systems to gain information about what political dissidents say, how they use the World Wide Web, and with whom they communicate. The organizations in China most likely to engage in these activities, however, are those responsible for internal security, repression, and control of the Chinese population, and control over the distribution of information. These are the Ministry of State Security, the Ministry of Public Security (MPS) and the system of Public Security Bureaus and People's Armed Police the MPS oversees, and organizations of the Communist Party such as the Central Propaganda Department.[67] Still, the PLA has the expertise to conduct such operations and is sometimes involved.[68]

The second type of malicious activity essentially is intelligence gathering designed to collect information of military, technical, scientific, or economic value. Gathering this intelligence information may speed the development and fielding of weapons in China, improve technology in sectors of China's industries while saving time and money in research and development, and often compromises valuable intellectual property. The organizations of the Chinese government with the missions and capabilities to conduct such activities span both military and civilian agencies in China, to include the PLA's Technology Reconnaissance Department (a.k.a. Signals Intelligence, or the Third Department), the Electronic Countermeasures and Electronic Countermeasures Department (a.k.a. the Fourth Department), the Ministry of State Security, and the state-owned companies in China's broad military-industrial complex.[69] Foreign business visitors to China with whom the author has had contact also have reported that in some localities Public Security Bureau personnel have cooperated with local authorities to gather information of economic value.

Reconnoitering, mapping, and gathering targeting information in foreign military, government, civil infrastructure, or corporate networks for later exploitation or attack may be the most dangerous cyber activity for American national security. This is where foreign intelligence or military services penetrate the computers that control our vital national infrastructure or our military, reconnoiter them electronically, and map or target nodes in the systems for future penetration or attack. Malicious code is often left behind to facilitate future entry. Regarding this third type of computer network penetration by China, the danger is that it could lead to a devastating computer attack. Gen. James Cartwright, then commander of the U.S. Strategic Command (USSTRATCOM) and recently vice chairman of the Joint Chiefs of Staff, said, "I don't think the [United States] has gotten its head around the issue yet, but I think that we should start to consider that [effects] associated with a cyber-attack could, in fact, be in the magnitude of a weapon of mass destruction."[70]

General Cartwright testified in 2007 before the U.S.-China Economic and Security Review Commission that China is actively engaging in cyber reconnaissance by probing the computer networks of U.S. government agencies as well as private companies.[71] A denial-of-service attack by China has the potential to cause cataclysmic harm if conducted against the United States on a large scale and could paralyze critical infrastructure or military command and control. China currently is thought by many analysts to have the world's largest denial-of-service capability.[72] In 2010 former National Security Agency director and director of National Intelligence Adm. Mike McConnell reinforced General Cartwright's admonition. He argued that just as in the Cold War when the United States aimed to protect itself against nuclear attack, today it must endeavor to protect its "power grids, air and ground transportation, telecommunications, and water filtration systems" against the chaos that could result from successful cyber attacks.[73]

PLA lieutenant general Liu Jixian, of the PLA's Academy of Military Science, writes that the PLA must develop asymmetrical capabilities against potential enemies, including space-based information support and networked-focused "soft attack."[74] Xu Rongsheng told a Chinese news reporter that "cyber warfare may be carried out in two ways. In wartimes, disrupt and damage the networks of infrastructure facilities, such as power systems, telecommunications systems, and education systems, in a country; or in military engagements, the cyber technology of the military forces can be turned into combat capabilities."[75] Other military strategists from China's military academies and schools of warfare theory have suggested that the PLA ought to have the capability to alter information in military command-and-control or logistics systems to deceive U.S. forces on resupply missions or divert supplies, as well as to be able to paralyze ports and airports by cyber or precision-weapon attacks on critical infrastructure.[76]

Although armed conflict between the United States and China is not a certainty, a cyberwar already is under way, and besides penetrations for intelligence collection, there are regular attacks on the United States from sites in China.[77] PLA organizations are being trained and prepared in military doctrine to "expand the types of targets or objectives for armed conflict to command and control systems, communications systems and infrastructure."[78] Military strategist Wang Pufeng argues that "battlefield situational awareness is the core of information age warfare, which means that one must be able to destroy or jam the systems that are fundamental to [an adversary's] situational awareness."[79]

With regard to information warfare, Wang Baocun, one of the leading information warfare specialists in the Chinese military, reminds readers in China that "the global information grid and global command and control systems are fundamental to the American defense system, including global positioning satellites."[80] In other Chinese military publications, there are suggestions that to be successful in information age warfare, one's own military must have certain capabilities and must be able to interfere with an adversary's ability to exploit the results of "reconnaissance, thermal imaging, ballistic missile warning, and radar sensing."[81]

PLA Responsibilities and Cyber Penetrations, Exploitation, Espionage, and Warfare

In terms of responsibilities and organizations, the PLA has divided responsibility for the conduct of electronic warfare, electronic defense, the collection of signals intelligence, and cyber operations. Notwithstanding the divided responsibilities, the Chinese military is well equipped and staffed to conduct such activities.[82]

The Third Department (Technical Reconnaissance Department, or Jishu Zhencha Bu) of the PLA's General Staff Department is responsible for technology reconnaissance, or signals collection, exploitation, and analysis, as well as communications security for the PLA.[83] It is often compared to the U.S. National Security Agency. Third Department intelligence officers are trained for various forms of electronic warfare and electronic espionage, but they apparently are also trained for similar activities in the realm of cyber operations.

The GSD's Fourth Department (Electronic Warfare and Electronic Countermeasures Department) is responsible for offensive electronic warfare and electronic countermeasures such as jamming and the counterjamming of various types of signals or communications.[84] Fourth Department personnel are skilled in electronic warfare and, according to a Northrop Grumman Corporation study, they are also probably charged with cyber penetrations.[85]

Given the Third Department's analytical and language capabilities, its personnel probably analyze and exploit the cyber information gathered in Fourth Department offensive actions. Each of China's military regions as well as the PLAAF, PLAN, and SAF has assigned to its headquarters department at least one technical reconnaissance bureau subordinate to the Third Department that monitors foreign communications (and cyber activity).[86] In addition to the technical reconnaissance bureaus assigned to the military regions, Project 2049 Institute also documents more Third Department organizations including three research institutes, four operational centers, and twelve operational bureaus that have a regional or functional orientation that can monitor phone, radio, satellite, or computer communications.[87] In the military regions, arms, and services, the technical research bureau alignment is:

- Beijing: 1
- Chengdu: 2
- Guangzhou: 1
- Jinan: 1
- Lanzhou: 2
- Nanjing: 2
- Shenyang: 1
- PLAAF: 3
- PLAN: 2
- SAF: 1[88]

In 2011 two Canadian journalists focused on published "Wikileaks" cables from the U.S. State Department that some attribute major cyber penetrations of U.S. websites in 2006 to the First Technical Reconnaissance Bureau of the Chengdu Military Region. The journalists quote one cable as saying "much of the intrusion activity traced to Chengdu is similar in tactics, techniques, and procedures to activity attributed to other electronic spying units of the People's Liberation Army."[89]

Penetrations of U.S. government agencies and defense contractors attributed to organizations in China had been detected for some time prior to the 2006 penetration. NASA suffered a series of other breaches attributed to Russia and China.[90] According to authors of an article on the breaches, "it's no secret that Beijing thirsts for missile and rocket technology. After a 2005 intrusion, investigators followed the e-trail to China."[91] But cyber penetrations traced back to China have plagued U.S. contractors and agencies for a year or so before this. A computer security analyst at a Department of Energy facility, Sandia National Laboratory, traced computer attacks and penetrations he detected to Guangdong Province.[92] Guangzhou Military Region, which includes Guandong Province, is the site of another of the PLA's technical reconnaissance regiments.

It is difficult at times to distinguish the origin of a cyber attack or penetration, and attribution of a cyber operation is not always possible. The PLA may be acting through its Third or Fourth Departments, the Ministry of State Security may be acting, the origin might be from groups known as "patriotic hackers" (even if the PLA sometimes uses such groups), or it could be some company or organization in China engaged in electronic espionage.[93] That said, it is clear that in terms of its military doctrine and approaches to modern warfare—whether one calls it the informational, electromagnetic, or cyber domain of war—the PLA has embraced the medium.

Three former U.S. officials—Admiral Mike McConnell; Michael Chertoff, former secretary of Homeland Security; and William Lynn, former deputy secretary of defense—said in a January 2012 *Wall Street Journal* opinion piece that "the Chinese government has a national policy of espionage in cyberspace. In fact, the Chinese are the world's most active and persistent practitioners of cyber espionage today." They pointed out in the same op-ed that "it is more efficient for the Chinese to steal innovations and intellectual property than to incur the cost and time of creating their own."[94]

Further, there are very clear linkages between China's traditional espionage efforts against military technologies and the targets of cyber espionage; the target sets are roughly the same. The U.S. Department of Justice has prosecuted a number of cases where long-term Chinese agents working for defense companies sent back to China information on naval propulsion systems, naval electronic control systems, and stealth aircraft design. For the most part, the agents were convicted of economic espionage, violation of laws prohibiting the transfer of military-related information to China.[95] These are some of the same targets of Chinese cyber espionage.

In a 2011 report, the U.S. National Counterintelligence Executive (NCIX), an agency subordinate to the Directorate of National Intelligence, made the point that cyberspace is unique because it provides foreign intelligence "collectors with relative anonymity, facilitates the transfer of vast amounts of information, and makes it more difficult for victim and governments to assign blame by masking geographic locations."[96] It added that "Chinese actors are the world's most active and persistent perpetrators of economic espionage."[97] The Northrop Grumman Corporation, in a second report for the U.S. China Economic and Security Review Commission in 2012, suggests that when "highly technical defense engineering information, operational military data, or government policy analysis" is the target of a cyber penetration from China," it probably is not the act of a criminal group.[98]

Implications for the United States

Considering how China is approaching war and the electromagnetic spectrum, the People's Liberation Army is a world-class player in the cyber domain. China's cyber warriors have been able to penetrate computer systems, steal or manipulate data, and engage in electronic warfare on a global basis. The governments of the United States, Australia, Japan, Germany, and Great Britain, to name a few, all have tracked cyber penetrations back to China. Much of this activity, given the nature of the defense-related systems that are being exploited, probably traces back to the PLA or goes to support defense production in China that helps the PLA. In addition, military publications in China make it clear that the PLA intends to use computer network operations in conflicts, along with integrated network electronic warfare.

PLA military planners and strategists are aware of the strengths and weaknesses in China's armed forces. There are limitations on how far the PLA, especially the PLA Army, can go in embracing information systems. PLA leaders understand that given the education base of many of the soldiers brought into the PLA, not every soldier will be able to function in a fully automated, computer-driven environment, nor will all soldiers be able to use or even have access to information systems. Still, the PLA is doing an excellent job of adapting these technologies to its forces. Moreover, China's military thinkers are developing their own doctrine and are no longer dependent on what they see happening in the U.S. armed forces or other militaries.

Two decades ago, in the wake of the U.S.-led coalition action in Iraq, the PLA woke up to realize that its military was not ready to take on a modern adversary that used networked C⁴ISR systems. Virtually all of the publications from PLA institutions, for almost a decade, quoted from or cited American military doctrine or manuals. Beginning in the mid-2000s, however, Chinese military thinkers began to develop indigenous doctrine on information systems and operations in the information age. Moreover, the PLA is fielding equipment, satellites, and communications systems to support information age operations.

The transition to information age operations has not reached down into every level of the PLA. In the Second Artillery Force, it appears that full automation, information flows, and data flows only extend down to the missile-firing brigades.[99] But one can be sure that individual missile batteries can take advantage of limited data links and satellite-based timing and positioning data. In the PLA Navy, as chapter 2 on C⁴ISR discusses, all of the major combat ships are networked and can share data. In the PLA Air Force, a majority of newer fighter aircraft are able to share data and be part of an information system managed by the PLA's own airborne early-warning aircraft. For the ground forces, it looks like automation and information age systems have penetrated down to the regimental level. By comparison, in the U.S. military data exchange and situational awareness extends to squads and weapon crews—in some cases to individual soldiers, sailors, marines, or airmen.

Some in the PLA believe that because the United States operates it forces over extended distances and is dependent on satellites and information systems, there is a weakness that can be exploited in conflict. They take comfort in the fact that the PLA is not as dependent on information sharing as is the U.S military. But what the PLA sees as one of its strengths is becoming a weakness, because as Chinese forces become dependent on information systems, they become more vulnerable to interference, manipulation, and jamming.

In a notional assessment of how the PLA could exploit some of the weaknesses it sees in the U.S. dependence on information systems, researchers at the Northrop Grumman Corporation point out weaknesses in the unclassified Internet systems used by the U.S. armed forces.[100] The U.S. military operates two forms of Internet protocols. The Secret Internet Protocol Router Network (SIPRNET) is part of the Defense Data Network that carries classified information. So far, DOD authorities do not believe that it has been penetrated. The Non-secure Internet Protocol Router Network (NIPRNET) carries sensitive, but unclassified information. It has suffered a number of penetrations, many of which have been traced back to China.

PLA publications consistently identify "U.S. logistics and C⁴ISR systems as the most important centers of gravity to target in a conflict."[101] Unfortunately vital logistical, personnel, and unit movement data are all carried on the nonsecure NIPRNET, and this network likely already has been mapped and penetrated by the PLA. This leaves the U.S. military open for exploitation by PLA forces in the event of a conflict. The PLA's emphasis on surprise, striking the enemy's center of gravity, and achieving information superiority, discussed in chapter 5, means that in the event of a conflict, the PLA would likely initiate cyber and electronic warfare first, in the Asia-Pacific region, in the United States, and around the globe.

The PLA is not solely focused on information superiority in the cyber and electromagnetic spectrum. As the next chapter describes, its General Political Department— often in coordination with the Communist Party's International Liaison Department, its Propaganda Department, and military intelligence—also has modernized traditional propaganda and psychological operations for wars in the information age.

9 The General Political Department and Information Operations

The General Political Department (GPD) is broadly responsible for Communist Party political and ideological training in the PLA. That covers a wide range of activities, from building troop morale through cultural shows, movies, the arts, and literature, to supporting museums and sports activities.[1] More importantly for the PLA and the Communist Party's internal security, the GPD serves as a personnel department, controlling dossiers on the political reliability of troops and officers, their training records, their security clearances, and their promotions. Internally, framing and molding public opinion through the media also falls to the GPD.[2] This department works closely with other Communist Party organizations, especially the International Liaison Department, the Propaganda Department, and the Organization Department, a central Chinese Communist Party organization that keeps track of the careers, advancement, and personnel dossiers of 70 million party members. In some cases the GPD also works hand in hand with the PLA's Second Department (Military Intelligence).

As if the GPD's responsibilities were not broad enough, in 2003 the Communist Party's Central Committee and the Central Military Commission approved a new warfare concept for the PLA, the "three warfares" (*san zhong zhanfa*, generally abbreviated in Chinese as *san zhan*).[3] These are (1) public opinion (media) warfare (*yulun zhan*), (2) psychological warfare (*xinli zhan*), and (3) legal warfare (*falu zhan*).[4] *PLA Daily* makes it clear that the three warfares doctrine is part of the PLA regulations for the conduct of "political work."[5] These three forms of political or information warfare can be performed in unison or separately, bringing into harmony the PLA's actions, the intent of the Communist Party, and the goals of the senior party leadership.

In the public opinion, or media, warfare effort, the PLA wants to influence both domestic and international public opinion in ways that build support for

China's own military operations, while undermining any justification for an adversary that is taking actions counter to China's interests. In the conduct of psychological warfare, the PLA seeks to undermine the will of foreign civil populations and the enemy's ability to conduct combat operations. The PLA's psychological warfare goals are to demoralize both enemy military personnel and their countrymen at home. In legal warfare, as described in chapter 7, the PLA seeks to use international law and domestic law to justify its own actions and assert its interests while it undermines the case for an adversary's actions. Legal warfare also tries to establish an argument by precedent in customary international law for China's position on an issue, when possible by tying the matter to domestic law in China.[6]

Media (Public Opinion) Warfare[7]

The idea in public opinion warfare is to use all forms of media to influence both domestic and international public opinion on the rectitude of China's policies and actions. This includes newspapers, television, radio, social media, and the use of front organizations to convey messages to foreigners. Some of these activities are close to traditional propaganda operations, but others border on sophisticated deception operations or perception management.[8] In this sense, psychological warfare and media warfare have similarities.

Inside China, the PLA (and the Communist Party) want to guide public opinion to conform to party policy and objectives, and to ensure that workers, the intelligentsia, and the populace understand and embrace the party's line on matters. When aimed at Taiwan, media warfare efforts are designed to promote a "united front" between the citizens of Taiwan and the Chinese Communist Party on specific policy issues. The Communist Party's International Liaison Department and the GPD take the lead on Taiwan-related "united front" operations.

Internationally, media warfare efforts seek to counter the dominance (hegemony) of the Western media while promoting the Communist Party's positions and views. These efforts are increasingly sophisticated and include such measures as inserting paid advertisements, written like news articles from Chinese publications, into American or other target foreign newspapers. In assessing this phenomenon, the U.S. China Economic and Security Review Commission's 2011 report to Congress noted as an example that *China Daily*, a Communist Party–affiliated state-owned newspaper, paid for inserts in newspapers such as the *Washington Post* and the *New York Times* making the argument that one-party rule in China benefits both American and Chinese economic policies because it keeps harmony in Chinese society and the steady production of goods at cheap prices for the U.S. economy.[9] The obvious objective of such advertising efforts is to attempt to discourage Americans and their elected representatives from putting any emphasis on human rights in China.

China Central Television (CCTV) also has a number of stations operating overseas, broadcasting in the native language of the host country and in Chinese, carrying the targeted messages of the Chinese Communist Party. Often these broadcasts feature military shows depicting PLA exercises or training and military life, documentaries on China's military history, and features that highlight how the PLA is contributing to international peace and stability.

In the broader national realm of perception management and image shaping, an initiative by the Chinese Communist Party's United Front Work Department and the PRC Ministry of Education to establish Confucius Institutes in foreign universities around the globe—with funding from China—is another sophisticated example of public opinion warfare that seeks to "use foreigners as a bridge" to promote and convey the message of the Chinese government and Communist Party. The institutes provide services, such as language and cultural instruction, on the campuses and in the communities where they are located. Some Americans, however, argue that Confucious Institutes are a way to engage in "soft power diplomacy," shaping opinions about China.[10]

Turning back to the PLA, one way the PLA contributes to perception management and image shaping is through senior officers' visits to other countries. Senior Chinese military leaders visiting the United States often use speeches and other forms of public diplomacy to develop themes consistent with China's defense and security interests. For example, when PLA Gen. Chen Bingde, the chief of the General Staff Department, delivered a speech in the United States in May 2011, he emphasized China's peaceful military tradition and the need for the United States to respect China's "core interests," such as its control over Taiwan.[11]

Another tactic in media warfare is to selectively open up for study the parts of the PLA that help deliver the message that the GPD and the Propaganda Department want delivered to foreign audiences while concealing other areas of PLA activity. This effort is designed to influence foreign observers' perceptions of China in a way that serves the purposes of the Communist Party and PLA. Domestically the effort is designed to reinforce stability and Communist Party control around China.

One way that the GPD seeks to shape messages to foreigners is to sponsor visits to China by foreign groups with military affiliations, by military retirees, and by veterans groups, visits that include tours and contact with selected PLA personnel. The group that is often used as a proprietary organization for such activities is the

China Association for International Friendly Contact (CAIFC). CAIFC is controlled by the General Political Department, but it also works closely with the CCP's International Liaison Department and the PLA's Military Intelligence Department in choosing its foreign targets. The author accompanied American groups invited or sponsored by CAIFC around China a few times as a military attaché in the 1980s and 1990s. American targets included businesspeople involved in heavy industry, electronics, aviation, or defense, and leaders of veterans organizations. Invariably, on the Chinese side, the escorts came from the PLA's Military Intelligence Department.[12] The GPD maintains its own liaison department, subordinate to which is an intelligence bureau and CAIFC.[13]

One recent propaganda and perception management initiative by the GPD and CAIFC involved a multiyear program to bring retired senior U.S. generals and admirals to China to meet with their retired PLA counterparts. In the Sanya Initiative, the meetings took place in the town of Sanya on Hainan Island, which has a climate similar to Hawaii's.[14] The lead for the Chinese side was Gen. Xiong Guangkai, the former PLA chief of military intelligence.[15] The Sanya Initiative sought to soften the views of the U.S. military toward China and to influence the United States to reduce arms sales to Taiwan. The American participants reportedly were encouraged to return home and meet with active military leaders, informing them of what they learned from the trip.

Media warfare, or public opinion warfare, generally is targeted against both domestic and foreign audiences. Both audiences are influenced to adopt the main line from the CCP's Liaison Department and General Political Department, sometimes acting through the latter's "loose" cover organization, CAIFC.

Psychological Warfare

The second of the three forms of warfare has a longer history and primarily targets enemies and potential adversaries. Psychological warfare has been a central responsibility of the GPD since the time it was established. The PLA targeted Nationalist forces and the Japanese with psychological operations and also used them in the Korean War. The PLA believes that this form of warfare serves national defense. It targets the adversary's will to fight and is designed to lower the efficiency of enemy forces by creating dissent, disaffection, and dissatisfaction in their ranks.[16]

Historically in China, psychological operations involved the use of stratagem (*moulue*) and deception. In its psychological warfare operations, the PLA may target an enemy's values, its motivation for fighting, and, in peacetime or wartime, the logic of an adversary's foreign policy, security policy, or national decisions.[17] In this sense, psychological operations my target an adversary's civil populace and its leaders, as well as military personnel. Historically, psychological warfare operations also were intended to divide alliances. The PLA's objectives were to cause an adversary's allies to take a neutral position or become disaffected from an ally. This is still the focus of psychological operations today.

Quoting a former U.S. military attaché to China, one study sums up the means and methods of PLA psychological operations this way: "Political signals may be sent through (1) public or private diplomacy at international organizations, such as the United Nations, and/or directly to other governments or persons; (2) the use of the Chinese and foreign media in official statements or 'opinion pieces' written by influential persons; (3) non-military actions, such as restrictions on travel or trade; or (4) by using military demonstrations, exercises, deployments, or tests, which do not involve the use of deadly force."[18]

In an analysis of the PLA's psychological warfare operations, Mark Stokes, a former U.S. Air Force attaché in China, quotes PLA strategist Yu Guohua saying in the journal *China Military Science* that the PLA "should sap the enemy's morale, disintegrate their will to fight, ignite the anti-war sentiment among citizens at home, heighten international and domestic conflict, weaken and sway the will to fight among its high level decision makers, and in turn lessen their superiority in military strength."[19]

When the PLA Navy or the maritime or coastal patrol organizations in China stage incidents with foreign navies or fishing fleets, they are engaging in psychological operations. Such actions intimidate neighbors and other claimants to disputed territories, whether in the South China Sea or the East China Sea. By creating the impression that acting counter to China's interests or desires may cause China to use force, the PLA is able to dissuade or deter an adversary without resorting to combat.

In 1996, just before the presidential election in Taiwan, the PLA engaged in a major psychological warfare operation that, at the same time, was a display of military force and a warning to Taiwan not to go too far in moves toward democracy and independence. China did not want to see Lee Teng-hui become the first popularly elected president of Taiwan. Chinese military officers sought to meet with foreign military attachés in Beijing, including the author, to tell them that if the election went to Lee, it could mean immediate war. The PLA then conducted a series of military exercises off the Taiwan coast, firing ballistic missiles into preannounced impact zones at sea in the vicinity of the Taiwan Strait, conducting an amphibious exercise, and leading artillery practice. Before the exercises, the PLA announced to international shipping and aviation that certain areas of airspace and the sea would be danger zones because of the exercises and that all aircraft and ships should avoid them.[20] The PLA's choice of the impact zones, which bracketed Taiwan and the Taiwan Strait, had the effect of a temporary blockade or embargo of shipping and air travel to Taiwan.

Beijing's message to the people of Taiwan was "Vote the wrong way, and you face a missile attack." To other countries, especially the United States, which has encouraged free elections in Taiwan, the message was that Taiwan was a major concern of China and if events went the wrong way, China would use military force.

Unfortunately for the PLA and the Communist Party leadership, this psychological warfare campaign backfired. On March 23, 1996, Lee became the first democratically elected president of Taiwan, with 54 percent of the vote. At the time the PLA missile-firing exercises began, March 8, 1996, President Clinton announced that two U.S. carrier battle groups would be dispatched to the area around Taiwan. The carriers stayed in the area throughout the PLA exercises, which ended on March 25, 1996, after Taiwan's presidential election.[21] The PLA sees psychological warfare as an integral part of the three warfares and modern information operations. Chinese legal scholars and members of the General Political Department also are active in what the PLA has named "legal warfare."

Preparation for War and Legal Warfare

While students of warfare are thinking through Beijing's military doctrine in space, other Chinese strategists and legal scholars are engaged in an internal debate on how traditional ideas of sovereignty and the laws of war apply in space. The authoritative PLA book *The Science of Military Strategy* puts the legal aspects of the three warfares at the top of its means to "influence and restrict international law and the conduct of modern war." The PLA sees war as a struggle in the military, political, economic, diplomatic, and legal domains. For the PLA, "international law is a powerful weapon to expose the enemy, win over sympathy and support of the international community [for China], and to strive to gain the position of strategic initiative." *The Science of Military Strategy* further argues that one must "publicize one's own humanitarianism and reveal a lot of the war crimes committed by the opponent in violation of law so as to win over universal sympathy and support from the international community . . . to compel [the] opponent to bog down in isolation and passivity."[22]

Those who follow China's military development cannot ignore this area of PLA activity. Often the arguments are nuanced and ahead of international customary law in an effort to establish a legal precedent for China's actions or policies. With respect to actions in the global commons such as the seas, international airspace, outer space, and cyberspace, the legal warfare precedents and arguments in China imply that, before using military force, China would telegraph its intentions or justify its planned operations through public opinion operations or legal action.

One authoritative volume on the military legal system, *The New Revolution in Military Affairs and Building a Military Legal System* (*Xin Junshi Geming yu Junshi Fazhi Jianshe*), explored the importance of ensuring that the PLA sets out legal justifications for military actions in advance of any conflict.[23] The essays in this volume imply that even now, as debates take place in China over the range of sovereignty and China's authority in the South China Sea or in space, the General Political Department of the PLA is developing ways to justify in domestic law its potential military actions with the ultimate objective of establishing positions in domestic law that can be used to create a precedent or to have an impact in the future on international law and international opinion. One reason for trying to ensure that the legal positions it seeks to take in the international arena are grounded in China's domestic laws is that the PLA believes that this strengthens its legal arguments. In disputes with Japan and Southeast Asian nations, Beijing now refers to its 1992 Territorial Seas Law adopted by the National People's Congress as justification for its territorial claims in disputes.[24] The Territorial Seas Law extended sovereign claims over 3 million square miles of area in the East and South China Seas, demarcating it as Chinese territory on its maps After that, when Chinese diplomats or legal representatives argued with officials of other nations, the domestic law was used as one of the justifications for the territorial claims. The 2005 Anti-Secession Law is another example of how domestic law is used by Beijing to justify potential military action in the future, in this case against Taiwan.

To reiterate a point made in chapter 7, PLA officers argue that setting forth legal arguments for military action is important if a nation is to get international support, setting out the justification for legal warfare.[25] PLA legal preparation for a military campaign complements the use of military force.[26] The major PLA text explaining this rationale was validated at a military-wide August 2004 critique session.[27]

One aspect of this is not new; since the establishment of the People's Republic of China, the Communist Party leadership has been careful to establish a casus belli before taking military action. Such justification has been in legal or political terms. Prior to the entry of PLA troops into the Korean War, the PRC telegraphed its actions publicly with a declaration from Mao Zedong and through the Indian government.[28] In the case of the 1962 Sino-Indian War, Chinese diplomats and military leaders carefully staked out their legal positions as early as three years before the conflict.[29] They did the same in 1969 with the Soviet Union and in 1979 prior to their attack on Vietnam. Thus this concept of legal warfare has roots in China's diplomatic practice that has been reinforced by its leaders' observation of modern war.

Zhang Shanxin and Pan Jiangang, two officers from the PLA's Xian Political Affairs College, believe that prior to any conflict, a nation must "muster public opinion in its favor" and conduct propaganda, psychological, and legal campaigns to ensure support for military action. They also suggest developing domestic law that justifies military action in international legal terms. These authors see this as a means of developing "comprehensive national power" and believe that the United States demonstrated the importance of such actions in the period before the 2003 attack on Iraq.[30]

Lu Hucheng and Zhang Yucheng, of the General Staff Department Political Department, classify "legal warfare" as a "special form of military operations" to be undertaken in preparation for a conflict. Lu and Zhang define these legal actions as "political preparation of the battlefield." They see legal arguments, propaganda, and international agreements worked in advance as justifying any necessary military action.[31]

Why is this concept of legal warfare important? In the recent past, Chinese scholars have set out their views on national sovereignty, sovereignty in space, and the need for "space control" in modern war. These actions are consistent with this concept of legal warfare, and, should any conflict come about in space, they would provide the outlines of any PLA justification for military action. Monitoring the outlines of the PLA's legal warfare arguments is important. It is also critical that American military theorists interact with Chinese scholars and diplomats when possible as a means to limit their ability to define the justifications for conflict and evolving international law on their own terms.

Justifying China's actions in international law and establishing positions in domestic law increasingly are important for the PLA as its strategists and planners think about space warfare (see chapter 7). Officers in the General Political Department are setting out positions now that China can use in the future to justify attacks on foreign satellites or other space bodies, while other scholars in China deal with the limits and range of national sovereignty in the global commons. These legal warfare efforts are designed to establish positions in domestic and international law as a legal basis for military action or to limit the freedom of action of other nations.[32]

China is developing its own ballistic missile defenses and has tested them against an incoming Chinese warhead. However, that does not mean it thinks the United

States should field missile defenses.[33] The PLA is very aware of the deep political schisms in the United States over renewed nuclear testing, over placing even defensive weapon systems in space, and over the foreign basing of American forces. Debate rages in Congress, the scientific community, academia, and the policy community on these issues, with near-theological disputes taking place on issues of nuclear testing and ballistic missile defense. PLA legal warfare efforts are applied in these areas at academic conferences and in meeting with foreigners to reinforce agreement with Chinese positions. It is likely that the concept of legal warfare will be applied to these disputes.

The author was once invited to an international conference in England run by a group of British pacifists to debate issues related to arms control and space. The English group's partner from China was the Chinese Association for Peace and Disarmament. However, when I met the members of the Chinese delegation, I saw that four of them were either PLA officers or Ministry of State Security (MSS) officers I had met in China at other arms control events. In England, however, they operated under cover and identified themselves as "disarmament researchers."

China's "Peaceful Rise" Theory as a Case Study of the Three Warfares

The PLA has managed to act globally in its media and propaganda campaigns and is increasingly able to do so in a nuanced way. The promulgation of China's "peaceful rise" as a new theory of international relations through a major propaganda campaign is a good example of a relatively successful effort designed to reassure China's neighbors and the world that China has peaceful intentions.[34]

In April 1998 four of China's national security scholars published a book discussing the theory of how China can rise peacefully as an international power without upsetting the international system.[35] (Earlier in their careers, some of these scholars were affiliated with the MSS.) Its focus is to examine how the rise of China as a world power (or superpower) can take place in such a way as to avoid war and another cold war.[36] The authors began their work on the theory in 1994 and, through the China Philosophy Society, further researched the topic. With respect to Southeast Asia, one of the scholars, Yan Xuetong, explained that the strategists who had developed the theory of China's peaceful rise designed it as a way to respond to the "China threat theory" advanced at the time by former prime minister and minister mentor Lee Kuan-yew of Singapore and Prime Minister Mahathir Mohamad of Malaysia.[37]

Later the Central Communist Party School was the major actor in promulgating the peaceful rise theory internationally, an effort led by its executive vice president, Zheng Bijian. When he moved on to chair the China Reform Forum, a Communist Party–affiliated organization, Zheng continued to discuss the theory, and he advanced it at the Bo'ao Forum on Hainan Island in 2003.[38] The Bo'ao Forum for Asia is a nonprofit, nongovernmental organization committed to regional economic integration in Asia and meets annually at its permanent site, Bo'ao, Hainan Island, China. In 2005 he published a version of his speech "China's Peaceful Rise" in the magazine of the Council on Foreign Relations, *Foreign Affairs*.[39] The peaceful rise theory is an interesting one. It suggests that China's rise as a great power is inevitable and that the different interests of a rising power and an existing superpower in the same region will create friction. Implicit, however, is the suggestion that it is up to the United States, as the lone superpower in the world, to accommodate China's rise.[40] Some American scholars have argued that the rise of great powers usually creates instability in the international system, particularly when those powers are nondemocratic states. The Americans cited the cases of Germany and Japan in the lead-up to the world wars as examples of the tension created by rising powers as they confront leading powers. Zheng responded with a new formulation:

> Our path is different from both the paths of Germany in World War I and Germany and Japan in World War II, when they tried to overhaul the world political landscape by way of aggressive wars. Our path is also to be different from that of the former U.S.S.R. during the reign of Brezhnev, which relied on a military bloc and arms race in order to compete with the United States for world supremacy.[41]

It was not only CCP intellectuals who put forth the formula. On December 10, 2003, Premier Wen Jiabao told an audience at Harvard University that, as a developing country, China would seek to rise peacefully as it resolves its natural resource and energy problems.[42] Sixteen days later, celebrating the 110th anniversary of Mao Zedong's birth, Hu Jintao told an audience that China would "develop along its own socialist course . . . and would follow a peaceful road to development."[43] Hu repeated the formulation on February 23, 2004, to a Politburo study meeting of senior CCP leaders, telling them that the peaceful development path would also follow a policy of self-reliance.[44] In addition, on March 14, 2004, Wen repeated the theory, telling a session of the National People's Congress that although China's peaceful rise would take a long time, it would not depart from the general interests of the world.[45]

The PLA and some in the Chinese Communist Party did not accept the peaceful rise formulation without some internal debate. In a meeting of senior PLA Air Force officers in May 2004, Jiang Zemin suggested that perhaps the formulation should be set aside, since the thesis potentially limited China's military development and modernization. His objection was both a manifestation of friction between himself and Hu Jintao in the transfer of his power to Hu and a demonstration of genuine concern within the PLA that it could continue to modernize and strengthen.[46] In the end, after some period of debate, the CCP arrived at the position that "there is no contradiction between military modernization or military strength and China's peaceful rise."[47] China's policymakers in the PLA and the CCP see military development as complementing China's peaceful rise and feel that accommodating this rise requires an adjustment in attitude by the United States and Southeast Asian nations.[48]

There are unspoken elements in the peaceful rise formulation. An analogy that illustrates Beijing's attitude on the peaceful rise debate is to imagine oneself walking down the middle of a sidewalk when another person comes unseen from around a corner and walks in your direction. That person's course does not deviate, as he or she expects you to shift your own course to accommodate his or hers. Failure to accommodate the new arrival could be interpreted as hostile and a direct challenge of the new arrival. Moreover, since the path of the new arrival is not shifting, any failure to adjust your route could result in a clash. In discussions in Beijing and Shanghai in 2004 and 2005, some Chinese scholars made it clear to the author that the peaceful rise thesis implied that China expected other powers such as the United States to shift policy to accommodate China. However, in Southeast Asia, the campaign to promote the peaceful rise theory was relatively successful and won Beijing increased diplomatic influence.

The PLA part of the action: a series of military-to-military dialogues around Southeast Asia reassured China's neighbors of its peaceful intentions. Unfortunately for the PLA and the makers of China's foreign policy, a generally more aggressive policy on disputed territories, resource claims, and fishing rights in the South China Sea by the PLA and China's maritime surveillance authorities undermined several years of diplomatic effort.[49]

Responding to the Three Warfares

Much of the PLA's campaign, whether in public opinion and media warfare or psychological warfare, depends on the fact that Westerners in general enjoy a free press. Thus the PLA seems to believe that by constantly repeating its message in the

Western press and in other forms of contact, it will be accepted. At home in China there is no free press, and the PLA uses the controlled media there and Hong Kong's Communist-controlled media to deliver its message to the Chinese populace.

In the United States and other Western countries, the free press remains the major counter to China and the PLA's controlled messages. Most reporters are careful enough or cynical enough not to accept every message they are given; they check facts. Still, many Americans have no idea that the China Association for International Friendly Contact is controlled by an intelligence bureau under the PLA's General Political Department. Nor are most Americans or others in the West aware of the relationships among the Military Intelligence Department of the PLA, its GPD counterpart, and CAIFC. Public education, therefore, also is an excellent way to counter the PLA's efforts at public opinion, or media, warfare, perception management, and psychological warfare.

The U.S. government is working to counter China's internal propaganda campaigns through broadcasts on media outlets such as Voice of America or Radio Free Asia as a means to keep Chinese citizens informed. The Internet and social media also make it more difficult to succeed with the type of controlled molding of public opinion conducted by the PLA. However, that does not stop the Chinese government from working to control social media and the internet as well as to identify internet activists.[50] This vying for public opinion and countering propaganda is an example of one area where the PLA has become more sophisticated, and its reach is global. In legal warfare, the PLA may be ahead. Few American legal or military scholars are engaging in arguments in legal journals that counter China's positions. At U.S. military schools and headquarters, there is no systematic effort to establish precedent or to counter some of the PLA's positions. International awareness of the PLA's strategy would be useful, making this another area where public education could be the most effective counter to propaganda.

10 Challenges Posed by the Chinese Military

China's entry into the World Trade Organization and the current level of foreign investment in, and trade with, the People's Republic of China mean that despite the military tensions between the United States and China, the two countries are more or less locked in a deep, interconnected relationship. The thought of creating some sort of containment strategy to limit China's military growth such as the one the United States, its European allies, and Japan maintained against the Soviet Union is not practical. Further, U.S. allies would object to such a strategy, as would the other states in Asia.

America's closest allies are committed to strong economic and trade relationships with China and, short of a war, would not favor a true containment strategy.[1] The United States has enough problems keeping in place the Tiananmen-related arms sales embargo in the European Union, as earlier chapters explained. According to the European Trade Commission, the European Union and China are two of the world's biggest trading partners.[2] As for the Southeast Asian nations, China's largest regional trade partners there are Malaysia, Thailand, and Singapore.[3] Thailand is an ally of the United States, and Singapore is such a close partner that the United States maintains a naval and air presence on the island. Another consideration is that collectively the Association of Southeast Asian Nations is China's third-largest trading partner and is projected to be China's top trading partner by 2012.[4] As for other major U.S. allies, Japan, South Korea, Germany, and Australia all have healthy trade balances with China. This means that there is a fine balance between "hedging" against China's military growth through a strong U.S. military presence in Asia and robust alliances, and maintaining economic, trade, and diplomatic relations.[5]

China has a powerful economy and is now a global manufacturer, consumer of energy resources and goods, and a financial powerhouse. Although China's gross domestic product is only $6.989 trillion, its total foreign exchange reserves are $3.232 trillion, the largest in the world. About 80 percent of that is invested in U.S. debt securities, a factor that makes for a deep and complicated bilateral relationship. The U.S. trade balance with China is negative, and the exchange rate between the yuan, China's currency, and the U.S. dollar is manipulated by China. Arguably the yuan also is undervalued. This means that China accumulates a lot of dollars in foreign exchange, and the U.S. bond market is still the best place to keep that money secure.

To a certain extent, that affects security calculations in China. In the event of a conflict with the United States, those foreign reserves likely would be frozen immediately. That does not mean there cannot be a conflict; China's leaders and its citizens are still quite prickly about certain issues and might well place some sovereignty or territorial issue ahead of financial interest. Also, there are potential points of conflict on the Korean Peninsula, where the Korean War is really not settled—only in an armistice—and North Korea is very unpredictable. China only has one security alliance in the world, and that is with North Korea.

Taiwan also is a potential flash point. For the past four years, tensions in Chinese-Taiwanese relations have been lower. Trends in trade, banking, bilateral tourism, and air traffic shipping have improved, even if there has been no change in the military threats China makes against Taiwan should Beijing perceive Taipei is moving toward independence.[6] A change in the elected leadership in Taiwan, however, could again create a military crisis, and Chinese leaders still threaten war if they perceive that Taiwan is moving toward independence. The Taiwan Relations Act does not bind the United States to Taiwan's defense, but if a conflict were to develop across the Taiwan Strait, it would seriously affect the political and security interests of the United States, and Japan's as well. After nurturing a democracy on Taiwan for decades and seeing the democratic system it encouraged become so vibrant, it is not likely that the United States would simply sit aside and watch how a China-Taiwan conflict played out.

The Air-Sea Battle strategy described in chapter 3 is a good example of the type of careful balance of "hedging" required of the United States. This involves maintaining a strong military presence in Asia, a cooperative security relationship between allies and partners in Asia, and keeping a realistic perspective on economic, diplomatic, and trade relations. It is a difficult balancing act, made more complicated by the fact that China is a permanent member of the United Nations Security Council. There are many times when the United States needs China's cooperation and would prefer that Beijing not exercise its veto power. The history of foreign intervention in China in the nineteenth and twentieth centuries also makes the PLA, China's leaders, and the populace very sensitive about sovereignty and territorial matters, producing constant tension for U.S. military forces in Asia. The disagreements between China and the Republic of Philippines over reefs and islands in the South China Sea complicates matters for the United States because of its defense treaty with the Philippines. In the East China Sea the dispute between China and Japan over the Senkaku Islands, which Japan administers, can involve U.S. forces because of U.S. treaty commitments to Japan.

Command, Control, Surveillance, and the PLA's Reach

As the discussion of the "historic missions of the People's Liberation Army" in chapter 3 points out, with its global economic interests, its dependence on imports of energy and natural resources, and its foreign investments, China is no longer an isolated, inward-looking country. It is building a military that can continue to respond to domestic problems and secure sovereign territory but also must patrol and keep open vital sea and air lines of communication while defending its economic and political interests long distances from home.[7] The PLA Navy's antipiracy/antiterrorism task force in the Gulf of Aden is only a precursor to future PLA operations in defense of national interest. Such operations necessarily require a global command, control, communications, intelligence, surveillance, and reconnaissance capacity. As the nation's interests widen and its economic strength provides for the required military capacity to defend those interests, it is natural for the Chinese military to grow and evolve.

The more troubling aspects of the PLA's developing C^{4}ISR capabilities are the way that they enable a longer reach. Already the PLA Navy can create conditions that may force the U.S. Navy to modify its activities and its strategies out to the "second island China," about two thousand kilometers from China's coast. The PLA's national command-and-control system is redundant, secure, and affects conventional and nuclear missile force readiness, alert status, and the capacity of the Second Artillery to respond to crisis. Perhaps the most troubling and volatile aspects of the PLA's understanding of how C^{4}ISR capabilities enable a range of military activities is that it has led China's military to directly target those same capabilities in the United States and supporting U.S. forces. This action has implications for nuclear deterrence and warning, for space systems, for electronic warfare, and for cyberwarfare.

It is the PLA's improved C^{4}ISR capability that allows China to project and control its limited forces into the western and southern Pacific. China's naval and air force modernization in particular is closely linked to this C⁴ISR capacity. Even if the PLA Army lags somewhat, it also is more effective because of this capacity.

Expanding Naval and Air Reach, but the Army Lags

In a relatively short time, perhaps a decade, the PLA Navy has made a transition from operating only around China's coast, to one that can conduct blue-water operations. China's navy is no peer of the U.S. Navy, and it is probably inferior to Japan's. However, no other nation in Southeast Asia is able to challenge the PLA Navy. This enables China's forceful posture about maritime rights, fishing rights, underwater resources, and disputed territory in the South China Sea. The ASEAN states are not willing to band together to counter China's improved navy; they have their own internal historical problems leading to mutual mistrust. Thus they tend to bandwagon with the United States on security issues.

China also is creating a series of places where the PLA Navy can stop to refuel, take on provisions, and do repairs. As China's naval modernization progresses, this "string of pearls" will facilitate longer reach for its fleets. As the PLA Navy improves its at-sea refueling capability and deploys more support ships and a greater amphibious capacity, it will range further abroad, to other continents, in defense of China's interests.

Improvements in nuclear submarines mean that the PLA Navy can conduct operations over a wider area with longer endurance. The ballistic missile submarines, once operational, will change China's deterrence posture, and provide new means to hold potential adversaries, especially the United States, at risk. The United States and Japan will need to improve their capabilities to monitor the movements of Chinese ballistic missile submarines and to detect them undersea.

The PLA Air Force is also improving its ability to conduct operations at a longer distance from the coast. The 2010 air exercises with Turkey demonstrated a willingness to use airpower outside China if necessary; the evacuation of citizens from Libya the next year demonstrated that China needs even more transport and refueling aircraft. The PLA Army lags behind the Navy and Air Force in its ability to project itself, but improved air and sealift will make it a player in the future. China's defense industries seem to have serious problems in aircraft engine design and manufacture, and they are impediments to modernizing air forces.

These developments also mean that other countries in Asia will improve their own navies. That is already the case for Vietnam, the Philippines, Japan, and India. Whether this fuels some kind of arms race or only means other countries are trying to approach parity with China, it still means that the security balance in the region is changing in response to China's increased reach.

The United States has serious disagreements with some of its allies, particularly in Europe, over military sales to China. Much of the recent PLA Air Force and Navy modernization depended on European assistance. The introduction of the East Asia Security Act of 2005 persuaded companies and governments among America's allies in Europe that profits from military sales to China dwarfed the financial opportunities that came from cooperative military development programs with the United States and reduced the level of sales to China.[8] However, after nearly a decade, perhaps that lesson should be renewed and Congress should consider again similar legislation.

The slowest change in broad posture in the PLA has been in the Army. The induction and training cycles mean that at most times, only one-third to two-thirds of any division is fully trained. Also, because many new recruits have lower levels of education than troops in the Air Force, Navy, and missile forces do, the Army seems to have problems with the move to an information-based planning and logistic system on a widespread basis. Finally, the Chinese Communist Party depends on the ground forces to maintain social stability should other security forces fail, so the Army is still focused on domestic security.

Nuclear Forces and Doctrine

The PLA Second Artillery Force no longer has only a handful of liquid-fueled ballistic missiles targeting the United States. Second Artillery reach, responsiveness, and nuclear strike capacity has expanded significantly and continues to grow. While Beijing repeatedly calls of dramatic cuts in U.S. and Russian nuclear forces, neither Washington nor Moscow can even agree on how many missiles are now in China's inventory. The Department of Defense thinks that "China's nuclear arsenal consists of approximately 55–65 intercontinental ballistic missiles (ICBM)," supplemented by both liquid-fueled and road-mobile intermediate range missiles.[9] The International Institute for Strategic Studies puts it at sixty-six ICBMs, and the Russians may have a higher figure. However, there is less clarity over how many nuclear weapons or warheads the PLA has. Estimates there vary from two hundred or so, all the way up to two thousand. In response, the U.S. Congress required the U.S. Strategic Command to report on the disparities in estimates of the size of China's nuclear forces, on the tunnel networks that support the Second Artillery, and on "the capability of the United States to use conventional and nuclear forces to neutralize such tunnels and what is stored within such tunnels."[10]

Certainly with such a wide variation, this is not the time to drastically reduce American nuclear forces. Rather, it is the time to ensure that the forces available to the United States are secure, reliable, and effective. Also, there is a problem with intermediate nuclear forces. Russia and the United States agreed on reductions, but the Chinese are not part of that agreement, and they are building so many missiles, including cruise missiles, that Russia may need to approach the United States about withdrawing from the 1987 Intermediate-Range Nuclear Forces Treaty.

Of course there also is the question of just how binding China's no-first-use policy may be on the PLA in its military responses to crises or military action. It would be a mistake to reduce American forces to the level China would like—in the hundreds—and then to find out that Beijing has two thousand warheads. If that were the case, any first use of nuclear weapons would benefit the PLA. The PLA's operational principles, discussed in chapter 5, also mean that surprise is very important to the PLA, undermining the credulity of the no-first-use pledge.

Strategic stability and the possibility to control nuclear escalation in a crisis also are threatened by the refusal of the PLA to engage in direct, government-to-government discussions with the U.S. military on nuclear crisis stability and confidence-building measures.

Between the Americans and the Soviets there were "standing taboos" in nuclear security matters—sort of a set of tacit agreements. Arrived at after years of defense talks and arms control negotiations, they formed a set of "red lines" that limited the likelihood of a nuclear war and also prevented the escalation of a conflict. Desmond Ball and his coauthors in a volume on crisis stability summarize these taboos this way:

1. Avoid the use of deadly force against a nuclear adversary.
2. Avoid creating a situation where an opponent is forced to either escalate or face complete humiliation in international affairs.
3. Avoid direct military action in an adversary's vital territorial areas.
4. Avoid using forces against an adversary's ally or protectorate [here think China and Taiwan, Philippines, South Korea, or Japan].
5. Avoid using military forces to alter the balance of power in an area that is status quo [think about China's anti-access (counter-intervention) strategies in the Western Pacific and South China Sea].
6. Avoid horizontal escalation [that is, if there is a crisis in one region, keep it focused there, do not escalate in another region changing a localized or regional conflict into a global conflict].[11]

Given what we know about the PLA's electronic warfare, space warfare, and cyberwarfare doctrine, to these the author would add avoid blinding an opponent by destroying his intelligence, surveillance, and warning assets. In other words, don't mess with the system of strategic warning of missile and nuclear crises. The Soviets were as serious as the United States about trying to avoid nuclear war and escalation. They believed discussions of these issues were useful and built both confidence and mutual understanding. The PLA is absent from any talks on the matter and has avoided invitation from the U.S. Strategic Command to engage in them.

Space and Satellites

As mentioned earlier, Congress already has passed legislation prohibiting NASA from spending money on cooperative programs with China in space. This was a reaction to China's cyber espionage and its destruction of its own satellite. There was a test of China's antiballistic missile system in 2010 that also showed improved ASAT capabilities and another ASAT test in January 2013. U.S. satellites, however, need to be hardened against jamming. Space surveillance and situational awareness programs should help to ensure that American satellites can avoid collisions with other objects in space.

China has a variety of imagery, reconnaissance, communications, and weather satellites, and all of them can be used by the military. Indeed, there is almost no discernible separation between China's civil and military space programs. Space activities all have a heavy military orientation, and the capabilities of the PLA's DF-21D antiship ballistic missile, for example, depend on these dual-use satellites. The General Armaments Department runs almost all astronaut training and space-related medical activities.[12] The China National Space Agency (created in 1993) may be the formal NASA equivalent, facilitating international agreements and cooperation, but it still operates in tandem with the PLA and is involved in the defense industry.[13] The China Aerospace Science and Industry Corporation, a state-owned company, specializes in tactical ballistic missiles, antiship missiles, land-attack cruise missiles, antisatellite interceptors, and small tactical satellites. The China Aerospace Science and Technology Corporation produces launch vehicles and large satellites. Both of these organizations operate closely together.

In short, there are no real advantages to space cooperation with China at the same time that the PLA is developing a robust counterspace capability. This explains why Congress prohibited such cooperation.

Some specialists in space advocate a "code of conduct" for activities in space that would help prevent certain destructive actions. Such a code, however, would likely be the first thing violated in a conflict given the PLA's doctrine on information warfare and counterspace activities. The Department of Defense should develop operationally responsive space capabilities and be prepared to substitute various forms of air-breathing platforms in the event of an attack on U.S. space assets. It also is wise to harden satellites against jamming and other forms of electromagnetic interference.

The Global Reach of Information and Electronic Warfare

In a research report cited in chapter 8, *Capability of the People's Republic of China to Conduct Cyber Warfare and Computer Network Exploitation*, the Northrop Grumman Corporation provided a case study of a multiday penetration into the computer systems of an American high-technology company and how the data acquired was transferred to an Internet protocol address in China.[14] The report also discussed the principal institutional and individual "actors" in Chinese computer network operations, as well as the characteristics of network exploitation activities that are frequently attributed to China. Cyberwarfare is a strategic issue that the U.S. and Chinese defense establishment must address in some form of confidence-building and threat-reduction measures, along with nuclear doctrine and space warfare doctrine.

China's computer network exploitation activities to support espionage opened rich veins of information that were previously inaccessible or could only be mined in small amounts with controlled human intelligence operations. China is using computer espionage to support its military and civilian modernization goals. Two departments of the PLA, the General Staff Department's Third and Fourth Departments, are organized to systematically penetrate communications and computer systems, extract information, and exploit that information.[15] It is far faster, cheaper, and more efficient for the PLA to steal new technology than to devote vast amounts of time and money to develop it.

The 2009 report to Congress of the U.S.-China Economic and Security Review Commission cited a *Wall Street Journal* article noting that "intruders, probably operating from China, exfiltrated 'several terabytes of data related to design and electronics systems' of the F-35 Lightning II," one of the most advanced fighter planes under development.[16] In addition, Lockheed Martin, Northrop Grumman, and British Aerospace and Engineering reportedly all have experienced penetrations from hackers based in China in the past three years.[17]

PLA integrated network electronic warfare doctrine is Soviet radio-electronic combat doctrine on Chinese steroids. Chinese doctrine has added in computer network operations that would disrupt not only command-and-control systems, but also logistics and resupply systems. This INEW doctrine is fully integrated with space warfare designed to degrade an adversary's space-based sensor and communications systems. And it also includes provisions for precision strikes on U.S. bases, forces, and embarkation areas in the homeland. To be effective, the strategy must be executed at the very first phase of any conflict.

The United States must deal with computer espionage and cyber attacks. China has made significant progress in its military technology development by hacking and stealing trade secrets and military technology. Moreover, this cyber espionage goes after the same targets as traditional human espionage, helping the PLA modernize. The J-20 stealth fighter may not be the equal of the American F-22 Raptor, but Chinese spies have been working to get F-22 technology, according to the Federal Bureau of Investigation, as well as technology for the E-2 Hawkeye naval AWACS aircraft.[18]

Former vice chairman of the Joint Chiefs of Staff Gen. James Cartwright has suggested that immediate steps be taken to address cyber penetrations as soon as they are detected. He suggested that when the Department of Defense detects a cyber penetration, it should go to the State Department to notify the government of the country from which the penetration was traced that its attack had been detected. Cartwright further suggested that this notification should be accompanied by a forty-eight-hour deadline and the threat to disrupt the malicious activity if no action was taken.[19]

In cases where U.S. counterintelligence or security officials are able to attribute an attack to a foreign person—whether in China or elsewhere—law enforcement authorities should be able to seek an arrest warrant in a closed federal court such as the Foreign Intelligence and Surveillance Court. And in the case of a foreign company involved in cyber espionage, there should be a statutory prohibition on that company doing business in the United States. The Department of State should also not be permitted to issue a visa to a person who is judged by the court to be involved in cyber espionage unless there is also a plan to bring that person to trial when he or she enters the United States. When companies or individuals are the subject of an arrest warrant or are denied the right to do business, the U.S. government also should notify its allies of the action.

To deal with cyber attacks of the type outlined in chapter 8, or attacks on satellites as outlined in chapter 6, the United States should have a clear policy that declares that attacks in cyberspace or outer space are acts of war and that the United States may respond with force, not necessarily in the same domain of war—that is, a cyber attack or a satellite attack may generate a weapon strike and a state of war.

Dealing with the three warfares is a more difficult issue. Public education in the United States helps make Americans aware of the nature and intent of the PLA's media warfare effort at molding public opinion and its perception-management activities. Exposure to scrutiny makes it more difficult for the PLA to succeed in these efforts. The same type of public education program is needed to make sure Americans understand the way that PLA military intelligence and the General Political Department use cover organizations such as the China Association for International Friendly Contact.

Basic Guidelines for U.S. Military Contacts and Exchanges with China

Military-to-military exchanges serve as confidence-building measures and enhance interoperability among allies or partners. China, however, is not a U.S. ally, and it takes the United States as its most likely foe. Many of the military modernization programs described in this book are specifically intended to be used in the event of conflict with the United States. The PLA also threatens U.S. interests in its aggressive activities in space, on the oceans against allies such as Japan and the Philippines, and across the Taiwan Strait against Taiwan.

All of this argues for carefully measured contacts that can help ensure that incidents do not escalate. It does not call for combined training. The National Defense Authorization Act of 2000 prohibits the secretary of defense from authorizing any military-to-military exchange or contact with the People's Liberation Army or China if such exchange or contact would create a national security risk. The legislation also makes these provisions inapplicable to search-and-rescue or humanitarian exercises, ensuring the U.S. military and PLA forces can do what is necessary for rescue, humanitarian relief, and to cooperate in certain UN peace-keeping efforts. The act also required the secretary of defense to certify annually to the defense committees whether any such exchange or contact was conducted. Also, the secretary of defense is required to submit an annual report to the defense com-mittees on the current state of such exchanges and contacts.[20] In 2001 Congress went a little further, requesting a report on Chinese military companies operating in the United States and creating the U.S.-China Economic and Security Review Commission to monitor and report on how U.S. China trade might affect U.S. security.[21]

There are other simple and practical guidelines the Department of Defense can use to guide its contacts with the PLA. Fundamentally, the United States should do nothing to improve the capability of the PLA to wage war against the United

States, Taiwan, or other friends and allies; do nothing to improve the PLA's ability to project force; and do nothing to improve the PLA's capability to suppress or threaten China's own people.[22]

China cannot project military force around the globe in all the domains of war at this time; but it is a global force in space, missile, and nuclear matters and in the cyber realm. The Navy and the Air Force are growing in the ability to project power. Regionally, the PLA is powerful and makes some of its neighbors wary. Over the next decade it is likely that China's military will proceed to grow, the quality of PLA's weapons and equipment will improve, and the PLA's orientation toward an increased capacity to support China's global interests will continue.

When Xi Jinping took over as general secretary of the Communist Party and chairman of the Central Military Commission in November 2012, his first address to the PLA was to the Second Artillery Force.[23] He made it clear that China intends to achieve great power status, and the Second Artillery is a pillar for achieving that goal. Further, there are no signs that the confrontational approach Beijing has taken in the waters it claims in the western Pacific or its ultimate posture on Taiwan will change. More likely, as the PLA becomes more powerful, China will become more assertive and less willing to compromise. All of this means that the barriers that Congress has erected against increased security cooperation with China will probably stay in place.

There is ample room for improvement in cooperation and dialogue in a number of areas, from direct discussions about cyber warfare to issues related to nuclear stability. Nonetheless, between China and the United States, a deep incongruity exists between the level of economic and trade engagement and the military postures of each country. And while each government professes that its military posture is not aimed at the other, the countries' respective programs suggest otherwise. Thus the United States will have to continue to monitor developments in the PLA carefully and continue hedging in its security posture.

NOTES

1. The PLA's Role in China's Foreign Policy

1. Larry M. Wortzel, *Dictionary of Chinese Military History* (Westport, CT: Greenwood, 1999), 176–77.
2. R. Keith Schoppa, *Revolution and Its Past: Identities and Change in Modern Chinese History,* 2nd ed. (Saddle River, NJ: Prentice Hall, 2006), 180–81, 194–95. For the PLA's official history, see Academy of Military Science, Military History Research Editorial Staff, *Zhongguo Renmin Jiefangjun Zhanshi* [Wartime history of the Chinese people's liberation army], vol. 1 (Beijing: Academy of Military Science Press, 1987). The Nanchang Uprising and the movement to the Jinggang Mountains are covered on pages 1–29.
3. Throughout this book, the pinyin system is used to transliterate the pronunciation of Chinese ideographs into English. On Taiwan (the Republic of China) and in many historical references, the Wade-Giles system is used for transliteration. "Guomindang" would be transliterated as "Kuomintang" in Wade-Giles, and "Jiang Jieshi" would be "Chiang Kai-shek."
4. Xiaobing Li, *A History of the Modern Chinese Army* (Lexington: University Press of Kentucky, 2007), 36–39.
5. These Communist officers were He Long, Ye Ting, Zhu De, Zhou Enlai, Liu Bocheng, Nie Ronbgshen, and Zhou Sidi, who formed a Guomindang Revolutionary Committee, also known as the Guomindang Left Wing. Wortzel, *Dictionary of Chinese Military History*, 176.
6. Ibid.
7. Ibid., 23–24.
8. Li, *History of the Modern Chinese Army*, 45.
9. Ibid.
10. Wortzel, *Dictionary of Contemporary Chinese Military History*, 152–53, 308. See also Jerome Ch'en, "Resolutions of the The Tsunyi Conference," *The China Quarterly*, no. 40 (October/ December 1969): 1–38.
11. Li, *History of the Modern Chinese Army*, 61.
12. This section relies heavily on a reference volume by the Rand Corporation that may well be the most complete description of the PLA and its organization available. See James C. Mulvenon and Andrew N. D. Yang, eds., *The People's Liberation Army as an Organization*, reference vol. v1.0 (Santa Monica, CA: Rand Corp., 2002). Another

excellent reference is David Shambaugh, ed., *The China Quarterly: China's Military in Transition*, no. 146 (June 1996); the entire issue is devoted to the PLA.

13. Law of the People's Republic of China on National Defense, adopted at the eighth session of the Fifth National People's Congress, March 14, 1997.

14. Tai Ming Cheung, "The People's Armed Police: First Line of Defense," *The China Quarterly* no. 146 (June 1996), 525–47. See also Dennis J. Blasko, *The Chinese Army Today: Tradition and Transformation for the 21st Century* (London: Routledge, 2006), 23.

15. Ellis Joffe, "Party-Army Relations in China: Retrospect and Prospect," in *The China Quarterly: China's Military in Transition*, no. 146 (June 1996): 305.

16. International Institute of Strategic Studies (hereafter cited as IISS), *The Military Balance: 2012* (London: Routledge, 2012), 233.

17. Ibid., 233–36.

18. Ibid. The size of the basic militia is from Blasko, *Chinese Army Today*, 24–25.

19. State Council Information Office, *China's National Defense in 2010* (Beijing, 2011), http://www.gov.cn/english/official/2011-03/31/content_1835499.htm.

20. Larry M. Wortzel, ed., *The Chinese Armed Forces in the 21st Century* (Carlisle, PA: Strategic Studies Institute, 1999). See also Ellis Joffe, *Party and Army: Professionalism and Political Control in the Chinese Officer Corps, 1949–1964* (Cambridge, MA: Harvard University Press, 1971), and Harlan Jencks, *From Muskets to Missiles: Politics and Professionalism in the Chinese Army, 1954–1981* (Boulder, CO: Westview, 1982).

21. State Council Information Office, *China's National Defense in 2010*.

22. Larry M. Wortzel, *China's Nuclear Forces: Operations, Training, Doctrine, Command, Control, and Campaign Planning* (Carlisle, PA: Strategic Studies Institute, 2007), 24–26; Defense Intelligence Agency, *Handbook of the Chinese Armed Forces*, DDI-2680-32-76 (Washington, DC: Defense Intelligence Agency, 1976), 2–1; and Blasko, *Chinese Army Today*, 27. See also David Shambaugh, "The Pinnacle of the Pyramid: The Central Military Commission," in Mulvenon and Yang, *People's Liberation Army*, 95–121.

23. Kenneth Allen, "Introduction to the PLA's Administrative and Operational Structure," in Mulvenon and Yang, *People's Liberation Army*, 35–39.

24. Wortzel, *China's Nuclear Forces*, 24–26.

25. This disagreement and firm insistence by Guo on the PLA's subordination to the CMC was emphasized by PLA officers in discussions with the author in August 2009.

26. State Council Information Office, *China's National Defense in 2010*.

27. Nan Li, "The Central Military Commission and Military Policy in China," in Mulvenon and Yang, *People's Liberation Army*, 45–94, and Shambaugh, "Pinnacle of the Pyramid," 95–121.

28. See Allen, "Introduction to the PLA's Administrative and Operational," 7–9, and David L. Finklestein, "The General Staff Department of the Chinese People's Liberation Army: Organization, Roles, and Missions," in Mulvenon and Yang, *People's Liberation Army*, 122–224.

29. Based on the author's experience as a military attaché escorting Chinese military officials in the United States and U.S. military officials in China.

30. See Larry M. Wortzel, "The General Political Department and the Evolution of the Political Commissar System," in Mulvenon and Yang, *People's Liberation Army*, 225–45.

31. Tian Peng, "Beijing Shi Jundui Shang, Bing, Can Tuixiu Ganbu Mingque Jianjie Shijian" [Retired sick, injured and incapacitated military cadre from Beijing meet and exchange their time], *Jiefangjun Bao*, July 6, 2011, http://chn.chinamil.com.cn/xwpdxw/2011-07/06/content_4460134.htm.

32. Susan M. Puska, "People's Liberation Army (PLA) General Logistics Department (GLD): Toward Joint Logistics Support," in Mulvenon and Yang, *People's Liberation Army*, 247–72.

33. Harlan W. Jencks, "The General Armaments Department," in Mulvenon and Yang, *People's Liberation Army*, 273–309.

34. Liu Wei, *Zhanqu Lianhe Zhanyi Zhihui Gailun* [Command and control of joint campaigns in theaters of war] (Beijing: National Defense University Press, 2003), 6.

35. A group army (*jituan jun*) is analogous to a U.S. or NATO corps, comprising at least two divisions or independent brigades, and supporting arms such as armor, artillery, intelligence, engineer, and air defense battalions or regiments. A group army has thirty thousand to sixty thousand personnel; divisions have six thousand to twelve thousand.

36. Jinan MR is generally considered the "strategic reserve" for China. The PLAAF Fifteenth Airborne Army is located there.

37. Dennis Blasko notes that this listing is in the protocol order assigned by the PLA based on the time that the region came under PLA control in the civil war. Blasko, *Chinese Army Today*, 32.

38. *Directory of PRC Military Personalities*, October 2010. This publication lists no author or publisher, but it is available to a number of specialists on the PLA in the United States and other NATO countries. The China Documentation Center at the Gelman Library, George Washington University, Washington, D.C., has one copy in its collection, http://findit.library.gwu.edu/item/4074485; the Federation of American Scientists also has a copy, but a posting on the FAS website says that all attempts to find an author or publisher failed, http://www.fas.org/nuke/guide/china/agency/pla-orbat.htm. The author's experience is that the publication is very reliable. A similar resource is *Zhongguo Jundui Xianren Zhuyao Zeren Minglu* [Record of China's important military personalities], Version 2011.4.3; this originally seems to have been published by the PRC website http://www.guancha.cn/; however, like the *Directory of PRC Military Personalities*, no author or publisher is given.

39. IISS, *Military Balance: 2010*, 230.

40. Ibid.

41. See Song Yuwei and Gao Tingting, "Jiayu Xin Zhangbei, Yanlian Xin Zhanfa" [Operating new equipment, practicing new tactics], *Jiefangjun Bao* [*PLA Daily*], July 15, 2011; and Hou Guorong and Gou Jianhong, "Duikang, Fuza Huanjing Kaoyan Zhong Junzhang [Confrontation, Testing the Command Tent in a Complex Environment]," *Jiefangjun Bao* [*PLA Daily*], July 18, 2011.

42. Liu, *Zhanqu Lianhe Zhanyi Zhihui Gailun*, 6–7.

43. See Harlan Jencks, "China's 'Punitive War' on Vietnam: A Military Assessment," *Asian Survey* 19, no. 8 (August 1979): 800–808.

44. Zhang Peigao, ed., *Lianhe Zhanyi Zhihui Jiaocheng* [Lectures on joint campaign command and control, 2nd edition] (Beijing: Military Science Press, 2001), 2–10. Also see Liu, *Zhanqu Lianhe Zhanyi Zhihui Gailun*, 6–7.

45. This section relies on Dennis J. Blasko, "PLA Ground Forces: Moving toward a Smaller, More Rapidly Deployable, Modern Combined Arms Force," in Mulvenon and Yang, eds., *People's Liberation Army as Organization*, 313–15.

46. Blasko, *Chinese Army Today*, 46–53.

47. An Bajie, "Military Takes Aim at Corruption," *Global Times*, September 28, 2010, http://www.globaltimes.cn/china/chinanews/2010-09/577869.html.

48. This section relies on Finklestein, "General Staff Department," 184–91.

49. State Council Information Office, *China's National Defense in 2002*, available at http://english.gov.cn/official/2005-07/28/content_18078.htm.

50. Ren Min, *Guofang Dongyuan Xue* [On national defense mobilization] (Beijing: Military Science Press, 2008), 341–55.

51. Blasko, *Chinese Army Today*, 35–36.

52. Ibid., 35.

53. State Council Information Office, *China's National Defense in 2002*.

54. A general description of the resources incorporated into the mobilization system described in the 2002 national defense white paper can be found in Jiang Luming, ed., *Xiandai Guofang Jingjixue Daolun* [Guide to modern national defense economics] (Beijing: National Defense University Press, 2002). The people's civil air defense system is described in Xiao Xingbo, *He Zhanzheng yu Renfang* [People's air defense and nuclear war] (Beijing: People's Liberation Army Press, 1989).

55. U.S.-China Economic and Security Review Commission (hereafter cited as USCC), *2009 Report to Congress of the U.S.-China Economic and Security Review Commission* (Washington, DC: Government Printing Office, 2009), 173.

56. Ye Youcai and Zhou Wenrui, "Jianshe Yi Zhe Gao Suzhi de Minbing Xinxi Jishu Fendui" [Building a high-quality militia information technology unit], *Guofang* [*National Defense*], no. 9 (2003): 45.

57. USCC, *2009 Report to Congress*, 173, 205n386, 205n387, 205n388.

58. Chin Chien-li, "Zhong Gong Di Yi Fu Can Mou Zhang, Ge Fengzhen" [Profile of communist China's first deputy Chief of General Staff Ge Fengzhen], *Chien Shao* [*Frontline*], May 1, 2005, 50–53.

59. Wu Tianmin and Liu Fengtian, "2009: Toushi Zhongguo Junyan" [Perspective on China's military exercises], *Jiefangjun Bao* [*PLA Daily*], December 23, 2009.

60. Liu Chengjun and Liu Yuan, "Xin Zhongguo 60 Nian Guofang he Jundui Jianshe Jiben Jingyan" [Fundamental experience of the 60 years of national defense and army building], *Zongguo Junshi Kexue* [*China Military Science*] 5, no 107 (2009): 9.

61. Academy of Military Science, *Zhongguo Renmin Jiefangjun Zhanshi*, 18–29.

62. Wang Yushan, "Heping Bushi Tianshang Diaoxia Laile" [Peace has not fallen from the sky], Xinhua Domestic Service, December 28, 2010, http://www/xinhua.com.cn\xhzss \XxjdzbC0230NT20101228N_simple.xml; this is an interview with Central Military Commission deputy and Minister of Defense General Liang Guanglie.

63. This section relies on IISS, *The Military Balance: 2011* (London: Routledge, 2011), 230–36; Defense Intelligence Agency, *Handbook of the Chinese Armed Forces* DDI-2680-32-76 (Washington, DC: Defense Intelligence Agency, July 1976), 2-1, 2-13, A-2, A-22; and Blasko, "PLA Ground Forces: Moving toward," 309–45.

64. Dabaike Quanshu Bianji Weiyuanhui, *Zhongguo Dabaike Quanshu: Junshi* [A complete encyclopedia of China: Military], 2 vols. (Beijing: Zhongguo Dabaike Quanshu Chubanshe, 1989), vol. 2, 1225.

65. Liu, *Zhanqu Lianhe Zhanyi Zhihui Gailun*, 6–7, 8–9. See also Blasko, *Chinese Army Today*, 33–34.

66. National Defense University Editorial Group, *Zhongguo Renmin Jiefangjun Zhanshi Bianji* [A brief history of the Chinese PLA Revolutionary War] (Beijing: PLA Press, 1983), 56–140. See also Wang Houqing, et al., *Zhanyi Fazhan Shi* [Campaign development history] (Beijing: National Defense University Press, 1996), 359–403.

67. *Zhongguo Dabaike Quanshu*, 1225. The formal encyclopedia translation of *zhanqu* is "theater."

68. Wang, *Zhanyi Fazhan Shi*, 531–32.

69. Wortzel, *Dictionary of Contemporary Chinese Military History*, 258–59.

70. Ibid. See also Edward C. O'Dowd and John F. Corbett Jr., "The 1979 Chinese Campaign in Vietnam: Lessons Learned," in Laurie Burkitt, Andrew Scobell, and Larry M. Wortzel, *The Lessons of History: The Chinese People's Liberation Army at 75* (Carlisle, PA: Strategic Studies Institute, 2003), 353–78; King C. Chen, *China's War with Vietnam, 1979: Issues, Decisions and Implications* (Stanford, CA: Stanford University Press, 1987; and Jencks, "China's 'Punitive War,'" 806–15.

71. Ding Bangyu, ed., *Zuozhan Zhihui Xue* [The study of operational command and control], (Beijing: Military Science Press, 2006), 69. This collective tradition is also outlined in Xiao Chaoren ed., *Zhonggong Dangshi Jianming Cidian* [A concise dictionary of the Chinese Communist Party's history] (Beijing: People's Liberation Army Press, 1986), 396, 397, 444 (the Gutian Meeting).

72. Ding, *Zuozhan Zhihui Xue*, 70.

73. Warren Kuo, ed., *A Comprehensive Glossary of Chinese Communist Terminology* (Taipei: Institute of International Relations, 1978), 121.

74. Ibid.

75. Ibid., 71.

76. Xiao, *Zhonggong Dangshi Jianming Cidian*, 448.

77. Ding, *Zuozhan Zhihui Xue*, 72.

78. Ibid., 73.

79. Ibid., 74.

80. Ibid., 75.

81. Ibid.

82. See also Shu Guangzhang, "Command, Control, and the PLA's Offensive Campaigns in Korea," in Mark A. Ryan, David M. Finklestein, and Michael A. McDevitt, eds., *Chinese Warfighting: The Experience of the PLA since 1949* (Armonk, NY: M. E. Sharpe, 2003), 91–122.

83. Ding, *Zuozhan Zhihui Xue*, 76.

84. Cheng Feng and Larry M. Wortzel, "PLA Operational Principles and Limited War: The Sino-Indian War of 1962," in Ryan et al., *Chinese Warfighting*, 173–97. On Vietnam, the deployment of forward commands was a key indication that the PLA was serious about offensive action, and a front headquarters was set up at Duyun. See Jencks, "China's 'Punitive' War," 806–15.

85. It is hard to find a copy, but the seminal English-language book on this is still William W. Whitson with Chen-Hsia Huang, *The Chinese High Command: The History of Communist Military Politics, 1927–1971* (New York: Praeger, 1973).

86. See Wortzel, *Dictionary of Chinese Military History*, 144–45, 165–66, 308.

87. Yu Ma, "Tai Zi Dang Ren Pai Guanxi Cang Zhang Da Gongkai" [A new list of offspring of high-ranking officials of China], *Ching Chi Jih Pao* [*Economic Daily*], November 12, 2004. See Ho P'in and Kao Hsin, *Zhonggong Taizi Dang* [Communist princelings] (Hong Kong: Times Publishers, 1992).

88. Xinhua News Agency, "PLA Celebrates 80th Anniversary," *China View*, August 2, 1007, http://news.xinhuanet.com/english/2007-08/02/content_6465779.htm. The website above has eleven links to different elements of Hu Jintao's full speech and the speeches of others. In his speech, Hu mentioned Mao Zedong, Zhou Enlai, Liu Shaoqi, Zhu De, Deng Xiaoping, Peng Dehuai, Liu Bocheng, He Long, Chen Yi, Luo Ronghuan, Xu Xiangqian, and Ye Jianying.

89. Ye Jianying, *Speech at the Meeting in Celebration of the 30th Anniversary of the Founding of the People's Republic of China*, September 29, 1979 (Beijing: Foreign Languages Press, 1979).

90. Ibid., 116–17.
91. Xinhua, "PLA Celebrates 80th Anniversary."
92. See Gary J. Bjorge, *Moving the Enemy: Operational Art in the Chinese PLA's Huai Hai Campaign*, Leavenworth Paper 22 (Fort Leavenworth, KS: Combat Studies Institute Press, 2004), 45.
93. Chen Yi was East China Field Army commander, but he had been temporarily detached to work with Liu Bocheng and Deng Xiaoping in the Central Plains Field Army area, to the southwest.
94. Mao Zedong, "The Present Situation and Our Tasks," December 25, 1947, in Mao Tse-tung, *Selected Works of Mao Tse-tung*, vol. 4 (Peking: Foreign Languages Press, 1975), 161–62.
95. Bjorge, *Moving the Enemy*, 48.
96. Larry M. Wortzel, *Mobility, Pace and Pauses in the Chinese People's Liberation Army: The Huai-Hai Campaign*, unpublished manuscript as a study for SAIC Corp., May 22, 2005. See also Larry M. Wortzel, "The Beiping-Tianjin Campaign of 1948–1949," in Ryan et al., *Chinese Warfighting*, 60–62.
97. Liu, *Zhanqu Lianhe Zhanyi Zhihui Gailun*, 6.
98. See Larry M. Wortzel, "China's Foreign Conflicts since 1949," in David A. Graff and Robin Higham, *A Military History of China* (Boulder, CO: Westview, 2002), 267.
99. Bernard D. Cole, *The Great Wall at Sea: China's Navy Enters the Twenty-First Century* (Annapolis, MD: Naval Institute Press, 2001), 2–3.
100. John W. Garver, *Foreign Relations of the People's Republic of China* (Englewood Cliffs, NJ: Prentice Hall, 1993), 10.
101. Ibid., 4–8. See also Alison A. Kaufman, "The 'Century of Humiliation' and China's National Narratives," testimony before the USCC, March 10, 2011. The hearing transcript can be found at http://www.uscc.gov/hearings/2011hearings/written _testimonies/hr11_03_10.php (accessed June 6, 2011).
102. Jonathan D. Spence, *The Search for Modern China* (New York: Norton, 1990), 230–35. See also Mary Hooker, *Behind the Scenes in Peking* (London: Oxford University Press, 1910 [Oxford Paperbacks, 1987]).
103. Garver, *Foreign Relations*, 4–8; Kaufman, "'Century of Humiliation'"; and Spence, *Search for Modern China*, 143–269.
104. See for instance, Kenneth Conboy and James Morrison, *The CIA's Secret War in Tibet* (Lawrence: University Press of Kansas, 2002), and James Lilley with Jeffrey Lilley, *China Hands: Nine Decades of Adventure, Espionage, and Diplomacy in Asia* (New York: PublicAffairs, 2004).
105. See Ellis Joffe, "People's War under Modern Conditions," *China Quarterly*, no. 112 (December 1987): 555–73, and Paul H. B. Godwin, "Changing Concepts of Doctrine, Strategy, and Operations in the Chinese People's Liberation Army," *China Quarterly*, no. 112 (December 1987): 578–81.
106. See Huang Dafu et al., *Jubu Zhanzheng Zhong de Zhanshu* [Tactics of limited war] (Beijing: National Defense University Press, 1989); and Dennis J. Blasko, "PLA Ground Forces Lessons Learned: Experience and Theory, in Burkitt et al., *Lessons of History*, 61–87. There is a good summary of these doctrinal shifts in David Shambaugh, *Modernizing China's Military: Progress, Problems, and Prospects* (Berkeley: University of California Press, 2002), 60–75.
107. See June Teufel Dreyer, "People's Liberation Army Lessons from Foreign Conflicts: The War in Kosovo," in Andrew Scobell, David Lai, and Roy Kamphausen, eds., *Chinese Lessons from Other Peoples' Wars* (Carlisle, PA: Strategic Studies Institute,

2011), 33–74, and Dean Cheng, "Chinese Lessons from the Gulf Wars," in Scobell, Lai, and Kamphausen, *Chinese Lessons from Other Peoples' Wars*, 153–200.

108. Shambaugh, *Modernizing China's Military*, 69–70.

109. The PLA generated books and studies designed to educate soldiers and officers about the new doctrine and the reforms it would institute to embrace this revolution in military affairs. See for instance Han Xiaolin, ed., *Gao Jishu Zhubu Zhanzheng Lilun Yanjiu* [Research and theory on limited war under high technology conditions] (Beijing: Military Friendship and Literature Press, 1998); Zhu Youwen, Feng Yi, and Xu Dechi., eds. *Gao Jishu Tiaojian Xia de Xinxi Zhan* [Information warfare under high technology conditions] (Beijing: Military Science Press, 1994); Chen Yong et al., *Gao Jishu Tiaojian Xia Lujun Zhanyi Xue* [The science of army (ground force) campaigns under high technology conditions] (Beijing: Military Science Press, 2003); Yu Yongzhe, ed., *Gao Jishu Zhanzheng Houqin Baozhang* [Ensuring logistics in high-technology war] (Beijing: Military Science Press, 1995); and Liu Mingtao and Yang Chengjun, eds., *Gao Jishu Zhanzheng Zhong de Daodan Zhan* [Ballistic missile battles in high technology warfare] (Beijing: National Defense University Press, 1993).

110. Two books that illustrate this trend are Cai Fengzhen and Tian Anping, eds., *Kongtian Yiti Zuozhan Xue* [Integrated aerospace operations] (Beijing: PLA Press, 2006), and Li Rongchang, Cheng Jian, and Guo Lianqing, eds., *Kongtian Yiti Zinxi Zuozhan* [Integrated, informationalized aerospace war] (Beijing: Military Science Press, 2003).

111. The first three Hu identified as "three big historical tasks" (*san da lishi renwu*). See Huang Yingxu, "Lun Zhongguo Gongchandang Red de Guojia Liyi Guan" [On CPC members' outlook on national interests], *Zhongguo Junshi Kexue* [*China Military Science*] 109, no. 6 (2009): 4.

112. Hu Jintao, "Renqing Xin Shiji Xin Jieduan Wojun Lishi Shiming" [Understand the new historic missions of our military in the new period of the new century], speech to the Central Military Commission of the Chinese Communist Party, December 24, 2004, http://gfjy.jiangxi.gov.cn/htmnew/11349.htm (accessed November 17, 2009).

113. Ibid. For a more detailed analysis and discussion of the "historic missions," see Daniel M. Hartnett, *Towards a Globally Focused Chinese Military: The "Historic Missions" of the Chinese Armed Forces*, CME D0018304.A1 (Alexandria, VA: Center for Naval Analyses 2008), 1; also see USCC, *2009 Report to Congress*, 114–16.

114. "CMC's Guo Boxiong Urges Improving PLA Capabilities to 'Fulfill Historic Missions,'" Beijing Xinhua Domestic Service, September 27, 2005, cited in Hartnett, *Towards a Globally Focused Chinese Military*, 3. Also see Cortez A. Cooper, *The PLA Navy's "New Historic Missions": Expanding Capabilities for a Re-emergent Maritime Power* (Arlington, VA; Rand, 2009), http://www.rand.org/content/dam/rand/pubs/testimonies/2009/RAND_CT332.pdf.

115. Hartnett, *Towards a Globally Focused Chinese Military*, 1, 10–12.

116. Ibid., 231.

117. Wang Lidong, *Guojia Haishang Liyi Lun* [A discussion of China's national maritime interests] (Beijing: Guofang Daxue Chubanshe, 2007), 248. See also Wang Zaibang, *Haishang Tongdao Anquan yu Guoji Hezuo* [Sea lane security and international cooperation] (Beijing: Current Events Press, 2005), 357–76. Hang Wuchao makes essentially the same point in "Shixi Guojia Liyi yu Zhanlue Fangxiang" [Analysis of national interests and strategic orientation], *Zhongguo Junshi Kexue* [China military science] 20, no. 1 (2007): 84–90.

118. On the need to develop the capacity to secure China's interests abroad, see Jiang Yamin, *Yuan Zhan* [Long distance operations] (Beijing: Academy of Military Science Press, 2007).

2. C⁴ISR

1. C⁴ISR is an acronym for command, control, communications, computers, intelligence, surveillance, and reconnaissance. ISR stands for intelligence, surveillance and reconnaissance when that acronym is used separately. In 2013, some U.S. military organizations started to use the acronym C⁵ISR for command, control, communications, computers, combat systems, intelligence, surveillance and reconnaissance. This book will use C⁴ISR, but the reader should understand that the term includes the combat systems that receive the data.

2. The Department of Defense defines antiaccess as "those capabilities, usually long-range, designed to prevent an advancing enemy from entering an operational area;" area-denial is defined as "those capabilities, usually of shorter range, designed not to keep the enemy out but to limit his freedom of action within the operational area." Department of Defense, *Joint Operational Access Concept (JOAC),* Version 1.0, January 17, 2012 (Washington, DC: Department of Defense, 2012), 40.

3. See James Mulvenon and David Finkelstein, eds., *China's Revolution in Doctrinal Affairs: Emerging Trends in the Operational Art of the Chinese People's Liberation Army* (Washington, DC: Rand Corp., 2005); Center for Technology and National Security Policy, *Coping with the Dragon: Essays on PLA Transformation and the U.S. Military* (Washington, DC: National Defense University, 2007), especially essays 4 and 9 (available on the web at http://www.ndu.edu/CTNSP/docUploaded/CopingwithDragon.pdf); Department of Defense, *Quadrennial Defense Review Report* (Washington, DC: Department of Defense, 2010), especially 31–34; and Jan Van Tol with Mark Gunzinger, Andrew Krepinovich, and Jim Thomas, *AirSea Battle: A Point-of-Departure Operational Concept* (Washington, DC: Center for Strategic and Budgetary Assessments, 2010), especially chapter 2, 17–47.

4. Gao Shijin and Zhang Peizhong, *Duo Yanghua Junshi Renwu Lun* [On [increasingly] multiple military missions] (Beijing: Long March Press, 2009), 64–65. See also Cortez A. Cooper, "Joint Anti-Access Operations: China's 'System-of-Systems' Approach," testimony before the U.S.-China Economic and Security Review Commission, Washington, January 27, 2010, www.uscc.gov/hearings/hearingarchive.php#hearings2011, and Roger Cliff, Mark Burles, Michael S. Chase, Derek Eaton, and Kevin L. Pollpeter, *Entering the Dragon's Lair: Chinese Anti-Access Strategies and Their Implications for the United States* (Santa Monica, CA: Rand Corp., 2007).

5. See the Chinese reaction to the U.S. characterization of antiaccess/area denial strategy in *China Daily* and *Huanqui Shibao*: http://www.chinadaily.com.cn/hqjs/jspl/2011-02 -18/content_1800254 (accessed April 4, 2011) and http://www.huanqiu.com /observation/2010-12/13503003.html (accessed April 4, 2011).

6. "Informationalized" and "informationalization" are awkward terms in English. In Chinese it makes more sense (*xinxihuade*), but the PLA uses both consistently in its own translations. Also, Chinese newpapers and publications sometimes use the term "informatized" to translate xinxihuade into English. The best English equivalents would be "information age warfare" or "war in the information age." This work will use the Chinese terms as well as English equivalents.

7. State Council Information Office, *China's National Defense in 2006*, http://www.china
.org.cn/english/features/book/194421.htm, in OSC, https://www.opensource.gov
/FEA20061230063508.

8. Wang Zhengde, ed., *Jiedu Wangluo Zhongxin Zhan* [Interpretation of network centric
warfare] (Beijing: National Defense Industries Press, 2004), 316–18. Wang follows the
evolution of U.S. Navy concepts of network-centric warfare and the application of the
concepts in the Gulf War, the Iraq War, and Afghanistan. See also Wang Zhengde, ed.,
Xinxi Duikang Lun [Information confrontation theory] (Beijing: Military Science
Press, 2007), 199–200, where Wang discusses the NATO attacks on Yugoslavia and
how the use of networked systems and bombing proved to be effective tools of war.
These concepts are formalized as doctrine in Peng Guangqian and Yao Youzhi, eds.,
The Science of Military Strategy (Beijing: Military Science Press, 2005), 256–57.

9. Liu Jingbo, ed., *21 Shiji Chu Zhongguo Guojia Anquan Zhanlue* [Chinese national
security strategy in the early 21st century] (Beijing: Current Affairs Press, 2006), 72–
73. Liu argues that the United States is using the 9/11 attacks and the subsequent war
on terrorism as a justification to increase military deployments in the western Pacific,
strengthen the Pacific Fleet, and increase deployed forces on Guam, all of which have
the capacity to threaten China.

10. Zhang Wannian, ed. *Dangdai Shijie Junshi yu Zhongguo Guofang* [China's national
defense and contemporary world military affairs] (Beijing: Military Science Press,
1999), 25. Zhang points out that even though the Soviet Union has broken up,
"hegemonism still looms on the international stage" and that the United States is
"primary among Western hegemonist nations."

11. Dong Ruifeng, "Hu-Ao Hui Qian Zhanwang Zhong-Mei Junshi Guanxi [Outlook for
Sino-U.S. military relations before the Hu-Obama meeting]," *Liaowang Xinwen
Zhoukan [Outlook Weekly]*, January 17–23, 2011, 25–27.

12. Min Zengfu, *Kongjun Junshi Sixiang Gailun* [An introduction to air force military
thinking] (Beijing: PLA Press, 2006), 376–77.

13. Zhang Kunping, "Mu Ji 'Bei Jian' – 0607' Yan Xi" [Eyewitness report on "North
Sword 0607" exercise], *Zhonguo Guofang Bao [China National Defense Report]*,
September 5, 2005, 1.

14. Min, *Kongjun Junshi Sixiang Gailun*, 379–80. See also Wang, *Jiedu Wangluo Zhongxin
Zhan*, 316–20.

15. Zhang, *Dangdai Shijie Junshi yu Zhongguo Guofang*, 80.

16. Ibid., 80–81.

17. Wei Fenghe and Zhang Haiyang, "Nuli Jianshe Qiangda de Xinxihua Zhanlue Daodan
Budui" [Strive to build a powerful informatized strategic missile force]," *Renmin Ribao
[People's Daily]*, December 13, 2012.

18. Sun Yiming and Yang Liping, *Xinxihua Zhanzheng Zhong de Zhanshu Shuju Lian*
[Tactical data links in information warfare] (Beijing: Beijing Post and
Telecommunications College Press, 2005), 5 and 276–314.

19. Wang Zhongquan, *Meiguo He Liliangyu He Zhanlue* [American nuclear [weapons]
strength and nuclear strategy] (Beijing: National Defense University Press, 1995), 73.

20. Ibid.

21. Ibid., 69–74.

22. William A. Owens, "JROC: Harnessing the Revolution in Military Affairs," *Joint Force
Quarterly* no. 5 (Summer 1994): 55–58. On the RMA, see William A. Owens, "The
Emerging System of Systems," *U.S. Naval Institute Proceedings* 121, no. 5 (May 1995):
35–39; Paul Bracken, "The Military after Next," *Washington Quarterly* 16, no. 4

(Autumn 1993): 157–74; Antulio J. Echevarria and John Shaw, "The New Military Revolution: Post-Industrial Change," *Parameters* 22, no. 4 (Winter 1992–1993): 70–79 and James R. FitzSimmonds and Jan M. van Tol, "Revolutions in Military Affairs," *Joint Force Quarterly* no. 4 (Spring 1994): 24–31.

23. William A. Owens, "The American Revolution in Military Affairs," *Joint Force Quarterly* no. 10 (Winter 1995–1996): 38.

24. Jeremy M. Boorda, "Leading the Revolution in C⁴I," *Joint Force Quarterly* no. 9, (Autumn 1995): 16.

25. Thomas G. Mahnken, "War in the Information Age," *Joint Force Quarterly* no. 10, (Winter 1995–1996): 40.

26. Guo Wujun, *Lun Zhanlue Zhihui* [On strategic command and control] (Beijing: Military Science Press, 2001), 226.

27. Ibid.

28. Ibid., 248.

29. Zhang Zhiwei, *Xiandai Huoli Zhan* [Modern firepower warfare] (Beijing: National Science and Technology Press, 2000).

30. Yun Shan, "Zhimian Xin Junshi" [Squarely facing the new military transformation], *Liaowang Xinwen Zhoukan* [*Clear Lookout News Weekly*] no. 28 (July 2003): 10–20.

31. Ibid., 15, 17.

32. Li Bingyan, *Da Moulue yu Xin Junshi Biange* [Grand strategy and the new revolution in military affairs] (Beijing: Military Science Press, 2004), 52.

33. Zhang, *Zhanyi Xue*, 167–69.

34. Li, *Da Moulue yu Xin Junshi Biange*, 50–55. See also Zhang, *Zhanyi Xue*, 155–56, 180–83.

35. Liang Biqin, *Junshi Zhexue* [Military philosophy] (Beijing: Military Science Press, 2004), 526–37.

36. Han, *Gao Jishu Zhubu Zhanzheng Lilun Yanjiu*, 183. See also Chen et al., *Gao Jishu Tiaojian Xia Lujun Zhanyi Xue*, 71. Chen et al. refer to the fifth domain of warfare as information, whereas Han sees it as the electromagnetic spectrum. Han's description is broader, and probably a more accurate description, since it comprises electronic warfare and information warfare.

37. Han, *Gao Jishu Zhubu Zhanzheng Lilun Yanjiu*, 184.

38. Xin Qin, *Xinxihua Shidai de Zhanzheng* [Warfare in the information age] (Beijing: National Defense University Press, 2000), 1, 10.

39. Shen Weiguang, *Xinxi Zhanzheng Lun* [The new "On War"] (Beijing: People's Press, 1997), 178.

40. Yun, "Zhimian Xin Junshi," 15–16.

41. Ibid., 16.

42. Song Yongxin and GuoYizhing, "Dimian Leida Zhan Fan Weixing Zhencha Duici Yanjiu" [Research into ground radar station countermeasures for satellite reconnaissance], *Hangtian Dianzi Duikang* [*Aerospace Electronic Warfare*] 22, no. 2 (July 19, 2006): 37–39, 64.

43. Jian Yun, "Weilai Zhanzheng: Da 'Bingli' Geng Da Zhihui" [Future warfare, command is a bigger issue that forces in future war]," *Beijing Qingnian Cankao* [*Beijing Youth Reference News*], February 6, 2002, 1.

44. Ibid.

45. Xin, *Xinxihua Shidai de Zhanzheng*, 41.

46. Wu Chao, Jia Zhaoping, and Chu Zhenjiang, "Jiejin Shenmi de Xinxihua Lanjun" [Getting close to the mysterious informatized blue force], *Beijing Zhanyou Bao* [*Beijing*

Battle Companion News], February 23, 2006. The PLA takes the enemy as blue forces, and the red forces are the PLA, harking back to the PLA's formation as the Communist Party's Red Army.

47. This is a lesson designed to reinforce the critique of Iraqi military decisions in the Gulf War.

48. Ibid.

49. Zhang, *Dangdai Shijie Junshi yu Zhongguo Guofang*, 80.

50. Ibid., 111–12.

51. Qiao Qingchen, "Quanmian Guanche Luoshi Kexue Fazhan, Tuidong Junshi Xunlian You Kuai You Hao Fazhan" [Resolutely and Completely Implement Scientific Development, Push Forward Excellent and Fast Military training], *Jiefangjun Bao* [*PLA Daily*], June 27, 2006.

52. Ibid.

53. Xue, *Zhanyi Lilun Xuexi Zhinan*, 161–62.

54. Ibid., 161.

55. Peng Guangqian and Yao Youzhi, *The Science of Military Campaigns* (Beijing: Military Science Press, 2005), 254.

56. Ibid., 253.

57. State Council Information Office, *China's National Defense in 2006* (Beijing: State Council Information Office, 2006). See Section III, "China's Leadership and Administrative System for National Defense."

58. Xue, *Zhanyi Lilun Xuexi Zhinan*, 161–62.

59. Ibid., 129–30.

60. Ibid., 162.

61. Wang Yongxiao and Liu Yidai, "Er Pao Muoni 'daodan zhan'" [Second artillery stages simulated 'missile war'], *Zhongguo Xinwen She* [*China News Service*], May 24, 2004.

62. Song Junfeng, Zhang Weiming, Xiao Weidong, and Tang Jiuyang, "Wangge Zhongxin Zhan de Zhishi Jichu Sheshi Goujian Yanjiu [Study of knowledge infrastructure construction for network centric warfare]," *Beijing Xitong Gongcheng Lilun yu Shijian* [Systems engineering theory and practice] no. 8 (2005): 103–13.

63. Si Laiyi, "Lun Xinxi Zuozhan Zhihui Kongzhi Jiben Yuanze" [On basic principles for command and control information warfare], in Military Science Editorial Group, *Wo Jun Xixi Zhan Wenti Yanjiu* [Research on questions about information warfare in the PLA] (Beijing: National Defense University Press, 1999), 245–51.

64. Wang Lu and Zhang Xiaokang, "Wangge Zhongxin Zhan C4ISR Xitong Yanjiu ji Xiaoneng Yingyong Fenxi" [Analysis of C4ISR system in NCW and analysis of its effectiveness], *Zhihui Kongzhi yu Fangzhen* [Command and control simulation] 28, no. 2 (April 2006): 22–25.

65. Nie Yubao, "Daji Haishang di Da Jianting Biandui de Dianzi Zhan Zhanfa" [Combat methods for electronic warfare attacks on heavily fortified enemy naval formations], in Military Science Editorial Group, *Wo Jun Xixi Zhan Wenti Yanjiu*, 183–87.

66. Li Xinqin, Tan Shoulin, and Li Hongxia, "Haishang Jidong Mubiao Chun Weishe Yujing Jianmo Ji Fangzhen Shixian" [Precaution model, simulation actualization on threat maneuver target group on sea], in *Qingbao Zhihui Kongzhi Xitong yu Fangzhen Jishu* [Information command and control systems and simulation technology] 27, no. 4 (August 2005): 28–32.

67. Fang Youpei, Wang Liping, Zhao Shuang, and Wang Bengde, "Tupo Hangmu Hudui Fangyu de Daodan Jishu Yanjiu" [Study of missile technology for the penetration of an aircraft carrier defense formation], *Hantian Dianzi Duikang* [Aerospace electronic

warfare] 22, no. 3 (2006): 4–8; Zhao Hongcha, Wang Fenglian, and Gu Wenjin, "Dailuo Jiaojun Shu de Fan Jian Daodan Bi Jiegou Zhong Zhidao" [Variable midcourse guidance law with angle constraint for anti-ship missiles], *Zhanshu Daodan Kongzhi Jishu* [Control technology and tactical missiles] 52, no. 1 (2006): 20–26; Lin Yuyang, Yao Xiaoxian, and Zhang Yan, "Dandao Daodan Mo Zhidao Bi Zhi Xin Xitong de Haubi Jiegou Kongzhi" [Sliding mode control of a moving-mass-center system for ballistic missile terminal guidance], *Zhanshu Dandan Kongzhi Jishu* [Control technology and tactical missiles] 52, no. 2 (2006): 11–13. Tan Shoulin and Zhang Daqiao, "Dandao Daodan Daji Hangjian Mo Zhidao Youxiao Qu de Jingque Pinggu" [Effective range for terminal guidance ballistic missile attacking aircraft carrier], in *Zhihui Kongzhi yu Fangzhen* [Command, control, and simulation] 28, no. 4 (August 2006): 6–9.

68. Ibid., 9.
69. Li, Tan, and Li, "Haishang Jidong Mubiao Chun Weishe Yujing Jianmo Ji Fangzhen Shixian," 32.
70. Ge Xinliu, Mao Guanghong, and Yu Bo, "Xinxi Zhanzheng Daodan Budui Mianlin de Wenti yu Duici" [Problems faced by guided missile forces in information warfare conditions and their countermeasures], in Military Science Editorial Group, *Wo Jun Xinxi Zhan Wenti Yanjiu*, 188–89.
71. Min, *Kongjun Junshi Sixiang Gailun*, 377–78.
72. Office of the Secretary of Defense, *Annual Report to Congress: Military and Security Developments Involving the People's Republic of China, 2011* (Washington, DC: Department of Defense, 2011), 3.
73. Luke Amerding of the National Bureau of Asian Research provided the research support for this section. Melanie Mickelson Graham of the Johns Hopkins University School of Advanced International Studies also assisted with information on PLA order of battle and weapon systems.
74. An excellent description of the PLA's theater of war battle command system is in Liu Wei, ed., *Zhanqu Zhanyi Zhihui Gailun* [An introduction to theater joint battle command] (Beijing, National Defense University Press, 2003).
75. On the way that the U.S. deployment surprised China, see Arthur S. Ding, "The Lessons of the 1995–1996 Military Taiwan Strait Crisis: Developing a New Strategy toward the United States and Taiwan," in Burkitt et al., *Lessons of History*, 379–402. Mark Stokes discusses the effort to use ballistic missiles and maneuvering warheads to attack U.S. naval formations in Mark A. Stokes, "Chinese Ballistic Missile Forces in the Age of Global Missile Defense: Challenges and Responses," in Andrew Scobell and Larry M. Wortzel, *China's Growing Military Power* (Carlisle, PA: Strategic Studies Institute, 2002), 107–68.
76. USCC, *2011 Report to Congress of the U.S.-China Economic and Review Commission* (Washington, DC: Government Printing Office, November 2011), 200–202. See also Roger Cliff, Chad Ohlandt, and David Yang, *Ready for Takeoff: China's Advancing Aerospace Industry* (contracted research for the USCC) (Arlington, VA: Rand Corp., 2011), http://www.uscc.gov/researchpapers/2011/Rand_Aerospace_Report%5B1%5D.pdf.
77. Bill Gertz, "China's Military Links Forces to Boost Power," *Washington Times*, March 16, 2000, http://taiwansecurity.org/News/WT-031600.htm.
78. K. K. Nair, "China's Military Space Program," in *Promoting Strategic and Missile Stability in Southern Asia*, Special Report 17, MIT/IPCS/CAPS Conference, New Delhi, March 28–29, 2006 (New Delhi: Institute of Peace and Conflict Studies, 2006), 9–10, www.ipcs.org.

79. For a description of JTIDS, see Sun and Yang, *Xinxihua Zhanzheng Zhong de Zhanshu Shuju Lian*, 48–50. The comparison between JTIDS and Qu Dian is in Hon. Bob Schaffer, "Remarks on China" in the House of Representatives," *Congressional Record*, March 14, 2002, E-360-E361, http://www.fas.org/irp/congress/2002_cr/h031402.html.

80. Schaffer, "Remarks on China."

81. Zhang Nenghua and Wang Gang, "Shuzi Shenjing Guantong Duowei Zhanchang" [A digital nerve connects a multi-dimensional battlefield], *Jiefanfjun Bao*, November 21, 2012.

82. Zheng Zonghui, "Jiyu Xinxi Xitong Tixi Duozhan Zhihui Yanjiu" [A study of systemic warfighting command based on information systems], *Zhongguo Junshi Kexue* [China military science] 126, no. 6 (2012): 116–25.

83. Wang Zhizhing and Sun Jicheng, "Xinxi Hua Houqin Zhihui Tizhi Wenti Yanjiu" [An exploration into informationized logistics command systems], *Zhongguo Junshi Kexue* [China military science] 126, no. 6 (2012): 92–100.

84. Carlo Kapp, "Sukhoi Flankers: The Shifting Balance Regional Air Power," *Air Power Australia*, January 2007 (updated April 2012), http://www.ausairpower.net/APA-Flanker.html.

85. "China Demonstrates Copy of Russian Su-30MK2 at Aircraft Factory SAC," *Naval Staff Today*, November 24, 2011. http://navaltoday.com/2011/11/24/china-demonstrates-copy-of-russian-su-30mk2-at-aircraft-factory-sac/; also see "Chinese Navy Commissioned Aircraft J-16 is a Copy of Russian Fighter," *Defence Forum India*, May 10, 2012, http://defenceforumindia.com/forum/china/36055-chinese-navy-commissioned-aircraft-j16-copy-russian-fighter-su-30mk2.html.

86. "Kongjing-2000 Airborne Warning and Control System," *Jin Ri Zhonguo Fangyu* [Today's Sino-Defense], January 4, 2009, http://www.sinodefence.com/airforce/specialaircraft/kj2000.asp.

87. Moin Ansari, "Pakistan-China Jointly Built Y-8/9 AWACS and Saab 2000," *Rupee News*, April 17, 2008, http://rupeenews.com/2008/04/pakistani-china-jointly-built-y-89-awacs-saab-2000/.

88. "Yun-8 Airborne Early Warning Aircraft," *Jin Ri Zhonguo Fangyu* [Today's Sino-Defense], September 3, 2007, http://www.sinodefence.com/airforce/specialaircraft/y8aew.asp.

89. Lt. Gen. David A. Deptula (ret.), "PLA Air Force Overview – 2010," *Second Line of Defense*, December 11, 2011, http://www.slideshare.net/robbinlaird/pla-air-force-overview-2010.

90. Stephen Saunders, ed., *Jane's Fighting Ships: 2005–2006*, 108th ed., (Surrey, UK: Jane's Information Group, 2005), 123.

91. Ibid., 124.

92. Ibid., 123.

93. James C. Bussert, "China Debuts Aegis Destroyers," *Signal*, July 2005, http://www.afcea/signal/articles/anmviewer.asp?a=992.

94. Zhang Kaide and Zhao Shubin, "Shimin Daji Zhihui Kongzhi Jishu Chutan" [The command and control technology of time critical strikes,]" in *Zhihui Kongzhi yu Fangzhen* [Command, control, and simulation] 28, no. 2 (April 2006): 1–5.

95. Bussert, "China Debuts Aegis Destroyers."

96. James C. Bussert, "China Builds Destroyers around Imported Technology," *Signal*, August 2004, http://www.afcea.org/signal/articles/anmviewer.asp?a=252. See also "New-Generation Warships for the PLA Navy," *Military Technology* 28, no. 2 (February 2004): 90–91.

97. The effect of the *qu dian* system and command and control technology on operations is discussed in Commentary (no author), "Zhongguo Xin Yin Shen Ting zuozhan Jiezhi Hen Gao" [The high value of China's operations with stealth light boats], *Tie xue Shijie* [The world of iron and blood], April 16, 2006, http://www.txsj.com/www/asp /news/list.asp?id=1242.

98. Maj. Gen. Wang Xiaotong, "Junshhi Cehui: Zuozhan Baozhang Fanwei de Liti Kuangzhan" [Military survey and mapping: The three-dimensional expansion of combat operations support]," *Guangming Ribao* [Brightness daily], January 4, 2006, http://www.gmw.cn/01gmrb/2006-01/04/content_355299.htm.

99. Ibid.

100. Tan Yanqi, Yan Jianbo, and Ding Jianmin, "Zuozhan Xitong Cehui Dimian yu Tiankong" [Operations network that measures the sky and maps the ground], *Jiefangjun Bao* [*PLA Daily*], October 31, 2005.

101. Peng Zecheng, "Lianhe Peixun, Lianhe Baozhang, Lianhe Yucai [Joint training, joint support, joint cultivation of talent]," *Jiefangjun Bao* [*PLA Daily*], March 2, 2006.

102. Pang Kun, Wang Yunsheng, and Huang Jiandong, "San Jun Lianpei: Xinxing Zhihui Yuan Cong Zheli Duoxiang Zhanchang" [Three services train jointly: A new model for command and control personnel to move to the battlefield], *Jiefangjun Bao* [*PLA Daily*], December 12, 2012.

103. Wu Tingyong, Wu Shiqi, and Ling Huang, "A MEO Tracking and Data Relay Satellite System Constellation Scheme for China," *Jounal of Electronic Science and Technology of China* 3, no. 4 (December 2005): 293–97, http://120.108.115.54/tjest/jest/0504 -PDF/0504-2.pdf.

104. Rui C. Barbosa, "Long-March 3C Launches China's Third Tracking and Data Relay Satellite," *NASA Spaceflight*, July 25, 2012, http://www.nasaspaceflight.com/2012/07 /long-march-3c-tracking-data-relay-satellite/.

105. Jeffrey T. Richelson, *The U.S. Intelligence Community*, 6th Edition (Boulder, CO: Westview Press, 2012), 192–93.

106. Wu, Wu, and Huang, in "A MEO Tracking and Data Relay Satellite System constellation Scheme for China," (see note 107) suggest that a system of tracking and data relay satellites in medium earth orbit may be a better solution for China than several TDRS in geosynchronous orbit.

107. Wu Jingjing and Yu Qingfeng, "China Has Established a Space to Earth Satellite Monitoring System, Xinhua [New China News Agency] http://news.xinhuanet.com /english/2006-08/11/content 4951600.htm; also see USCC, *2011 Report to Congress,* 201–2.

108. USCC, *2011 Report to Congress*, 200–206, 212–13; also see Union of Concerned Scientists, *UCS Satellite Database*, July 31, 2012, http://www.ucsusa.org/nuclear_weapons _and_global_security/space_weapons/technical_issues/ucs-satellite-database.html.

109. At the time of publication of this book, China will have achieved regional coverage in the East Asia-Pacific region with six satellites in orbit. Over the next decade, China plans global coverage, adding forty more satellites. BBC, "Beidou GPS-Substitute Opens to Public in Asia," December 27, 2012, http://www.bbc.co.uk/news/technology -20852150. Also see USCC, *2011 Report to Congress* (Washington, DC: Government Printing Office, 2011), 200–202. The initial reporting on the Beidou system can be found in James A. Lewis, *China as a Military Space Competitor* (Washington, DC: Center for Strategic and International Studies, 2004).

110. Lewis, *China as a Military Space Competitor*, 4, and BBC, "Beidou GPS Substitute."

111. See USCC, *2011 Report to Congress*, 198–217.

112. Richard D. Fisher Jr., *China's Military Modernization: Building for Regional and Global Reach* (Westport, CT: Praeger Security International, 2008), 167–68.

113. Office of the Secretary of Defense, *Annual Report to Congress*, 2011, 29. In the author's view, one stimulus to the PLA for developing this anti-ship ballistic missile system was its embarrassment over its inability to respond to two U.S. aircraft carrier battle groups dispatched off Taiwan in 1996. At that time, as an attempt to intimidate Taiwan and perhaps influence the presidential election in Taiwan, China notified sailors and aviators that it would test ballistic missiles in two areas, just north and south of Taiwan, between March 8 and 15, 1996 establishing an "exclusion or danger zone." In response, the United States dispatched the *Independence* and *Nimitz* carrier battle groups to the area. The author was army attaché at the U.S. Embassy in Beijing at the time, and senior PLA officers were visibly angry over this development. The incident is discussed in some detail in John W. Garver, *Face off: China, The United States, and Taiwan's Democratization* (Seattle: University of Washington Press, 1997).

114. This estimate is based on the author's discussions with crews of U.S. Air Force and Navy refueling, fighter, and reconnaissance aircraft. It represents their "best guess" of what can be done given requirements for crew rest, refueling missions, and time of station for a force the size of what China can field.

115. 109th Cong., 1st sess., H.R. 3100, East Asia Security Act of 2005: To Authorize Measures to Deter Arms Transfers by Foreign Countries to the People's Republic of China, http://www.gpo.gov/fdsys/pkg/BILLS-109hr3100ih/pdf/BILLS-109hr3100ih.pdf.

3. Naval Modernization, Strategy, Programs, and Policies

1. See Louise Levanthes, *When China Ruled the Seas: The Treasure Fleet of the Dragon Throne, 1405–1433* (New York: Oxford University Press, 1994); Edward L. Dreyer, *Early Ming China: A Political History, 1355–1435* (Stanford, CA: Stanford University Press, 1982); Lo Jung-Pan, "The Emergence of China as a Sea Power in the Late Sung and Early Yuan Periods," *Far Eastern Quarterly* 14, no. 4 (August 1955): 489–503, http://www.upf.edu/materials/fhuma/himemoxi/mat/losea.pdf; and Bruce Swanson, *Eighth Voyage of the Dragon: A History of China's Quest for Sea Power* (Annapolis, MD: Naval Institute Press, 1982).

2. Cole, *Great Wall at Sea*, and John L. Rawlinson, *China's Struggle for Naval Development 1839–1895* (Cambridge, MA: Harvard University Press, 1967).

3. Lu Zhangtao, "Zhongguo Haijun Jiajin Zhuangxing yi Beizhan" [China's navy intensifies its transformation to take a stand and be Prepared for Battle], *Guoji Xianqu Daobao* [China international herald leader], December 19, 2011, http://www.xinhuanet.com/herald/. In this story, Lu discussed a speech by PRC president Hu Jintao to delegates attending the Eleventh Congress of the PLA Navy's Communist Party Committee. At this gathering of the senior Communist Party members of the PLA Navy, Lu reviewed Hu Jintao's comments about the Navy's strategic missions. An integrated look at how the future Navy fits in with China's other armed forces is published in Wang Kehai, Shen Jianhua, and Yu Weichao, "Hu Jintao Jun Bing Zhong Jianshe Sixiang Yanjiu [A study of Hu Jintao's thinking on building services and arms of the PLA]," *Zhongguo Junshi Kexue* [China military science] 112, no. 4 (2011): 28–36.

4. Bernard Cole, "China's Naval Modernization: Cause for Storm Warnings?," Comments at the Institute for National Strategic Studies 2010 Pacific Symposium, Hosted by the U.S. National Defense University, June 16, 2010, http://www.ndu.edu/inss

/docuploaded/PLAN_Cole_Remarks.pdf; "Hu Jintao Tells Chinese Navy to Prepare for War, *Asia News*, December 7, 2011, http://www.asianews.it/news-en/Hu-Jintao-tells -Chinese-Navy-to-prepare-for-war-23380.html. Hu Jintao's speech of December 6, 2011, urged the Navy to "prepare for military struggle" and meet its historic strategic missions. Some journalists took Hu's words as telling the PLA to be ready for "urgent combat," but the words he used, *junshi douzheng*, literally mean military struggle and is a common exhortation that senior PLA leaders use to encourage forces to work and train harder. China's party- and state-controlled English-language newspaper, *China Daily*, created some alarm in the West when it translated Hu's words as "prepare for urgent military combat" instead of a more common translation, "prepare for military struggle." See *China Daily*, http://bbs.chinadaily.com.cn/thread-721650-1-1.html.

5. Wortzel, *China's Nuclear Forces*, 3–8. See also Yun, "Zhimian Xin Junshi," 20, and Wang, *Jiedu Wangluo Zhongxin Zhan*, 316–20.

6. Levanthes, *When China Ruled the Seas*, 42–43.

7. Cole, *Great Wall at Sea*, 2.

8. See John K. Fairbank, Edwin O. Reischauer, and Albert M. Craig, *East Asia: Tradition and Transformation* (Boston: Houghton Mifflin, 1973), 365–68.

9. The Northern Song dyasty ruled from 960 to 1127; the Southern Song from 1127 to 1279. The latter years under attack by Kublai Khan, who established the Yuan dynasty in 1271.

10. Paul K. Davis, *100 Decisive Battles from Ancient Times to the Present* (New York: Oxford University Press, 1999), 145–51. See also Levanthes, *When China Ruled the Seas*, 49–53. Cole, in *Great Wall at Sea*, puts the strength of Chinese invading forces at 250,000 (p. 3), but this is probably a typographical error.

11. Levanthes, *When China Ruled the Seas*, 52.

12. Ibid., 54.

13. Cole, *Great Wall at Sea*, 3.

14. An excellent description of the expeditions is in Levanthes, *When China Ruled the Seas*, 87–172.

15. Geoff Wade, *The Zheng He Voyages: A Reassessment, ARI Working Paper no. 34,* Asia Research Insitute, National University of Singapore, October 2004. http://www.ari.nus .edu.sg/docs/wps/wps04_031.pdf. According to Wade, there is still some debate about the exact dates and size of each of the seven expeditions.

16. Ibid., 175–81.

17. Spence, *Search for Modern China*, 54–56.

18. Wortzel, *Dictionary of Chinese Military History*, 197–98.

19. Ibid., 178–79.

20. Ibid., 225–28.

21. Office of Naval Intelligence, *China's Navy 2007* (Washington, DC: Office of Naval Intelligence, 2007), 1.

22. Ibid.

23. *Directory of PRC Military Personalities*, October 2011, 40–51.

24. Cole, *Great Wall at Sea*, 165–72, and Nin Li, "The Evolution of China's Naval Strategy and Capabilities: From 'Near Coast' and 'Near Seas' to 'Far Seas,'" in Phillips C. Saunders, Christopher Yung, Michael Swaine, and Andrew Nien-Dzu Yang, eds., *The Chinese Navy: Expanding Capabilities, Evolving Roles* (Washington, DC: National Defense University Press, 2011), 109–40. Liu Huaqing started research on the new strategy in 1982, according to Cole.

25. Jing-dong Yuan, "China's Defense Modernization: Implications for Asia-Pacific Security," *Contemporary Southeast Asia* 17, no. 1 (June 1995): 67–84, and Toshi

Yoshihara and James R. Holmes, *Red Star over the Pacific: China's Rise and the Challenges to U.S. Maritime Strategy* (Annapolis, MD: Naval Institute Press, 2010), 20–21, 32–33, 52–55.

26. Cole, *Great Wall at Sea*, 166.

27. Ibid., 167.

28. Two books that discuss these long-term goals and China's comprehensive national power are Liu, *21 Shijichu Zhongguo Guojia Anquan Zhanlue*, and Yan Xuetong, *Zhongguo Guojia Liyi Fenxi* [Analysis of China's national interest] (Tianjin: Tianjin People's Press, 1997).

29. See Hartnett, *Towards a Globally Focused Chinese Military*, 1.

30. Hu Jintao, "Renqing Xinshiji Xinjieduan Wojun Lishi Shiming."

31. See Hu Jintao, "Hu Jintao zai Kaocha Haijun Nanhai Dui zhu Sanya Budui Shi Qiangidao: Zhenru Xuexi Guanche Dang de Shiqi Da Jingshen" [Hu Jintao on reviewing the South Sea Fleet Sanya Units urges: Deeply study and thoroughly grasp the spirit of the Party's Seventeenth Congress], *Jiefangjun Bao*, April 4, 2011, 1.

32. Tong Haibin, "Haijun Wenhua Jianshe de Zhenli Nian he Jingshen Zhuiqiu" [Values and morals for development of naval culture]," *Zhongguo Junshi Kexue* [China military science] no. 6 (2012): 19.

33. USCC, *2009 Report to Congress*, 128, http://www.uscc.gov/annual_report/2009/09 _annual_report.php.

34. Jeremy Page, "China Says Jet Made Landing on New Carrier," *Wall Street Journal,* November 26, 2012.

35. Department of Defense, *Annual Report to Congress*, (hereafter, *DOD Report to Congress*), 59, http://www.defense.gov/pubs/pdfs/2011_cmpr_final.pdf.

36. Ibid., 3.

37. IISS, *The Military Balance: 2012* (London: Routledge, 2012), 235–37.

38. "Taiwan Relations Act, Public Law 96-8, United States Code Title 22, Chapter 48, Sections 3301-3316, enacted April 10, 1979, http://www.taiwandocuments.org /tra01.htm.

39. Eleni Ekmenktsioglou, "U.S. Military's A2/AD Challenge," *The Diplomat*, January 18, 2012, http://the-diplomat.com/new-leaders-forum/2012/01/18/u-s-militarys-a2ad -challenge/. See also Andrew Krepinevich, "Why AirSea Battle," Center for Strategic and Budgetary Assessment (CSBA), February 9, 2010, http://www.csbaonline.org /publications/2010/05/airsea-battle-concept/; and Jan Van Tol, *AirSea Battle: A Point- of-Departure Operational Concept* (Washington, DC: CSBA, 2010).

40. National Legislation, United Nations, "People's Republic of China, Law in the Territorial Sea and the Continuous Zone of 25 February 1992, http://www.un.org/depts /los/LEGISLATIONANDTREATIES/PDFFILES/CHN_1992_Law.pdf.See article 2, in particular. See also the Central Intelligence Agency's site on China's territorial disputes, https://www.cia.gov/library/publications/the-world-factbook/fields/2070.html.

41. See Yao Wenhuai, "Jianshe Qiangda Haijun, Weihu Woguo Haiyang Zhanlue Liyi" [Build a powerful navy, safeguard China's maritime strategic interests], *Guofang* [National defense] 7 (2007): 6.

42. John Wilson Lewis and Xue Litai, *China's Strategic Seapower: The Politics of Force Modernization in the Nuclear Age* (Stanford, CA: Stanford University Press, 2006), 23– 128, and Ronald O'Rourke, "PLAN Force Structure: Submarines, Ships, and Aircraft," in Saunders et al., *Chinese Navy*, 141–73.

43. James C. Bussert, "New Missile Destroyers Deploy for Blue Water Operations," SignalOnline, (November 1999) http://www.afcea.org/content/?q=node/797.

44. Bussert, "China Builds Destroyers."
45. May-Britt Stumbaum, "Testimony before the U.S.-China Economic and Security Review Commission," hearing on the "China-Europe Relationship and Transatlantic Implications," U.S. Capitol, JVC-210, April 19, 2012 (archived at www.uscc.gov).
46. Ibid. See also Bates Gill, "Managing Tensions and Promoting Cooperation in US-China-EU Relations: US-Europe Approaches on Security Issues with China," in Robert Ross, Oystein Tunsjo, and Zhang Tuosheng, *US-China-EU Relations: Managing a New World Order* (London: Routledge, 2010), 276–78.
47. 109th Cong., H.R. 3100, East Asia Security Act of 2005.
48. Stumbaum, "Testimony before the U.S.-China Economic and Security Review Commission."
49. Office of the National Counterintelligence Executive (hereinafter NCIX), *Foreign Spies Stealing US Economic Secrets in Cyberspace: Report to Congress on Foreign Economic Collection and Industrial Espionage, 2009–2011* (Washington, DC: NCIX, October 2011), 4–5, and USCC, *2011 Report to Congress*, 88–106, 155–82.
50. Ronald O'Rourke, *China's Naval Modernization: Implications for U.S. Navy Capabilities; Background Issues for Congress* (Washington, DC: Congressional Research Service, July 17, 2009), 17.
51. Su Shiliang, "Persistently Follow the Guidance of Chairman Hu's Important Thought on Navy Building, Greatly Push Forward Innovations and Development in the Navy's Military Work," *Renmin Haijun* [People's Navy], June 6, 2009, 3, in OSC, http://www.opensource.gov, CPP20090716478009.
52. IISS, *Military Balance: 2012*, 237.
53. Cole, *Great Wall at Sea*, 106–8.
54. Brian Hsu, "China to Acquire TU-22 Supersonic Bombers?," *AIOnline*, January 4, 2013, http://www.ainonline.com/aviation-news/ain-defense-perspective/2013-01-04/china-acquire-tu-22-supersonic-bombers.
55. USCC, *2009 Report to Congress*, 139–40.
56. USCC, *2012 Report to Congress* (Washington, DC: Government Printing Office, 2012), 127.
57. Ibid., 127–28.
58. This point is made in several places by Jiang Yamin in *Yuan Zhan*.
59. USCC, *2009 Report to Congress*, 139.
60. "Type 920 Hospital Ship," *SinoDefense.com*, http://www.sinodefence.com/navy/support/type920.asp. Also see Peter W. Mackenzie, *Red Crosses, Blue Water: Hospital Ships and China's Expanding Naval Presence*, CAN Studies, CRM D002784.a1/final (Alexandria, VA: Center for Naval Analyses, September 2011).
61. James Bussert, "China Builds Modern Marine Corps Force," *Signal Online*, April 2006, http://www.afcea.org/signal/articles/templates/SIGNAL_Article_Template.asp?articleid=1115&zoneid=181. There also is an excellent article on the PLA Navy Marine Corps in *Nanfang Zhoumo* [Southern weekend], Yao Yijiang, Tang Zhongping, and Zeng Qing, "Tezhong Zuozhan Zhengming Yizhao-Haijun Luzhandui Teshi Zhan" [A critical move in special operations-PLA Marine Corps special warfare], *Nanfang Zhoumo* [Southern weekend], May 20, 2010, http://www.infzm.com/content/45147.
62. Cole, *Great Wall at Sea*, 114–15.
63. Yao, Tang, and Zeng, "Tezhong zuozhan Zhengming Yihao," 1.
64. Ibid.
65. *Directory of PRC Military Personalities*, October 2011, 221, 243.
66. *Zhongguo Dabaike Quanshu, Junshi* [China complete encyclopedia, military affairs], vol. 2 (Beijing: China Complete Encyclopedia Press, 1989), 1091.

67. Wortzel, *Dictionary of Chinese Military History*, 282–83.
68. Ibid., 180–81.
69. See the UN Convention on the Law of the Sea, http://www.unlawoftheseatreaty.org/. See also Peter Dutton, ed., *Military Activities in the EEZ: A U.S.-China Dialogue on Security and International Law in the Maritime Commons* (Newport, RI: U.S. Naval War College, 2010), http://www.usnwc.edu/Research—-Gaming/China-Maritime -Studies-Institute/Publications/documents/China-Maritime-Study-7_Military -Activities-in-the-.pdf.
70. Ibid., 58. See also John J. Tkacik Jr., testimony before the Committee on Foreign Affairs, U.S. House of Representatives, "Investigating the Chinese Threat, Part 1: Military and Economic Aggression," March 28, 2012, http://www.strategycenter.net/include /docFormat_list.asp?docRecNo=1181&docType=0.
71. USCC, *2009 Report to Congress*, 144.
72. Ibid., 48.
73. Ibid., 145. See also Shambaugh, *Modernizing China*, 336–37.
74. Tony Capacio, "Chinese Vessels Harass U.S. Navy Ship, Pentagon Says," *Bloomberg*, March 9, 2009, http://www.bloomberg.com/apps/news?pid=newsarchive&sid =aUMS9YLJ2OmM.
75. See Tkacik, "Investigating the Chinese Threat."
76. Capacio, "Chinese Vessels Harass U.S. Navy Ship."
77. Larry Wortzel, "China's Peaceful Rise," *Asian Wall Street Journal*, September 5, 2005.
78. Larry M. Wortzel, "China and Southeast Asia: Building Influence and Addressing Fears," in Andrew Scobell and Larry M. Wortzel, *Shaping China's Security Environment: The Role of the People's Liberation Army* (Carlisle, PA: Strategic Studies Institute, 2006), 289–92.
79. Quoted in 112th Cong., 1st sess., H.R. 352, http://thomas.loc.gov/cgi-bin/query/z?c112 %3AH.RES.352%3A.
80. Ibid.
81. Abdul Khalik, "Panetta to Woo ASEAN to Balance China, *The Jakarta Post*, October 22, 2011, http://www.thejakartapost.com/news/2011/10/22/panetta-woo-asean -balance-out-china.html.
82. Ministry of Foreign Affairs of Japan, "Q&A on the Senkaku Islands," http://www.mofa .go.jp/region/asia-paci/senkaku/qa_1010.html.
83. Department of State, "Remarks with Vietnamese Foreign Minister Pham Gia Khiem" (Washington, DC: October 29, 2010), http://www.state.gov/secretary/rm /2010/10/150189.htm. Cited in USCC, *2012 Report to Congress* (Washington, DC: Government Printing Office, 2012), 135, 193.
84. Daniel M. Hartnett and Frederic Velucci Jr., *Continental or Maritime Power? A Summary of Chinese Views on Maritime Strategy since 1999* (Alexandria, VA: Center for Naval Analyses, 2007), 4–7.
85. Robert Kagan, "The Obama Administrations's Pivot to Asia," *Foreign Policy*, undated transcript, http://www.foreignpolicyi.org/files/uploads/images/Asia%20Pivot.pdf.
86. Joseph S. Nye, "A Pivot that is Long Overdue, *New York Times*, November 21, 2011, http://www.nytimes.com/roomfordebate/2011/11/21/does-the-us-need-troops-in -australia/marines-in-australia-its-about-time.
87. Jonathan Masters, "The Pentagon Pivots to Asia," *Analysis Brief*, Council on Foreign Relations, January 6, 2012, http://www.cfr.org/united-states/pentagon-pivots-asia /p26979.
88. USCC, *2011 Report to Congress*, 182–96.

89. The terms "AirSea Battle" and "Air-Sea Battle" are the same concept. The original publication from the Center for Strategic and Budgetary Assessments used the former, while the Pentagon has used the latter.
90. Van Tol et al., *AirSea Battle*, http://www.csbaonline.org/publications/2010/05/airsea -battle-concept.
91. Department of Defense, *Joint Operational Access Concept (JOAC)*, version 1.0 (Washington, DC: Joint Chiefs of Staff, 2012), 4.
92. Peng Kuang and Peng Guangqian, "Kong-Hai Yi Ti Zhan de Hulu Li" [What is [concealed] inside 'Air-Sea Battle' concept], *Liaowang Xinwen Zhoukan* [Outlook weekly], March 19, 2012, 46–47.
93. See the discussion by Prime Minister Yoshiko Noda of Japan in Yuka Hayashi, "Japan Leader in U.S. Visit to Pledge Security Efforts," *Wall Street Journal*, April 30, 2012.

4. The PLA Air Force and China's Approaches to Aerospace

1. Kenneth W. Allen, Glenn Krumel, and Jonathan D. Pollack, *China's Air Force Enters the 21st Century* (Santa Monica, CA: Rand Corp., 1995), 139.
2. Dennis J. Blasko, "The PLA from 1949 to 1989," in Graff and Higham, *Military History of China*, 250.
3. Xiaobing Li, *History of the Modern Chinese Army*, 108.
4. Xiaoming Zhang, "Air Combat for the People's Republic: The People's Liberation Army Air Force in Action, 1949–1969," in Ryan et al., *Chinese Warfighting*, 278.
5. Ibid., 279.
6. Ibid.
7. Ibid.
8. Ibid., 280–82.
9. Allen et al., *China's Air Force Enters the 21st Century*, 61.
10. Ibid., 67.
11. Ibid., 68.
12. IISS, *Military Balance: 2012*, 237–38.
13. Allen et al., *China's Air Force Enters the 21st Century*, 76–78. See also Zhang, "Air Combat for the People's Republic, 288–93.
14. Wortzel, "China's Foreign Conflicts since 1949," 275–77 and 279–80.
15. Wang Wei and Zhang Shufeng, "Luolun Kang–Mei Yuan-Chao Zhanzheng Zhong Mao Zedong de Zhanzheng Kongzhi Yishu" [A discussion of Mao Zedong's "war control" arts in the war to resist America and aid Korea], in *Jinian Kang Mei Yuan Chao Zhanzheng Shengli 50 Zhounian Lun Wenji* [Discussion collection to commemorate the 50th anniversary of victory in the war to resist America and aid Korea] (Nanjing: Nanjing Army Command Academy, 2003), 16–25.
16. See the discussion on "war control" in Peng and Yao, *Science of Military Strategy*, 192–210. Another useful source on how to prevent the escalation of conflict is Xiao Tianliang, *Zhanzheng Kongzhi Wenti Yanjiu* [On war control] (Beijing: National Defense University Press, 2002).
17. Cliff et al., *Ready for Takeoff*, 64–65.
18. Ibid.
19. Ibid., passim.
20. USCC, *2010 Report to Congress of the U.S. China Economic and Security Review Commission* (Washington, DC: Government Printing Office, 2010), 74.
21. Ibid.
22. Office of the Secretary of Defense, *Annual Report to Congress, 2011*, 24.

23. Murray Scott Tanner and Larry Ferguson II, *The Future Missions of the People's Liberation Army Air Force* (Alexandria, VA: Center for Naval Analyses, 2010), iii–v.

24. State Council Information Office, *China's National Defense in 2008* (Beijing: State Council, 2009), http://www.china.org.cn/government/central_government/2009 -01/20/content_17155577_9.htm (accessed January 13, 2013).

25. See Roger Cliff, John Fei, Jeff Hagen, Elizabeth Hague, Eric Heginbotham, and John Stillion, *Shaking the Heaven and Splitting the Earth: Chinese Air Force Employment Concepts in the 21st Century* (Santa Monica, CA: Rand Corp., 2011). See also the discussion on evolving PLAAF strategy in Kenneth W. Allen and Collins Elt, *Overview of the PLA Air Force, 2002–2006* (Alexandria, VA: Center for Naval Analyses, 2008), 19.

26. Cliff et al., *Shaking the Heaven*, 47.

27. See Li Rongchang, Cheng Jian, and Zheng Lianqing, eds., *Kong-Tian Yiti Xinxi Zuozhan* [Informatized, integrated aerospace operations] (Beijing: Academy of Military Science Publishers, 2003); and Cai Fengzhen and Tian Anping, eds., *Kongtian Zhanchang yu Zhongguo Kongjun* [The aerospace battlefield and China's Air Force](Beijing: PLA Press, 2003).

28. Cai et al., *Kongtian Yiti Zuozhan Xue*, 287–301; and Chang Xianqi, ed., *Junshi Hangtian Xue* [Military astronautics], 2nd ed. (Beijing: National Defense Industries Press, 2004), 129–64, 266, 433–47.

29. Cliff et al., *Shaking the Heaven*, 1–4.

30. Allen et al., *China's Air Force Enters the 21st Century*, 143.

31. The Jian-20 (J-20) is undergoing flight testing. It appears to be based on the U.S. F-22 stealth fighter. Apparently a stealth strike fighter, the Jian-31 (J-31) also is underdevelopment and in the prototype phase. See USCC, *2012 Report to Congress* (Washington, DC: Government Printing Office, 128–30).

32. Allen et al., *China's Air Force Enters the 21st Century*, 235.

33. Ibid.

34. Cliff et al., *Shaking the Heaven*, 34–54.

35. USCC, *2012 Report to Congress*, 128–30.

36. Larry M. Wortzel, "Deterrence and Presence in Beijing's Aerospace Revolution," in *Chinese Aerospace Power: Evolving Maritime Roles*, ed. Andrew S. Erickson and Lyle J. Goldstein (Annapolis, MD: Naval Institute Press, 2011), 423–24.

37. Cai et al., *Kongtian Yiti Zuozhan Xue*, 58.

38. Cai and Tian, *Kongtian Zhanchang yu Zhongguo Kongjun*, 207–12.

39. Wortzel, "Deterrence and Presence," 434.

40. Cai and Tian, *Kongtian Zhanchang yu Zhongguo Kongjun*, 285–87.

41. IISS, *Military Balance: 2012*, 254.

42. "IL-76MD Transport Planes Delivered to China," *Moscow Times*, January 25, 2013, http://www.themoscowtimes.com/business/article/il-76md-transport-plane-delivered -to-china/474560.html; also see Kim Noedskov, *The Return of China: The Long March to Power; The New Historic Mission of the People's Liberation Army* (Copenhagen: Royal Danish Defense College, 2009), 142–43. China will buy twenty-four new IL-76 MD aircraft and also a dozen used aircraft, plus the four IL-78 tankers.

43. Cliff et al., *Shaking the Heaven*, 56–57.

44. Tanner and Ferguson, *Future Missions of the People's*, 10–11.

45. Cliff et al., *Shaking the Heaven*, 55.

46. Tanner and Ferguson, *Future Missions of the People's*, 26.

47. Cai et al., *Kongtian Yiti Zuozhan Xue*, 289–90.

48. Tanner and Ferguson, *Future Missions of the People's*, 32.

49. Cliff et al., *Shaking the Heaven*, 17.
50. The information in this paragraph is drawn from IISS, *Military Balance: 2012*, 238–41. For more detail on PLAAF structure down to the small-unit level, see Ken Allen, "PLA Air Force Organization," in Mulvenon and Yang, *People's Liberation Army*, 346–457; and Allen et al., *China's Air Force Enters the 21st Century*, 189–210.
51. Abraham M. Denmark, "PLA Logistics, 2004–2011: Lessons Learned in the Field," in *Learning by Doing: The PLA Trains at Home and Abroad*, ed. Roy Kamphausen, David Lai, and Travis Tanner (Carlisle, PA: Strategic Studies Institute, 2012), 297–335.
52. Denmark, "PLA Logistics, 2004–2011," 315–18.
53. Ibid., 311–15.
54. Ibid.
55. Ibid., 315; and Royston Chan and Tom Miles, "Libya Evacuation: China Evacuates 12,000 Nationals via Naval Frigate," *Christian Science Monitor*, February 25, 2011.
56. IISS, *Military Balance: 2012*, 238.
57. Dennis Blasko, "PLA Exercises March toward Trans-regional Joint Training," *China Brief* 9, no. 22 (November 4, 2009), http://www.jamestown.org/single/?no_cache=1&tx_ttnews%5Btt_news%5D=35690.
58. Xue, *Zhanyi Lilun Xuexi Zhinan*, 238.
59. Ibid., 239.
60. Ibid., 240.
61. Ibid., 246.
62. Ibid.
63. Blasko, "PLA Exercises March."
64. Denmark, "PLA Logistics, 2004–2011," 303–9.
65. Noedskov, *Return of China*, 142.
66. Ibid., 147.
67. IISS, *Military Balance: 2012*, 238.
68. Ibid.
69. Ibid., 234.
70. Cai et al., *Kongtian Yiti Zuozhan Xue*, 58.
71. Cai and Tian, *Kongtian Zhanchang yu Zhongguo Kongjun*, 207–12.
72. Zhang Jiali and Min Zengfu, "Shilun Jubu Zhanzheng Kongtian Zhong Hua" [On extending the regional war into the air and space], *Zhongguo Junshi Kexue* [China military science] 18, no. 1 (January 2005): 41.
73. Tan Jie, "Kuai Su, Yuan Cheng, Gao Xiao" [Be fast and highly efficient in covering long distances], *Jiefangjun Bao* [PLA Daily], March 11, 2009, 8.
74. Cliff et al., *Ready for Takeoff*, 41–45.
75. Office of the Secretary of Defense, *Annual Report to Congress, 2011*, 33.

5. Modernized Ground Forces, Doctrine, and Missions

1. Wortzel, *Dictionary of Chinese Military History*, 203.
2. Ibid., 152–53.
3. William W. Whitson with Chen-Hsia Huang, *The Chinese High Command: A History of Communist Military Politics, 1927–71* (New York: Praeger, 1973), 70–74.
4. Wortzel, *Dictionary of Chinese Military History*, 273.
5. Ibid., 130, 150, 290–91.
6. Academy of Military Science History Research Group, ed., *Zhongguo Renmin Jiefangjun Quanguo Jiefang Zhanzheng Shi* [History of the war of liberation of the Chinese People's Liberation Army], vol. 4 (Beijing: Military Science Press, 1997), 368.

To put the equipment captures into perspective, in the civil war between July 1946 and June 1950, the PLA captured 54,430 artillery pieces, 3,162,000 rifles, 320,000 machine guns, 1,000 railroad engines, 622 tanks, 389 armored vehicles, and 195,000 horses.

7. Ibid., 134–35.
8. Wortzel, "China's Foreign Conflicts since 1949," 275–77.
9. Ibid., 277.
10. Ibid., 279–80.
11. Henry J. Kenny, "Vietnamese Perceptions of the 1979 War with China," in Ryan et al., *Chinese Warfighting*, 235.
12. See Wortzel, "China's Foreign Conflicts since 1949," 280; and O'Dowd and Corbett, "1979 Chinese Campaign in Vietnam," 353–78.
13. O'Dowd and Corbett, "1979 Chinese Campaign in Vietnam," 366.
14. Blasko, *The Chinese Army Today*, 146–49.
15. State Council Information Office, *China's National Defense in 2010*.
16. Dennis Blasko, "PLA Ground Forces: Moving toward a Smaller, More Rapidly Deployable, Modern Combined Arms Force," in *The People's Liberation Army as an Organization*, Reference Volume v1.0, ed. James C. Mulvenon and Andrew N.D. Yang (Santa Monica, CA: Rand Corporation, 2002), 315.
17. IISS, *Military Balance: 2011*, 230.
18. Blasko, "PLA Ground Forces: Moving toward," 316.
19. IISS, *Military Balance: 2010*, 230.
20. Blasko, *Chinese Army Today*, 39.
21. Ibid., 38.
22. For two excellent discussions of the PLA's operational concepts and strategic guidelines, see David M. Finkelstein, "China's National Military Strategy: An Overview of the 'Military Strategic' Guidelines," in *Right-Sizing the People's Liberation Army: Exploring the Contours of China's Military*, eds. Roy Kamphausen and Andrew Scobell (Carlisle, PA: Strategic Studies Institute, 2007), 69–140; and Mulvenon and Finkelstein, *China's Revolution in Doctrinal Affairs*.
23. Mao Zedong, "Strategy in China's Revolutionary War," *Selected Military Writings of Mao Tse-Tung* (Peking: Foreign Languages Press, 1963), 144–45.
24. This is also expressed in other sets of operating principles as "Concentrate superior force to destroy the enemy forces one by one." See Mao Zedong, *Selected Military Writings*, 315–19.
25. Mao, "The Present Situation," 161–62.
26. China's ancient military strategist is often referred to as "Sun-Tsu," using a different and older transliteration system than that adopted in the People's Republic of China. China's pinyin transliteration system to English uses "Sunzi."
27. For instance, in January 1999 the PLA promulgated its guidance for joint operations as a set of *gangyao* (principles) that were approved by the CMC chairman and party general secretary Jiang Zemin. See *Jiefangjun Bao* [*PLA Daily*], January 8, 1999.
28. See Roger Ames, trans., *Sun-Tzu: The Art of War* (New York: Ballantine, 1993); D. C. Lau and Roger T. Ames, *Sun Pin: The Art of Warfare* (New York: Ballantine, 1996); and Harro Von Senger, *The Book of Stratagems: Tactics for Triumph and Survival* (New York: Penguin, 1991). Note that many books in China and some Chinese strategists often refer to "the thirty-six strategems," or *san shi liu ji*, see for instance, Guan Meifen, *San Shi Liu Ji* [The thirty-six strategems] (Tainan: National Library Press, 1996).

29. A discussion of U.S. principles of war and Chinese operations in the conflict against India in 1962 is in Cheng and Wortzel, "PLA Operational Principles," 188–95.

30. Ibid., 194.

31. Mao Zedong, "Problems of Strategy in Guerilla War against Japan: May 1938," in Mao Tse-Tung, *Selected Works of Mao Tse-Tung*, vol. 2 (Beijing: Foreign Languages Press, 1967), 79–112.

32. Ibid.

33. Lau and Ames, *Sun Pin*, 16.

34. Ssu-MaCh'ien et al., *Records of the Historian* [Shi ji] (Peking: China Bookcase, 1959), cited in Lau and Ames, *Sun Pin,* 12 and 334. See also Mao, "Problems of Strategy," 104 and 110n10.

35. Wang Wenrong et al., eds., *Zhan Lue Xue* [The science of military strategy] (Beijing: National Defense University Press, 1999); Zhang et al., *Zhanyi Xue*; and Yang Zhiyuan et al., eds., *Zhan Shu Xue* [The science of military tactics] (Beijing: Academy of Military Science Press, 2002). A variety of reading guides and explanatory volumes supplement these books, some with an emphasis on ground, air, naval, or Second Artillery forces.

36. This summary of contemporary operational concepts with brief explanations is drawn from Zhang et al., *Zhanyi Xue*; Cliff et al., *Entering the Dragon's Lair*; and Mulvenon and Finkelstein, *China's Revolution in Doctrinal Affairs*.

37. The operational principles are drawn from Andrew Scobell, David Lai, and Roy Kamphausen, *Chinese Lessons from Other Peoples' Wars* (Carlisle, PA: Strategic Studies Institute, 2011).

38. Ren, *Guofang Dongyuan Xue*, 333–51.

6. Strategic Rocket Forces, Nuclear Doctrine, and Deterrence

1. Two excellent references on the Second Artillery Force are Mark A. Stokes, *China's Strategic Modernization: Implications for the United States* (Carlisle, PA: Strategic Studies Institute, 1999); and Mark A. Stokes, *China's Nuclear Warhead Storage and Handling System* (Arlington, VA: Project 2049 Institute, 2010), http://project2049.net/documents /chinas_nuclear_warhead_storage_and_handling_system.pdf.

2. USCC, *2012 Report to Congress,* 176–77.

3. V. I. Esin, "Nuclear Might of the PRC," in *Prospects for China's Participation in Nuclear Arms Limitation*, ed. Aleksey Arbatov, Vladimir Dvorkin, and Sergey Oznobischchev (Moscow: Institute of the World Economy and International Relations, Russian Academy of Sciences, 2012), 24.

4. The author acknowledges the strategic analysis and assessment division of the Scitor Corp. for providing support for the research in this chapter. An earlier version of this chapter was published by the Strategic Studies Institute of the U.S. Army War College. The views expressed here are those of the author and do not represent the official policy or position of the Department of Defense or the U.S. government.

5. The Second Artillery Force is often referred to as "the Second Artillery Corps" or "the Strategic Rocket Forces" in some literature. The State Council most recently has referred to it as "the Second Artillery Force."

6. State Council Information Office, *China's National Defense in 2010*, 10–11.

7. There also are a number of copies of Yu Jixun, ed., *Di Er Paobing Zhanyi Xue* [The science of second artillery campaigns] (Beijing: PLA Press, 2004), circulating among American and Taiwanese policy analysts and academics. This book is a PLA classified document, making it somewhat puzzling that so many outside China have gained

access to it. However, the likelihood that the copies circulating are simply deception efforts by the PLA is lowered by the fact the books *A Guide to the Study of Campaign Theory* and *The Science of Campaigns* are largely consistent with the contents of *The Science of Second Artillery Campaigns*. That would be a very elaborate deception measure. See Larry M. Wortzel, "China's Nuclear 'Leakage,'" *The Diplomat*, August 7, 2012, http://thediplomat.com/china-power/chinas-nuclear-leakage/.

8. Xue, *Zhanyi Lilun Xuexi Zhinan*.
9. Zhang Yuliang, ed., *Zhanyi Xue* [*The science of campaigns*] (Beijing: National Defense University Press, 2000). *Zhanyi Lilun Xuexi Zhinan*, the reading guide to the book, is available in PLA bookstores and explains many of the concepts in this seminal volume.
10. Wortzel, *China's Nuclear Forces*, 26–30. See also Mark B. Schneider, testimony before the USCC, hearing on "Developments in China's Cyber and Nuclear Capabilities," George Mason University, Manassas, VA, March 26, 2012, archived at http://www.uscc.gov /hearings/2012hearings/transcripts/March_26_2012_USCC_Hearing_Transcript.pdf. Schneider believes that the Chinese no-first-use commitment is ambiguous enough that it "commits them to nothing."
11. Yu, *Di Er Paobing Zhanyi Xue,* 115.
12. Chen Nuoyan, "Zhonggong Beizhan yi Mei wei Di" [CCP treats the U.S. as enemy in war preparations], *Cheng Ming* [Contend] 7, no. 345 (July 1–July 31, 2006): 15. *Cheng Ming* has served as an outlet for information released by the Chinese Communist Party for decades, although it is a private magazine that is not owned by the PRC government.
13. Yan Xuetong, "The Problem of 'Mutual Trust,'" *New York Times*, November 15, 2012, http://www.nytimes.com/2012/11/16/opinion/the-problem-of-china-and-u-s-mutual -trust.html?_r=0.
14. B. Cruetzfield, "Theory Talk #51: Yan Xuetong on Chinese Realism, the Tsinghua School of International Relations, and the Impossibility of Harmony," *Theory Talks*, http://www.theory-talks.org/2012/11/theory-talk-51.html (accessed November 28, 2012).
15. Wang, *Meiguo He Liliang yu He Zhanlue*, 125–26.
16. Yun, "Zhimian Xin Junshi," 20.
17. Zhang, *Dangdai Shijie Junshi yu Zhongguo Guofang*, 107–8. Although this book is fourteen years old, it is perhaps the most authoritative statement of China's defense posture published by the PLA in many years. It stands as a future defense posture statement for the PLA and contains guidance for military doctrine and acquisition, much of which has been accomplished in the years since it was published.
18. Ibid., 202.
19. Li Jijun, *Junshi Zhanlue Siwei* [Thinking about military strategy] (Beijing: Military Science Press, 1996).
20. Ibid., 188–89.
21. Ibid., 210–12.
22. Information Office of the State Council, *China's National Defense in 2006*.
23. State Council Information Office, *China's National Defense in 2010*, 3–4.
24. Xia Liping, "Jiji Fangyu de Zhongguo Junshi Zhanlue" [China's military strategy of active defense], *Xuexi Shibao* [Study times], December 12, 2005, available at http://www.china.com.cn/xxsb/txt/2—0/12/14/content_6060925.htm. *Study Times* is published by the Communist Party's Central Party School.
25. Chen Zhou, "Xin Shiqi de Jiji Fangyu Junshi Zhanlue" [The military strategy of active defense for the new period], *Xuexi Shibao* [Study times], March 18, 2008,

http://www.china.com.cn/xxsb/txt/2008-03/18/content_12996594.htm.

26. Huang Yingxu, "Shixian Jiji Fangyu Junshi Zhanlue yu Shi Ju Jin" [The time is come to realize the military strategy of active defense], *Xuexi Shibao* [Study times], December 31, 2001.

27. Based on author's discussions with military officers in Beijing and scholars in Shanghai and Beijing, June 2006 and 2010.

28. There are two types of missile campaigns: the nuclear counterattack campaign and the conventional guided-missile attack campaign. The latter involves surprise and sudden preemptive action; Xue, *Zhanyi Lilun Xuexi Zhinan*, 148. Two points in contemporary PLA doctrine are relevant here. The first emphasizes that "in modern warfare the application of firepower involves the use of precision guided missiles" and the second that "sudden attacks and surprise attacks are the route to success in warfare." See Li, *Da Moulue yu Xin Junshi Biange*, 52 and 56.

29. Xue, *Zhanyi Lilun Xuexi Zhinan*, 393.

30. Ibid., 394.

31. Ibid., 393–94.

32. Ibid., 153.

33. Esin, "Nuclear Might of the PRC," 28–29.

34. Jiang Ning and Guo Fengkuan, "Haiba 4500 Mi Kong-Di Yiti Huoju" [A "Live Show" of Integrated Air-Land Operations Performed at 4,500 meters Above Sea Level], *Jiefangjun Bao* [*PLA Daily*], August 15, 2012, 5.

35. Zhang, *Dangdai Shijie Junshi yu Zhongguo Guofang*, 114.

36. Xin, *Xinxihua Shidai de Zhanzheng*, 298–99.

37. Ibid., 94–95.

38. Xin, *Xinxihua Shidai de Zhanzheng*, 88.

39. Ibid., 88–89.

40. USCC, *2009 Report to Congress*, 240.

41. Ibid.

42. Liu et al., *Gao Jishu Zhanzheng Zhong de Daodan Zhan*, 15.

43. Ibid., 11.

44. DF stands for *Dong Feng*, or East Wind.

45. Esin, "Nuclear Might of the PRC," 32; and Wendell Minnick, "China Ramps Up Missile Threat with DF-16," *Defense News, March 21, 2011,* http://www.defensenews.com/article/20110321/DEFFEAT06/103210308/China-Ramps-Up-Missile-Threat-DF-16.

46. Hu Yinan Li Xiaokun and Cui Haiping, "Official Confirms China Building Aircraft Carrier," *China Daily,* July 12, 2011, http://www.chinadaily.com.cn/china/2011-07/12/content_12881089.htm.

47. Guo, *Lun Zhanlue Zhihui*, 226.

48. Nie, "Daji Haishang di Da Jian Jianting Biandui de Dianzi Zhan Zhanfa," 183–87.

49. Ibid.

50. Cited in USCC, *2011 Report to Congress,* 159–60.

51. Ge et al., "Xinxi Zhan Zhong Daodan Budui Mianlin de Wenti yu Duici," 188–89.

52. Min, *Kongjun Junshi Sixiang Gailun*, 377–78.

53. Office of the Secretary of Defense, *Annual Report to Congress: Military and Security Developments Involving the People's Republic of China 2011* (Washington, DC: Department of Defense, 2011), 34–37; IISS, *The Military Balance 2012*, 223–24.

54. See accounts of the research by students of Phillip A. Karber of Georgetown University on China's underground tunneling at William Wan, "Georgetown Students Shed Light on China's Tunnel System for Nuclear Weapons," *Washington Post*, November 29, 2011, http://www.washingtonpost.com/world/national-security/georgetown-students

-shed-light-on-chinas-tunnel-system-for-nuclear-weapons/2011/11/16/gIQA6AmKAO
_story.html. Karber makes it clear that he does not know how many missiles or
warheads may be in these tunnels but points out how difficult they make strikes
against China's ballistic missile force. See his testimony at the USCC hearing on
"Developments in China's Cyber and Nuclear Capabilities."

55. Xue, *Zhanyi Lilun Xuexi Zhinan*, 387–88.

56. The Central Military Commission's confidence that it would get advanced warning of
an attack has serious counterintelligence implications for the United States. At present,
the PLA may have just achieved a real-time, national technical intelligence collection
capability. It will probably take at least five years for China to deploy sufficient real-
time global surveillance assets and to be effective at interpreting what it learns from the
surveillance systems. The PLA's confidence, therefore, implies that it has sufficient
human intelligence assets in place in the United States to provide such warning.

57. Andrew Scobell, *China's Use of Military Force: Beyond the Great Wall and Beyond* (New
York: Columbia University Press, 2003), 34–35.

58. Xue, *Zhanyi Lilun Xuexi Zhinan*, 148–53.

59. Xia, "China's Military Strategy of Active Defense."

60. Ibid. See also Xue, *Zhanyi Lilun Xuexi Zhinan*, 384.

61. Xue, *Zhanyi Lilun Xuexi Zhinan*, 267. See also Zhang, *Dangdai Shijie Junshi yu
Zhongguo Guofang*, 202.

62. Xue, *Zhanyi Lilun Xuexi Zhinan*, 385.

63. Ibid., 384.

64. Ibid. According to the IISS, the PLAAF has one nuclear-ready regiment of up to
twenty H-6 (Tu-16) Badger bombers on standby. See IISS, *The Military Balance: 2012*
237.

65. Peng and Yao, *Science of Military Strategy*, 218. This is the English-language
translation, with some updates, of Peng Guangqian et al., eds., *Zhanlue Xue 2001* [On
strategy, 2001] (Beijing: Military Science Press, 2001).

66. Ibid.

67. On this doctrine, see Feng and Wortzel, "PLA Operational Principles," 180–83, 194–
95.

68. Xin Qin reinforces this, writing that "one must attack the C⁴ISR network that
supports the command-and-control system of an enemy, particularly one that is
fighting a war on external lines"—in other words, an enemy fighting a power-
projection war. Xin, *Xinxihua Shidai de Zhanzheng*, 90.

69. Ibid., 384–85. These targeting priorities are repeated in a basic-level PLA publication
intended to educate enlisted soldiers and junior officers on high technology in war.
This book says that nuclear-tipped intercontinental ballistic missiles are aimed at
enemy political and economic centers, military bases, important defense industrial base
areas, nuclear weapons storage depots, key communications hubs, and other such
strategic targets. See Guo Yanhua et al., eds., *Jusnhi Jishu Aomi Jieyi* [Explaining the
"mysteries" of military high technology] (Beijing: National Defense University Press,
2005), 123.

70. Xue, *Zhanyi Xuexi Lilun Zhinan*, 385. See also Liu et al., *Gao Jishu Zhanzheng Zhong
de Daodan Zhan*, 116. Ge Xinliu, Mao Guanghong, and Yu Bo, *Wo Jun Xinxizhan
Wenti Yanjiu* [PLA research on problems of information warfare] (Beijing: National
Defense University Press, 1999), 188–92.

71. Xue, *Zhanyi Xuexi Lilun Zhinan*, 387.

72. Ibid., 388.

73. U.S. Defense Threat Reduction Agency, "U.S.-China Strategic Dialogue," conference report, Honolulu, HI, August 1–3, 2005, executive summary, 1.
74. Ibid.
75. Xu Jing, Chen Xianping, and Ge Song, "Jia Yu Chang Jian yu Zhanchang" [Controlling the long sword and the battlefield], *Huojianbing Bao* [Rocket soldiers daily], August 12, 2012, 3.
76. Xue, *Zhanyi Xuexi Lilun Zhinan*, 153, 390–91, 394.
77. Xin, *Xinxihua Shidai de Zhanzheng*, 16.
78. Xue, *Zhanyi Lilun Xuexi Zhinan*, 387.
79. Ibid., 387–88.
80. Ibid., 389.
81. Ibid., 391.
82. Ibid.
83. Ibid., 153.
84. Ibid., 390.
85. Zhang Junsun and Wang Qingyong, "Mou Jidi Zhanshi Liangpin Gongji Yanjiu Chengguo Jianbu Erpao Kong Bai" [Results of combat food supply research by Second Artillery fills the gap], *Huojianbing Bao* [Rocket soldiers daily], November 26, 2005, 1. *Note: Rocket Soldiers Daily* is available in print in the Chinese language collection of the Gelman Library at George Washington University.
86. Esin, "Nuclear Might of the PRC," 30.
87. Zhang and Wang, "Mou Jidi Zhanshi Liangpin Gongji Yanjiu Chengguo Jianbu Erpao Kong Bai," 1.
88. Meeting with General Esin at the Potomac Foundation, Vienna, VA, December 10, 2012. Also See Bill Gertz, "Missile Mania: China Conducts Mobile ICBM Test Just Days ahead of North Korean Launch," *Washington Free Beacon*, December 4, 2012, http://freebeacon.com/missile-mania-2/.
89. USCC, *2012 Report to Congress*, 178–80.
90. Han Huifeng and Tang Xudong, "Gan zuo 'Guo Bao' Yunshu 'Baoxian Si'" [Happy to be the safety fuse in the transport of national treasure], *Huojianbiing Bao* [Rocket soldiers daily], November 3, 2005, 2.
91. Zhang Ligang and Kang Fushun, "Kua Qu Jidong Shunlian Chengwei Shandou Li Jianshe Zhutui Qi" [Trans-regional mobile training becomes booster of combat capabilities], *Huojianbing Bao* [Rocket soldiers daily], June 13, 2006, 1.
92. He Junbo, Zou Yilu, He Tianjin, "Ming Pai Sheji Zao Fouding Zhi Hou" [Prestigious design after disaster and debate], *Huojianbing Bao* [Rocket soldiers daily], April 1, 2006, 2.
93. Sun Jiamin and Ding Wen, "She Bai Fuza Huanjing, Shishi Quancheng Duikang" [Set up a complex environment, implement a full course (entire route) confrontation], *Huojianbing Bao* [Rocket soldiers daily], July 11, 2006, 2.
94. Xue, *Zhanyi Lilun Xuexi Zhinan*, 387.
95. Ibid., 392.
96. Zhang Nenghau and Wang Gang, "Shuzi shenjing Guantong Duowei Zhanchang" [Digital nerve connects multi-dimensional battlefield], *Jiefangjun Bao* [*PLA Daily*], November 21, 2012, 2.
97. State Council Information Office, *China's National Defense in 2008*.
98. Liu et al., *Gao Jishu Zhanzheng Zhong de Daodan Zhan*, 107.
99. Ibid., 108.
100. Yu, *The Science of Second Artillery Campaigns*, 209, 298–301.

101. Office of the Secretary of Defense, *Annual Report to Congress 2011*, 35–36; and Esin, *Nuclear Might of the PRC*, 27–30.
102. The level of tolerance for the risk of nuclear war is explored in Xiao, *He Zhanzheng yu Renfang*, a book "for internal distribution only." The questions of preparations, civil defense, and nuclear calculus can also be found in Zhu Mingquan, *He Kuosan: Weixian yu Fangzh* [Nuclear proliferation: Danger and prevention] (Shanghai: Science and Technology Literature Press, 1995); and Yao Yunzhu, *Zhanhou Meiguo Weishe Lilun yu Zhengce* [Post-war American deterrence theories and policies] (Beijing: National Defense University Press, 1998).
103. Xiao Tianliang, *Zhanzheng Kongzhi Wenti Yanjiu* [Research on the problem of war control] (Beijing: National Defense University Press, 2002), 219–20.
104. See Wu, Wu, and Huang, "A MEO Tracking and Data Relay Satellite System Constellation Scheme"; Barbosa, "Long-March 3C Launches China's Third Tracking and Data Relay Satellite"; Richelson, *U.S. Intelligence Community*; Wu and Yu, "China Has Established a Space to Earth Satellite Monitoring System"; and USCC, *2011 Report to Congress*.
105. See Karber, testimony, USCC hearing on "Developments in China's Cyber and Nuclear Capabilities"; Schneider, testimony, USCC hearing on "Developments in China's Cyber and Nuclear Capabilities"; and Mark Schneider, "The Nuclear Doctrine and Forces of the People's Republic of China," *Comparative Strategy* 28, no. 3 (2009): 244–70. According to Schneider, estimates of China's nuclear force range from two hundred to two thousand warheads.

7. Space Warfare, Systems, and Space Control

1. Larry M. Wortzel, "The Chinese People's Liberation Army and Space Warfare," *Astropolitics* 6 (2008): 1–26. See also Cliff et al., *Ready for Takeoff*, 89–113. Also see Ian Easton, *The Great Game in Space: China's Evolving ASAT Weapons Programs and Their Implications for Future U.S. Strategy* (Arlington, VA: Project 2049 Institute, 2009); and Ian Easton and Mark A. Stokes, *China's Electronic Intelligence (ELINT) Satellite Developments: Implications for U.S. Air and Naval Operations* (Arlington, VA: Project 2049 Institute, 2011).
2. USCC, *2011 Report to Congress*, 198–240; and USCC, *2010 Report to Congress*, 73–91.
3. Office of the Secretary of Defense, *Annual Report to Congress 2011*, 35.
4. Department of Defense, *National Security Space Strategy: Unclassified Summary* (Washington, DC: Department of Defense, 2011), 1.
5. Ibid., 2.
6. "Security in Space: The Cluttered Frontier," *The Economist*, February 12, 2011, 87; and Mark Stokes and Dean Cheng, *China's Evolving Space Capabilities: Implications for U.S. Interests* (Arlington, VA: Project 2049 Institute, 2012), http://www.uscc.gov/RFP/2012/USCC_China-Space-Program-Report_April-2012.pdf.
7. Turner Brinton, "Will U.S. Space Agencies Follow New Policy?," *Defense News*, February 21, 2011, 48.
8. Senate Armed Services Committee, *Hearing on Current and Future World-wide Threats*, testimony of the director of the Defense Intelligence Agency Ronald L. Burgess Jr., 112th Cong., 2nd sess., February 16, 2012, http://www.armed-services.senate.gov/Transcripts/2011/03%20March/11-11%20-%203-10-11.pdf.
9. Cai et al., *Kongtian Yiti Zuozhan Xue*, 58.

10. USCC, *2008 Report to Congress of the U.S.-China Economic and Security Review Commission* (Washington, DC: Government Printing Office, 2008), 156–62, www.uscc.gov.

11. Zhao Dexi and Xie Chaohui, "Junshi Taikong Liliang de Fazhan" [The development of military space power]; *Zhongguo Junsho Kexue* [China military science] 21, no. 3 (June 2008): 90–92.

12. See, for example, U.S. Joint Chiefs of Staff, *Joint Publication 3-14: Joint Doctrine for Space Operations* (Washington, DC: Joint Staff, 2002); Secretary of the Air Force, *Air Force Doctrine Document 2-2: Space Operation* (Washington, DC: Department of the Air Force, 2006, superseding a 2001 publication); and Secretary of the Air Force, *Air Force Doctrine Document 2-2.1: Counterspace Operation* (Washington, DC: Department of the Air Force, 2004).

13. See, for instance, Yu Kunyang, Mao Zhaojun, and Li Yunzhi, "Mei, E, Hangtian Budui Zuzhi Tizhi Fenxi Ji Qishi" [Analysis of U.S.'s and Russia's space organization systems and their inspiration], *Zhuangbei Zhihui Jishu Xueyuan Xuebao* [Journal of the Academy of Equipment Command and Technology] 16, no. 6 (2005): 70–75, www.wangfangdata.com.cn. Another good example is Meng Lang, *Weilai Zhanzheng Shenma Yang* [What is happening on the future battlefield], http://www.people.com .cn/GB/junshi/62/20010108/372946.html. See also Tian Taoyun, "Yingjie Xin Tiaozhan: Zhongguo Junshi Zhuanjia Tichu Junshi Hangtian Lilun" [Meeting a new challenge: China's military experts propose military aerospace theory], *Xinhuawang* [China News Agency net], December 13, 2002, news.xinhaunet.com/newscenter/2002-12/13/content_659248.html.

14. Dipindra Nalan Chakravarthi, "Future Aerospace Power," *New Delhi Force*, September 1, 2007, in OSC, https://www.opensource.gov, SAP20070912342003.

15. See Daniel O. Graham, *High Frontier: A New National Strategy* (Washington, DC: High Frontier, 1982).

16. Cai et al., *Kongtian Yiti Zuozhan Xue*, 58. An earlier work on aerospace doctrine by Cai explored the issue of control of outer space as analogous to control of territorial seas. Cai et al., *Kongtian Zhanchang yu Zhongguo Kongjun*.

17. Huang Zhicheng, "Taikong Wuqihua yu Taikong Weishe" [The weaponization of space and space threats], *Guoji Jishu Jingji Yanjiu* [Studies in international technology and economy] 9, no. 1 (January 2006): 27.

18. Liu Jixian, "Junshi Hangtian Lilun de Yanjiu yu Chaungxin-dui *Junshi Hangtian Xue* de Renshi yu Pingjia" [Study and originality in military space theory: Understanding and commentary on *military space theory*], *Zhongguo Junshi Kexue Kexue* [China military science] 19, no. 6 (June 2006): 147.

19. Alan J. Wasser, "LBJ's Space Race: What We Didn't Know Then (Part 1)," *The Space Review*, June 20, 2005, http://www.thespacereview.com/article/396/1.

20. An excellent summary of what the PLA learned from observing foreign military operations during conflicts is available in Daniel Alderman and Joe Narus, *Other People's Wars: PLA Lessons from Foreign Conflicts*, colloquium brief, U.S. Army War College and National Bureau of Asian Research (Carlisle, PA: Strategic Studies Institute, 2010), http://www.strategicstudiesinstitute.army.mil/pubs/display.cfm?pubID =1062. See also Fu Quanyou, "Chuangjin Tansuo yu Jiashen Gaige Tisheng Guangfan de Junshi Fazhen" [Aggressively explore and deepen reform to promote comprehensive development in military work], *Qiushi* [Seek truth] no. 6 (March 16, 1998): 2–6; Shen Weiguang, "Xinxizhan: Mengxiang yu Xianshi" [Information warfare: Dreams and reality], *Zhongguo Guofang Bao* [China defense news], February 14, 1997; Wang Huyang, "Xinxi Zuozhan, Wuge Fangfa" [Five methods in information warfare],

Jiefangjun Bao [*PLA Daily*], November 7, 1995; Deng Raolin, Qian Shi Xu, and Zhao Jincun, eds., *Gao Jishu Jubu Zhanzheng Lilun Yanjiu* [Theory and research in high technology warfare under limited conditions] (Beijing: Military Friendship and Literature Publishers, 1998); and Li Jijun, "Xin Shiqi Jundai Jianshe de Zhidao Gangling" [Guiding doctrine on military building in the new age], in his *Junshi Lilun yu Zhanzheng Shijian* [Military theory and practice in war] (Beijing: Military Science Publishers, 1994).

21. Lyle Goldstein, "China's Falklands Lessons," *Survival* 50, no. 3 (June/July 2008): 65–82. See also Alderman and Narus, *Other People's Wars.*

22. Tan Baoping, "Zai Keji Lianbing de Jujiao Dianshang Zhuoli Xin" [Make fresh efforts to focus science and technology in troop training], *Jiefangjun Bao* [*PLA Daily*], November 23, 1999.

23. *Chinese Military Encyclopedia*, vol. 7 (Beijing: PressAcademy of Military Science Press, 1997), 404, and State Council Information Office, *China's National Defense in 2004* (Beijing: State Council Information Office, 2004).

24. See Zhao Erquan, "Lun Xinxihua Zhanzheng dui Wuzhuang Chongtu Fa de Shenyuan Yinxiang" [A Discussion of the far-reaching effects of informationalized warfare on the laws of armed conflict], in *Xin Junshi Geming yu Junshi Fazhi Jianshe* [The new revolution in military affairs and building a military legal system], ed. Liu Jixian and Liu Zheng (Beijing: PLA Press, 2005), 498–505, and Pan Youmu, "Zhuoyan Kongtian Yitihua Tansuo Guojia Kongtian Anquan Zhanlue" [Focus on air-space integration and exploring a national air-space strategy], *Zhongguo Junshi Kexue* [*China military science*] 19, no. 2 (2006): 64.

25. Zhang Qinghai, Ji Xiaohai, "Tai kong zhan: You gouxiang dao xianshi" [Space warfare: From vision to reality], *Zhongguo Junshi Kexue* [China military science] 18, no. 1 (2005): 34–6. See also Huang Tie Gang, Zhou Xin Chu, Chen Jun, and Liu Ya Jing, "Weilai de si zhanchang: Taikong" [The fourth battlefield in future: Outer space], *Xiandai Fangyu Jishu* [*Modern Defence Technology*] 32, no. 1 (February 2004): 8–14. A similar position can be found in Zhang Zhiwei and Feng Zhuanjiang, "Weilai Yiti Kongtian Zuozhan Fenxi [Analysis of future integrated air and space operations]," *Zhonguo Junshi Kexue* [China military science] 19, no. 2 (2006): 23–25.

26. Yang Jinhui and Chang Xianqi, "Kongjian Xinxi Duikang Wenti Yanjiu" [Research and problems of space information warfare], *Wu Xiandian Gongcheng* [Radio engineering] 36, no. 11 (2006): 9.

27. Zhang Jiali and Min Zengfu, "Shi lun jubu zhanzheng kong zhong hua" [On Extending the regional war into the air and space], *Zhongguo Junshi Kexue* [China military science] 18 no. 1 (January 2005): 41.

28. Pan, "Zhuoyan Kongtian Yitihua Tansuo Guojia Kongtian Anquan Zhanlue," 60.

29. Xinhua, "China's PLA Eyes Future in Space, Air: Air Force Commander," *People's Daily Online,* November 2, 2009, http://english.people.com.cn/90001/90776/90786 /6799960.html.

30. Cheng Yong and Guo Yanlong, "Fan Weixing Jiguang Wuqi Fazhan Xianzhuang yu Dongtai Fenxi" [An analysis of present day trends in anti-satellite laser weapons], *Dimian Fangkong Wuqi* [Ground air defense weapons] 312, no. 4 (2004): 51–54, www.cnki.net.

31. Li Daguang, "Mei Yanfa Kongtian Feiji de Zhanlue Kao Liang" [Strategic considerations in the united states' research and development of space planes], *Liaowang Xinwen Zhoukan* [Outlook weekly] no. 21 (March 21–27, 2011): 59.

32. Li Naiguo, *Xinxizhan Xinlun* [A new discussion on information warfare] (Beijing: National Defense University Press, 2004), 67–68.

33. Shen Shilu, Feng Shuxing, and Xu Xuefeng, "Tian Ji Dui Di Daji Dongneng Wuqi Zuozhan Nengli yu Kexing Xing Fenxi" [The analysis of the operational capability and feasibility of space-to-ground kinetic weapons], *Zhuangbei Zhihui Jishu Xueyuan Xuebao* [Journal of the Academy of Command and Technology] 17, no. 1 (February 2006): 33–37.

34. Zhang and Feng, "Analysis of Future Integrated Air and Space Operations," 1.

35. Liu, "Junshi Hangtian Lilun de Yanjiu yu Chaungxin-dui *Junshi Hangtian Xue* de Renshi yu Pingjia," 145.

36. The Chinese Ministry of Foreign Affairs (MFA) seems to be operating on the practice that if China establishes a position on an issue in its domestic law, it can then use that argument to advance its own position in international law. For example, China now uses the Law on the Territorial Sea and the Contiguous Zone of 1992 as part of the basis for defending its territorial claims in the South China Sea and East China Sea. Once the National People's Congress passed the domestic law, the MFA then included the language in its legal declarations to United Nations bodies and international courts or adjudication bodies, as well as in negotiations with foreign countries.

37. Staff Writers, "Stability and Security in Space," *Space Daily,* April 25, 2011, http://www.spacedaily.com/reports/Stability_And_Security_In_Space_999.html.

38. Peter Dutton of the U.S. Navy War College discusses this in "At Sea with China," *Wall Street Journal*, May 4, 2010, http://online.wsj.com/article /SB10001424052748704608104575221130565188088.html. See also Ren Xiaofeng, "Zhuanyu Jingjiqu Junshi Liyong de Falu Wenti: Zhongguo de Guanjiao" [Legal issues regarding military and intelligence gathering activities in the eez and adjacent airspace: A Chinese perspective], http://vip.chinalawinfo.com/newlaw2002/slc/slc.asp?db=art&gid =33557856.

39. On military activities in the exclusive economic zone, see Dutton, *Military Activities in the EEZ*, in which participants from China set forth the PLA's objections to military reconnaissance in the EEZ.

40. Liu and Liu, *Xin Junshi Geming yu Junshi Fazhi Jianshe*. See also Zheng Shenxia and Liu Yuan, eds., *Guofang he Jundui Jianshe Guanshe Luoshi Kexue Fazhan Guan Xuexi Tiyao* [Study materials for completely building the military and national defense] (Beijing: PLA Press, 2006), 192–94.

41. Beijing did this in its 1992 Maritime Law, adopted by the National People's Congress, and it extended sovereign claims over some 3 million square miles of area in the East and South China Seas, demarcating it as Chinese territory on its maps. See Law of the People's Republic of China on the Territorial Sea and the Continuous Zone, adopted February 25, 1992, effective the same day, http://www.zhb.gov.cn/english/law _detail.php3?id=32.

42. See the discussion of sovereignty security in Liu Jingbo, *21 Shijichu Zhongguo Guojia Anquan Zhanlue* [China's national security strategy in the early 21st century] (Beijing: Facts Press, 2006), 2–3. John Garver has an excellent discussion on this sensitivity and relates it to what he calls the "myth of national humiliation." See Garver, *Foreign Relations*, 4–8.

43. Cai and Tian, *Kongtian Zhanchang yu Zhongguo Kongjun*, 2. The two editors make essentially the same point in their 2006 text, Cai et al., *Kongtian Yiti Zuozhan Xue*, 58.

44. Aria Pearson, "China's New Submarine Spotted on Google Earth," *NewScientist Tech*, July 6, 2007, http://technology.newscientist.com/article/dn12204.

45. Mao Yuan, "'Gegediqiu' yinfa de Sikao" [Thoughts prompted by "Google Earth"], *Huojianbing Bao* [*Rocket soldiers daily*], June 1, 2007, 2. Later a PLA Air Force newspaper published comments on blogs by soldiers complaining that China's secrets were open to observation from space. See Wang Guobo and Yang Chen, "'Gegediqiu' Yinfa Jiceng Guanbing Reyi" ["Google Earth" prompts heated discussion among grassroots level military personnel] *Kongjun Bao* [Air Force daily], April 19, 2007.

46. Wei Liping, "Shan yu Zhencha Weixing, 'Zhuo Mi Cang'" [About reconnaissance satellites, be good at hiding and secrecy], *Kongjun Bao* [PLA Air Force daily], April 19, 2007.

47. Ibid.

48. Li Yong, Wang Xiao, Yi Ming, and Wang Long, "Tianji Guangdian chengxiang Yaogan Shebei Mianlin de Weixie" [Threats to spaceborne optoelectronic imaging and telemetry systems and countermeasures technology], *Hongwai yu Jiguang Gongcheng* [Infrared and laser engineering] 34, no. 6 (2005): 631–35, 640. See also Huang Shiqi and Liu Daizhi, "Fan Chengxiang Weixing Zhencha Jishu yu Fangfa Celue Yanjiu" [Study anti-imaging spy satellite technology and tactical methods research], *Xitong Gongcheng yu Dianzi Jishu* [Systems engineering and electronics] 28, no. 7 (2006): 104–7.

49. Ren, "Zhuanyu Jingjiqu Junshi Liyong de Falu Wenti."

50. Zhang Hualiang and Song Huaren, "Luelun Xinxihua Zhanzheng Zhu Zhanchang Xiang Taikong Zhuanyi de Biranxing" [Discussion on the inevitability of the main battlefield in information war transferring to outer space], *Zuangbei Zhiui Jishu Xueyuan Xuebao* [Journal of the Academy of Equipment Command and Technology] 15, no. 5 (October 2004): 14, 17.

51. Ren, "Zhuanyu Jingjiqu Junshi Liyong de Falu Wenti."

52. Cheng and Guo, "Fan Weixing Jiguang Wuqi Fazhan Xianzhuang yu Dongtai Fenxi," 51–54.

53. *U.S. National Space Policy*, White House, August 31, 2006. See the website of the Federation of American Scientists (FAS) at http://www.fas.org/irp/offdocs/nspd/space.pdf.

54. Dean N. Reinhardt, *Vertical Limit of State Sovereignty*, McGill University, Montreal, Canada, June 2005, 19, http://www.dtic.mil/cgi-bin/GetTRDoc?AD=ADA436627.

55. Ibid., 21.

56. R. Cargill Hall, "The Evolution of U.S. National Security Space Policy and Its Legal Foundations," *Journal of Space Law* 33, no. 1 (Summer 2007), 8–10, 16–18.

57. Reinhardt, *Vertical Limit of State Sovereignty*, 22–24.

58. Ibid., 38–40.

59. See Michel Bourbonniere, "National Security Law in Outer Space: The Interface of Exploration and Security," *Journal of Air Law and Commerce* 70, no. 1 (Winter 2005): 3–62, http://www.smu.edu/lra/Journals/JALC.

60. Liu Yijian, "Zhihai Quan Lilun Ji Fazhan Qushi" [Theory of outer space policy and trends in its development], *Zhongguo Junsi Kexue* [China military science] no. 1 (January 1, 2005): 42–46.

61. Nima Nayebi, "The Geosynchronous Orbit and the Outer Limits of Westphalian Sovereignty," *Hastings Science and Technology Law Journal* 3, no. 2 (2011): 471–98.

62. Pan, "Zhuoyan Kongtian Yitihua Tansuo Guojia Kongtian Anquan Zhanlue," 60–66.

63. Cai et al., *Kongtian Yiti Zuozhan Xue*, 90–91.

64. Ibid., 91–92.

65. Ibid., 57, 216–17.

66. Jerome Morenoff, *World Peace through Space Law* (Charlottesville, VA: The Michie Co., 1967), 159–65. Also see Robert A. Ramey, "Armed Conflict on the Final Frontier: The Law of War in Space," in the *Air Force Law Review* 48, (2000): 44, http://www .afjag.af.mil/shared/media/document/AFD-081204-031.pdf.

67. The author has served as notetaker in many meetings between members of the Central Military Commission and visiting American members of the Joint Chiefs of Staff. The Chinese side invariably complains about U.S. reconnaissance missions.

68. Ramey, "Armed Conflict on the Final Frontier," 52 and note 454.

69. Li Daguang, "Taikong Zuozhan de Zhidao Sixiang" [Thoughts on aerospace operations command and control], *Guoji Taikong* [International aerospace] no. 3 (2004): 27–30, www.cnki.net. See also Liu, "Junshi Hangtian Lilun de Yanjiu yu Chaungxin-dui *Junshi Hangtian Xue* de Renshi yu Pingjia," 145–47; and Cai et al., *Kongtian Yiti Zuozhan Xue*, 57–58.

70. Cai et al., *Kongtian Yiti Zuozhan Xue*, 57.

71. Zheng and Liu, *Guofang he Jundui Jianshe Guanshe Luoshi Kexue Fazhan Guan Xuexi Tiyao*, 25. Zheng and Liu lump Japan in with the United States and label it as a country that seeks to contain China. Liu was promoted and made political commissar of the General Logistics Department after this article was published.

72. Ibid., 25–26.

73. Cai et al., *Kongtian Yiti Zuozhan Xue*, 90–91.

74. Cai et al., *Kongtian Zhanchang yu Zhongguo Kongjun*, 76.

75. Cai et al., *Kongtian Yiti Zuozhan Xue*, 90–91.

76. Zhang and Song, "Luelun Xinxihua Zhanzheng Zhu Zhanchang Xiang Taikong Zhuanyi de Biranxing," 14–17.

77. Ren, "Zhuanyu Jingjiqu Junshi Liyong de Falu Wenti."

78. See, for example, M. J. Peterson, "The Use of Analogies in Developing Outer Space Law," *International Organization* 541, no. 2 (Spring 1997): 254–74; Nina Tannenwald, "Law Versus Power on the High Frontier: The Case for a Rule-Based Regime for Outer Space," *Yale Journal of International Law* 29, no. 263 (Summer 2004), 363–42, http://drum.lib.umd.edu/bitstream/1903/7902/1/tannenwald.pdf; and Haile Jayson, "The New Age of Conquest and Colonialism: How Admiralty Will Be Used on the Final Frontier," *Tulane Maritime Law Journal* 29, no. 2 (Summer 2005): 353.

79. See the earlier note on Ren, "Zhuanyu Jingjiqu Junshi Liyong de Falu Wenti."

80. See Yu Zhirong, "Jurisprudential Analysis of the U.S. Navy's Military Surveys in the Exclusive Economic Zones of Coastal Countries," in Dutton, *Military Activities in the EEZ*, 37–48.

81. Chen Qiang, "Chinese Practice in Public International Law," *Chinese Journal of International Law* 3, no. 591 (2003): 17–28. During the years the author was a military attaché in Beijing (1988 to 1990 and from 1995 until the end of 1997), there were a number of meetings where senior Chinese Navy and other defense officials complained to U.S. commanders or defense officials about peacetime reconnaissance by the United States inside China's EEZ.

82. Wang Pufeng, "Xinxizhan Yanjiu zhong Ruogan Wenti de Wo Jian" [My views on basic questions in research on informationalized warfare], in *Zhongguo Xinxi Zhan* [China's Information Warfare], ed. Shen Weiguang, Jie Xijiang, Ma Ji, and Li Jijun (Beijing: Xinhua Press, 2005, 42–43).

83. Li, *Xinxizhan Xinlun*, 35–45, especially 43.

84. There is an excellent discussion of this disagreement and the U.S., Soviet, and Chinese positions in Bourbonniere, "National Security Law in Outer Space," 3–62. A good

overview can be found in Ramey, "Armed Conflict on the Final Frontier," 41–42. The Chinese position is outlined in Chen, "Chinese Practice in Public International Law," 5–8.

85. For data on Chinese satellites, see *Jane's Space Directory: 2006–2007* (Surrey, UK: Jane's, 2006), http://www.ucsusa/global_security/space_weapons/satellite _database.html.

86. Cheng and Guo, "Fan Weixing Jiguang Wuqi Fazhan Xianzhuang yu Dongtai Fenxi," 51–54.

87. Yang Yonghui and Xiao Siwei, "Weixing Ce Kong Lian Ganrao Jishu Yanjiu" [Jamming Technique against Satellite TTC Channel], *Hangtian Dianzi Duikang* [Aerospace electronic countermeasures] 22, no. 5 (October 1, 2006): 22–24; Zhang Liying, Zhang Xixin, and Wang Hui, "Fan Weixing Wuqi Jishu Ji Fangyu Cuoshi Qianjin" [Preliminary analysis of anti-satellite weapon technology and defensive measures], *Feihang Daodan* [Winged missile journal] no. 3 (March 2004): 28–30; Xu Xiaofeng, Zhu Xiaosong, and Liu Liyuan, "Jiyu Mou Weixing Tongxin Xitong de Ganrao Yanjiu" [Jamming analysis based on a certain satellite communications system], *Hangtian Dianzi Duikang* [Aerospace electronic countermeasures] 22, no. 5 (October 2006): 28–29, 45; Chen Yong and Guo Yanlong, "Fan Weixing Jiguang Wuqi Fazhan Xianzhuang yu Dongtai" [Present status and trend in antisatellite laser weapons], *Guangxue yu Guangdian Jishu* [Optics and optoelectronic technology] 16, no. 3 (August 2003): 1–4; Tang Yuyan and Huang Peikang, "Jiaohui Duijie Zhong Leida Celiang Xinxi de Zui You Guji" [Optimal estimation of radar measurement information in rendezvous docking], *Xiandai Fangwei Jishu* [Modern defence technology] 34, no. 6 (December 2006): 98–102; China National Space Administration, *China's Space Activities (White Paper)*, October 2006), Beijing, http://www.cnsa.gov.cn/n615709/n620681/n771967/69198.html; and Information Office of the State Council, *China's Space Activities in 2011* (Beijing, December 2011), http://news.xinhuanet.com/english/china/2011-12/29/c_131333479.htm. These programs are summarized in USCC, *2011 Report to Congress*, 213–14. For a more in-depth assessment of China's space activities, including antisatellite programs prepared for the U.S.-China Economic and Security Commission, see Stokes and Cheng, *China's Evolving Space Capabilities*.

88. Mao Zedong, *Mao Tse-tung on Guerilla Warfare*, trans. Samuel B. Griffith (New York: Praeger, 1961), 52–53. See also Peng and Yao, *Science of Military Strategy*, 280–82. See also Zhang Xingye and Wang Chaotian, eds. *Zhanyi Sixiang Fazhan Shi* [The history of the development of campaign thought] (Beijing: National Defense University Press, 1997, 336–41.

89. See Schneider and Saunders, testimony before the USCC. See also David C. Gompert and Phillip C. Saunders, *The Paradox of Power: Sino-American Strategic Restraint in an Age of Vulnerability* (Washington, DC: National Defense University Press, 2011).

90. Yang Hua, Chen Changming, Ling Yongshun, and Ma Donghui, "Tianji Daodan Yujing Xitong Ji Dui Qi de Gongji He Ganrao Fenxi" [Analysis of attack and jamming of spaceborne missile early warning system], *Hangtian Dianzi Duikang* [Aerospace electronic warfare] 21, no. 4 (2006): 5–7, 37; Tao Benren, "Dui Dimian Junshi Dianzi Xinxi de Tianji Fanghu Xitong" [Space defense system for ground military electromagnetic information], *Hangtian Dianzi Duikang* [Aerospace electronic warfare] 22, no. 4 (August 1, 2006): 15–18; and Lu Jiuming and Zhu Kai, "Junshi Tongxin Weixing Ji Qi Xinglian Lu Xingneng Yanjiu" [Research on military communications

satellites and the performance of downlinks], *Xiandai Fangwei Jishu* [Modern defence technology] 34, no. 3 (June 2006): 48–51.

91. Yang, Cheng, Ling and Ma, "Tianji Daodan Yujing Xitong," 5.
92. Ibid., 6.
93. Ibid., 7.
94. Ibid., 7, 37.
95. Ibid., 37.
96. Peng Mei, "Er Pao Zhanlue Yanjiu Zhongxin Chengli" [Second artillery center for strategic studies established], *Jiefangjun Bao* [*PLA Daily*], December 24, 2012, http://epaper.oeeee.com/A/html/2012-12/24/content_1781813.htm.
97. Huang, "Taikong Wuqihua yu Taikong Weishe," 24.
98. Ibid.
99. Ibid., 26.
100. Ibid., 26–27.
101. Ibid.
102. Warren Ferster and Colin Clark, "NRO Confirms Chinese Laser Test Illuminated U.S. Spacecraft," *Defense News*, October 2, 2006.
103. Sun Haiping and Chang Jin'an, "Junshi Weishe de Xinxingshi: Taikong Weishe" [Space deterrence: A new form of military deterrence], *Junshi Xueshu* [Journal of military art] 10 (2003): 32–33.
104. USCC, *2011 Report to Congress,* 206.
105. Ibid., 207.
106. See Larry Wortzel and Dean Cheng, *China's Military Ambitions in Space* (Washington, DC: George C. Marshall Institute, 2006), http://www.marshall.org/pdf/materials/488.pdf (accessed April 27, 2011).
107. Jefffrey Mervis, "Spending Bill Prohibits U.S.-China Collaborations," *Science Insider,* April 21, 2011, http://news.sciencemag.org/scienceinsider/2011/04/spending-bill-prohibits-us-china.html.
108. Cliff et al., *Ready for Takeoff,* 112.
109. Ibid., 108.
110. Ibid.
111. Ibid., 101.
112. Alex Kane Rudanski, "U.S. Keeps Wary Eye on China's Space Program," *McClatchy,* July 17, 2012, http://www.mcclatchydc.com/2012/07/17/156473/us-keeps-wary-eye-on-chinas-space.html.
113. Barry Wain, "All at Sea over Resources in East Asia: Competing Claims over the South China Sea among China and Its Neighbors Could Destabilize the Region," *YaleGlobal Online,* August 14, 2007, www.yaleglobalyale.edu.

8. Information Age Warfare and INEW

1. Zhang, *The Science of Military Campaigns,* 155.
2. Jeffrey T. Richelson, *The U.S. Intelligence Community,* 6th ed. (Boulder, CO: Westview, 2012), 88–89.
3. Li Wuchao and Wang Yonggang, "Fen Jin de Bu Dai Yong bu Tingxie" [The Pace of progress never stops], *Kongjun Bao* [Air Force daily], August 13, 2012, 2.
4. Nair, "China's Military Space Program."
5. Li, *Xinxizhan Xinlun,* 35–45.
6. "Laolao Bawo Guofang he Jundui Jianshe de Zhidao Fangzhen" [Firmly grasp the imporant guidelines for national defense and army building], *Jiefangjun Bao* [*PLA*

Daily], January 1, 2006, 1, http://www.chinamil.com.cn/site1/zbxl/2006-01/01 /content_374878.htm.

7. Liu Mingfu, Cheng Gang, and Sun Xuefu, "Renmin Jundui Lishi shiming de You Yi Ci yu Shi Jujin" [The historic missions of the People's Army again adavnces with the times], *Jiefangjun Bao* [*PLA Daily*], December 8, 2005.

8. Li and Wang,"Fen Jin de Bu Dai Yong bu Tingxie."

9. Wang, *Jiedu Wangluo Zhongxin Zhan*, 316.

10. Wang Xianhui, Yuan Jianquan, and Lu Junjie, "Zhencha Duikang Daji Yiti Hua Xitong Yanjiu" [Reconnaissance, electronic warfare and strike integrated system], *Hangtian Dianzi Duikang* [Spaceflight electronic confrontation] 25, no. 1 (July 28, 2008): 37–39.

11. Peng and Yao, *Science of Military Strategy*, 337.

12. Ibid., 338.

13. See Blasko, *Chinese Army Today*, 12–14. On PLA history, see Wortzel, *Dictionary of Chinese History*, 132–36, 224–25, 258–59. See also Li, *History of the Modern Chinese Army*, 94–112, 198–204, 250–59.

14. Ye Zheng, *Xinxihua Zuozhan Gailun* [An introduction to informationalized operations] (Beijing: Military Science Press, 2007), 17–18.

15. Shen et al., *Zhongguo Xinxi Zhan*, 2–3.

16. Ibid., 86–87. The authors seem to adapt the formulation used by the United States. See National Security Agency, "Global Information Grid," November 14, 2008, http://www.nsa.gov/ia/programs/global_information_grid/index.shtml.

17. Ibid., 122.

18. Ibid.

19. This refers to the Communications Department of the General Staff Department, or *Zongcanmoubu Tongxinbu*. Tongxinbu, "Zhanqu Xinxi Hua Jianshe Chubu Gouxiang" [The initial concept of theater informatization efforts], *Junshi Xueshu* [Military art] no. 7 (July 1, 2004): 20.

20. Ibid., 21.

21. Ibid., 20.

22. Ibid., 126.

23. Wang Yeming, "Zhiming Diqiu: Rang Weilai Zhanchang Geng 'Touming'" [Smart planet makes future battlefields more "transparent"], *Jiefangjun Bao* [*PLA Daily*], December 16, 2010.

24. Shen et al., *Zhongguo Xinxi Zhan*, 122, 126.

25. Ye et al., *Xinxi Hua Zuozhan Gailun,* 19.

26. Ibid., 23.

27. Wei Yufu and Zhao Xiaosong, *Junshi Xinxi Youshi Lun* [Theory of military information superiority] (Beijing: National Defense University Press, 2008), 249–51.

28. Shen et al., *Zhongguo Xinxi Zhan*, 227–29.

29. Dai Qingmin, "Lun Duoqu Zhi Xinxi Quan" [On seizing information supremacy], *Zhongguo Junshi Kexue* [China military science] 16, no. 2 (April 2002): 11–13. Also see Dai Qingmin, *Wangdian Yiti zhan Yinlun* [Introduction to integrated network and electronic warfare] (Beijing: PLA Press, 2002), 112–17.

30. Minnie Chan, "PLA Eyes Talent Pool to Expand Capability," *South China Morning Post*, April 20, 2011, http://www.scmp.com/portal/site/SCMP/menuitem .2af62ecb329d3d7733492d9253a0a0a0/?vgnextoid =f0d7cc9cc2e6f210VgnVCM100000360a0a0aRCRD&ss=china&s=news.

31. Tongxinbu, "Zhanqu Xinxi Hua Jianshe Chubu Gouxiang," 22.

32. The Chinese term for INEW is *wangdian yiti zhan*.

33. Ye et al., *Xinxi Hua Zuozhan Gailun*, 229.

34. Ibid., 231.

35. David G. Chizum, *Soviet Radioelectronic Combat* (Boulder, CO: Westview, 1985), 3–4; Department of Defense, *Soviet Military Power: Prospects for Change—1989* (Washington, DC: Department of Defense, 1989); and David R. Beachley, "Soviet Radio-Electronic Combat in World War II," *Military Review* 61, no. 3 (March 1981): 66–72. See also David M. Glantz, *Soviet Military Operational Art: In Pursuit of Deep Battle* (London: Cass, 1991), 295 and especially chapter 5.

36. Dai, "Lun Wangdian Yiti Zhan, 113.

37. Wang Chang-Ho, *Chueh-chi I Tong Ya: Chu-chiao Shin Shih-chi Chieh Fang Chun* [East Asia rising: Focus on the People's Liberation Army in the new century] (Taipei: LiveABC Interactive Corp., 2009), 219–20. Because this study originated in Taiwan, which uses the Wade-Giles transliteration system, the Chinese is rendered in Wade-Giles rather than pinyin. A similar point is made in Wang Wowen, "Chuan Tou Xinxihua Zhanzheng 'Mi Wu' de Li Qi" [Sharp weapons for penetrating the "dense fog" of information warfare], *Jiefangjin Bao* [*PLA Daily*], May 16, 2006.

38. Wang Zhengde, ed., *Jiedu Wangluo Zhongxin Zhan* [Interpretation of network centric warfare] (Beijing: National Defense Industries Press, 2004), 316–18.

39. Timothy L. Thomas, *The Dragon's Quantum Leap: Transforming from a Mechanized to an Informatized Force* (Fort Leavenworth, KS: U.S. Army Foreign Military Studies Office, 2009), 38–39. See also Timothy L. Thomas, *Decoding the Virtual Dragon: Critical Evolutions in the Science and Philosophy of China's Information Operations and Military Strategy* (Fort Leavenworth, KS: U.S. Army Foreign Military Studies Office, 2007); and Timothy L. Thomas, *Dragon Bytes: Chinese Information-War Theory and Practice* (Fort Leavenworth, KS: U.S. Army Foreign Military Studies Office, 2004).

40. Wang, *Jiedu Wangluo Zhongxin Zhan*, 317–18. See also Thomas, *Dragon's Quantum Leap*, 39.

41. Ding, *Zuozhan Zhihui Xue*, 4.

42. Wang, *Jiedu Wangluo Zhongxin Zhan*, 319.

43. Wang, *Xinxi Duikang Lun*, 174.

44. Ibid., 199.

45. Defense Intelligence Agency, *Future Soviet Threat to U.S. Airbreathing Reconnaissance Platforms: A Special Defense Intelligence Estimate*, DDE-2623-1-86 (Washington, DC: Defense Intelligence Agency, 1986), 4.

46. For studies on informatized operations or information age warfare in the PLA, see Che Yajun and Xue Xinglin, eds., *Zhanchang Huanjing yu Xinxihua Zhanzheng* [The battlefield environment and informatized warfare] (Beijing: National Defense University Press, 2010); Shen et al., *Zhongguo Xinxi Zhan*; and Laiyi, "Lun xinxi zuozhan zhihui kongzhi jiben yuanze."

47. Wang et al., "Zhencha Duikang Daji Yiti Hua Xitong Yanjiu," 39.

48. Chizum, *Soviet Radioelectronic Combat*, 3–4; Beachley, "Soviet Radio-Electronic Combat in World War II," 66–72; Gordon, "Evolution of Soviet Fire Support," 18–21; and Glantz, *Soviet Military Operational Art*, 295.

49. Extract from chapter 1, *U.S. Army Field Manual FM 24-33*, www.fas.org/irp/doddir/army/fm24-33/fm243_2.htm (accessed February 10, 2010).

50. Ibid.

51. Wang et al., "Zhencha Duikang Daji Yiti Hua Xitong Yanjiu," 39.

52. Jeffery W. Long, *The Evolution of U.S. Army Doctrine: From Active Defense to AirLand Battle and Beyond* (Fort Leavenworth, KS: Command and General Staff College, 1991), http://www.stormingmedia.us/47/4771/A477142.html (accessed March 7, 2011).

53. Ibid.

54. Peng and Yao, *Science of Military Strategy*, 410–12; and Zhu et al., *Gao Jishu Tiaojian Xia de Xinxi Zhan*, 56–62.

55. Ye et al., *Xinxi Hua Zuozhan Gailun*, 229–30.

56. Wang, *Jiedu Wangluo Zhongxin Zhan*, 316–18. See also Wang et al., "Zhencha Duikang Daji Yiti Hua Xitong Yanjiu," 39–41.

57. Dai, "Lun Wangdian Yiti Zhan," 113.

58. Zhang Zhiwei, *Xiandai Huoli Zhan* [Modern firepower warfare] (Changsha, Hunan: National Defense Science and Technology Press, 2000).

59. Thomas, *Dragon Bytes*, 57.

60. Dai Qingmin, "Lun Duoqu Xinxi Quan" [On seizing information supremacy], *Zhongguo Junshi Kexue* [China military science] 16, no. 2 (February 2003): 12–13.

61. Ibid., 13.

62. Zhang Ying, "Zhanlue Pouxi: Zhonguo Bixu An Junshi Duikang Yuanze Yanjiu Wangge Zhan" [Strategic analysis: China must research cyberwarfare according to the principles of military confrontation], *Dongfang Zaobao* [Oriental morning post], July 9, 2009, http://www.dfdaily.com/node2/node23/node102/userobject1ai178135.shtml (accessed July 9, 2009).

63. See Qiao Liang and Wang Xiangsui, *Chaoxian Zhan* [Unrestricted warfare] Beijing: PLA Arts and Literature Press, 1999).

64. U.S. Joint Chiefs of Staff, Office of the Chairman, *The National Military Strategy for Cyberspace Operations* (Washington, DC: Department of Defense, 2006), 5, http://www.dod.gov/pubs/foi/ojcs/07-F-2105doc1.pdf. Cited in Robert Sheldon, "China's Great Firewall and Situational Awareness," *Strategic Insights* 10, no. 1 (Spring 2011): 36–51.

65. Magnus Hjortdal, "China's Use of Cyber Warfare: Espionage Meets Strategic Deterrence," *Journal of Strategic Security* 4, no. 2 (2011): 1.

66. Larry M. Wortzel, "China's Approach to Cyber Operations: Implications for the United States," testimony before the Committee on Foreign Affairs, U.S. House of Representatives, hearing on "The Google Predicament: Transforming U.S. Cyberspace Policy to Advance Democracy, Security and Trade," March 10, 2010, http://www .internationalrelations.house.gov/111/wor031010.pdf; also available at http://www.uscc .gov/10_03_10_wortzel_statement.php.

67. USCC, *2009 Report to Congress*, 289–309.

68. Wortzel, "China's Approach to Cyber Operations: Implications for the United States," March 10, 2010, and Bryan Krekel et al., *Capability of the People's Republic of China to Conduct Cyber Warfare and Computer Network Exploitation* (McLean, VA: Northrop Grumman Corporation, 2009), http://www.uscc.gov/.../NorthropGrumman_PRC_Cyber _ Paper_FINAL_Approved%Report_16Oct2009.pdf.

69. Ellis L. Melvin, "A Study of the Chinese People's Liberation Army Military Region Headquarters Department Technical Reconnaissance Bureau," June 19, 2005. Melvin is a private citizen who served in the U.S. military in Taiwan and undertakes a great deal of personal research on PLA organizations in the Chinese language. He provided a copy of this study to the author. See also James Mulvenon, "PLA Computer Network Operations: Scenarios, Doctrine, Organizations, and Capability," in *Beyond the Strait: PLA Missions Other than Taiwan*, ed. Roy Kamphausen, David Lai, and Andrew

Scobell (Carlisle, PA: Strategic Studies Institute, 2009); Wang, *Jiedu Wangluo Zhongxin Zhan*; Wei Baofu and Zhao Xiaosong, *Junshi Xinxi Youxiu Lun* [Theory of military information superiority] (Beijing: National Defense University Press, 2008); and Larry M. Wortzel, "China Goes on the Cyber-Offensive," *Far Eastern Economic Review*, vol. 172, Issue 1, (January/February 2009): 56.

70. USCC, *2007 Report to Congress of the U.S.-China Economic and Security Review Commission* (Washington, DC: Government Printing Office, 2007) 95–96, www.uscc.gov, 110th Cong., 1st sess.

71. Ibid.

72. Robert Marquand and Ben Arnoldy, "China's Hacking Skills in Spotlight," *Seattle Times,* September 16, 2007.

73. Mike McConnell, "How to Win the Cyber-War We're Losing," *Washington Post*, February 28, 2010, http://www.washingtonpost.com/wp-dyn/content/article/2010/02/25/AR2010022502493.html.

74. Liu Jixian, "Chuangxin he Fazhan Lianhe Zuozhan Yanjiu de Ruogan Wenti" [Innovation and development in the research of basic Issues of joint operations], *Zhongguo Junshi Kexue* [China military science] 93, no. 3 (March 2009): 1–17.

75. Zhang, "Zhanlue Pouxi: Zhonguo Bixu An Junshi Duikang Yuanze Yanjiu Wangge Zhan," July 10, 2009.

76. Min, *Kongjun Junshi Sixiang Gailun*, 175–76. See also Jiang, *Yuan Zhan*, 133–40.

77. Krekel et al., *Capability of the People's Republic of China.*

78. Zhao Erquan, "Lun Xinxihua Zhanzheng dui Wuzhang Chongtu fa de Shenyaun Sixiang," in Liu and Liu, *Xin Junshi Geming yu Junshi Fazhi Jianshe*, 498–505.

79. Shen et al., *Zhongguo Xinxi Zhan*, 82–83.

80. Ibid., 86–87.

81. Wei and Zhao, *Junshi Xinxi Youshi Lun*, 287–90.

82. Krekel et al., *Capability of the People's Republic of China*, 30–50.

83. Ibid., 30–32.

84. Ibid.

85. Bryan Krekel, Patton Adams, and George Bakos, *Occupying the Information High Ground: Chinese Capabilities for Computer Network Operations and Cyber Espionage* (McLean, VA: Northrop Grumman Corporation, March 7, 2012), 45–55, http://www.uscc.gov/RFP/2012/USCC%20Report_Chinese_CapabilitiesforComputer_Network OperationsandCyberEspionage.pdf#xml=http://www.dmssearch.gpo.gov/PdfHighlighter .aspx?DocId=41&Index=D%3a%5cWebsites%5cUseIndex%5cUSCC&HitCount =2&hits=1f+9d4b+.

86. Melvin, "Study of the Chinese People's Liberation Army," 1–2. See also *Directory of PRC Military Personalities*, 2008, 18–19.

87. Mark A. Stokes, Jenny Lin, and L.C. Russell Hsiao, "The Chinese People's Liberation Army Signals Intelligence and Cyber Reconnaissance Infrastructure" (Arlington, VA: Project 2049 Institute, November 11, 2011), http://project2049.net/documents/pla_third _department_sigint_cyber_stokes_lin_hsiao.pdf.

88. Larry M. Wortzel, "The Chinese Way of (Cyber) War: The PRC Boasts an Extensive Cyber Strategy for Espionage and Battlefield Dominance," *Defense Dossier* 4 (August 2012): 3, American Foreign Policy Council, http://www.afpc.org/files/august2012.pdf.

89. Brian Grow and Mark Hosenball, "In Cyber-spy vs. Cyber-spy, China Has the Edge," *Globe and Mail*, April 14, 2011, http://www.theglobeandmail.com/news /technology/tech-nes/in-cyberspy-vs-cyberspy-china-has-the-edge-/article1985224 /singlepage/#articlecontent (accessed April 15, 2011).

90. Keith Epstein and Ben Elgin, "The Taking of NASA's Secrets," *BusinessWeek*, December 1, 2008, 72–79.
91. Ibid., 78.
92. Nathan Thornburgh, "The Invasion of the Chinese Cyberspies (and the Man Who Tried to Stop Them)," *Time*, August 29, 2005, http://www.time.com/time/printout /0,8816,1098961,00.html (accessed December 17, 2008).
93. Hjortdal, "China's Use of Cyber Warfare," 1–24. See also Shane Harris, "China's Cyber Militia," *National Journal*, May 31, 2008, http://www.nationaljournal.com/magazine /china-s-cyber-militia-20080531.
94. Mike McConnell, Michael Chertoff, and William Lynn, "China's Cyber Thievery Is National Policy—and Must Be Challenged," *Wall Street Journal*, January 27, 2012, http:// online.wsj.com/article/SB10001424052970203718504577178832338032176.html.
95. Interested readers can explore these cases by searching out indictments on the Department of Justice website at http://www.justice.gov/usao/. Another excellent compendium of espionage cases in the United States is maintained by the CI Centre, a Washington-based security education company, http://www.cicentre.com/?page=asset _prc_cyber.
96. NCIX, *Foreign Spies Stealing US Economic Secrets in Cyberspace*, 1.
97. Ibid., i.
98. Krekel et al., *Occupying the Information High Ground*, 96.
99. Huang Luwei, Bi Yiming, and Yang Jifeng, "Daodan Budui Wangge Zhongxin Zhan Wenti Yanjiu" [Research on problems of network-centric warfare for the missile forces]," *Zhihui Kongzhi yu Fangzhen* [Command, control and simulation] 28, no. 2, (April 2006): 18–21.
100. Krekel et al., *Occupying the Information High Ground*, 27–43.
101. Ibid., 31.

9. The General Political Department and Information Operations

1. Wortzel, "General Political Department and Evolution of Political Commissar System," 229–33.
2. Liu Gaoping, *Yulun Zhan Zhishi Duben* [Textbook on media warfare] (Beijing: National Defense University Press, 2005), 83–100.
3. An excellent discussion of the three warfares is an article about training in a group army in Shenyang Military Region is Mei Yushen and Yan Yongfeng, "Shenyang Junqu Mou Jituanjun Lakai 'San Zhan' Xumu" [A certain shenyang military region group army opens the curtain on "three warfares"], *Zhongguo Qingnian Bao* [China youth daily], July 17, 2004, http://zqb.cyol.com/gb/zqb/2004-07/17/content_910023.htm. See also Hou Baocheng, "Zhengzhi Gongzuo Weishenme Yao Jiaqiang dui 'San Zhan' de Yan Jiu" [The need to step up the study of 'three warfares' in political work"], *Jiefangjun Bao* [*PLA Daily*], July 29, 2004, http://www.pladaily.com.cn/gb/pladaily /2004/07/29/20040729001087.html. There is a good summary of the three warfares in English in Timothy A. Walton, *China's Three Warfares* (Herndon, VA: Delex Systems, 2012).
4. Bhaskar Roy, "China: The Military and Leadership Power," South Asia Analysis Group, paper no. 4052, September 20, 2010, http://www.southasiaanalysis.org /%5Cpapers41%5Cpaper4052.html.
5. Hou, "Zhengzhi Gongzuo Weishenme Yao Jiaqiang dui 'San Zhan' de Yan Jiu."

6. See Peter Dutton, "Three Disputes and Three Objectives," *Naval War College Review* 64, no. 4 (Autumn 2011): 43–67. See also Office of the Secretary of Defense, *Annual Report to Congress, 2011*, 26.

7. A direct translation of *yulun* is "public opinion," thus in many English translations the term "public opinion warfare" is used. In some PLA translations of book titles and articles, however, it is called "media warfare."

8. In perception management, a nation or organization undertakes conscious actions to convey certain information or indicators of intent to foreign audiences to influence their emotions and reasoning. Perception management also may deny specific items of information to foreign audiences for the same reasons. The goal is to influence foreign public opinion, leaders, and intelligence systems, and to influence official assessment. The goal of perception management operations often is to mold foreign behavior in ways that favor the original actor's objectives. See Stephen Collins, "Mind Games," *NATO Review* (Summer 2003), http://www.nato.int/docu/review/2003/issue2/english/art4.html.

9. USCC, *2011 Report to Congress*, 322–23.

10. Alan H. Yang and Michael Hsiao, "Confucious Institutes and the Question of China's Soft Power Diplomacy," *China Brief* 12, no. 13 (July 6, 2012), http://www.jamestown.org/programs/chinabrief/single/?tx_ttnews%5Btt_news%5D=39592&cHash=ccbda5a33d17f73e50a7a3d92be5233b. For a counterargument, see Peter Mattis, "Reexamining the Confucius Institutes," *The Diplomat: Diplomat Blogs*, August 2, 2012, http://thediplomat.com/china-power/reexamining-the-confucius-institutes/.

11. Chen Bingde, "Speech Presented at the National Defense University [of the United States]," Washington, May 20, 2011. This point is made in ibid., 333.

12. See Nicholas Eftimiades, *Chinese Intelligence Operations* (Annapolis, MD: Naval Institute Press, 1994), 92–93.

13. Shambaugh, *Modernizing China's Military*, 131–36. See especially the chart on page 135.

14. Bill Gertz, "China Using Retired U.S. Officers to Influence Policy," *Washington Times*, February 7, 2012, http://times247.com/articles/china-using-retired-u-s-officers-to-influence-policy. See also Bill Gertz, "Chinese Communists Influence U.S. Policy through Ex-Military Officials," *Washington Free Beacon*, February 6, 2012, http://freebeacon.com/chinese-government-influencing-policy-through-ex-military-officials/. A copy of the Sanya Initiative's own report on its 2008 program is available at http://freebeacon.com/wp-content/uploads/2012/02/Sanya-Initiative-08-smaller.pdf.

15. USCC, *2011 Report to Congress*, 338–40, and 352–53, notes 141, 142, 143.

16. Mark A. Stokes, "The Chinese Joint Aerospace Campaign: Strategy, Doctrine, and Force Modernization," in Mulvenon and Finkelstein, *China's Revolution in Doctrinal Affairs*, 271–74.

17. Zhu Wenquan and Chen Taiyi, *Xinxi Zuozhan* [Information operations] (Beijing: National Defense University Press, 1999), 349–50; and Li Rongchang, Cheng Jian, and Zheng Lianqing, eds., *Kongtian Yiti Xinxi Zuozhan* [Integrated aerospace information operations] (Beijing: Academy of Military Science Press, 2003), 156–62.

18. Walton, *China's Three Warfares*, 5. Walton cites personal communication with Dennis Blasko, author of *The Chinese Army Today*.

19. Stokes, "Chinese Joint Aerospace Campaign," 273.

20. Ibid., 272–73.

21. See Andrew Scobell, *Show of Force: The PLA and the 1995–1996 Taiwan Strait Crisis* (January 1999), Asia-Pacific Research Center, http://iis-db.stanford.edu/pubs/10091/Scobell.pdf.

22. Peng and Yao, *Science of Military Strategy*, 79.

23. Liu and Liu, *Xin Junshi Geming yu Junshi Fazhi Jianshe*. See also Zheng and Liu, *Guofang he Jundui Jianshe Guanshe Luoshi Kexue Fazhan Guan Xuexi Tiyao*, 192–94.

24. Law of the People's Republic of China on the Territorial Sea and the Continuous Zone, adoption date February 25, 1992, archived by the United Nations at http://www.un.org /Depts/los/LEGISLATIONANDTREATIES/PDFFILES/CHN_1992_Law.pdf. For a discussion of how domestic laws are used by China to justify its position in international law see Hyun-soo Kim, "The 1992 Chinese Territorial Sea Law in Light of the UN Convention," *International and Comparative Law Quarterly* Vol. 43, no. 4 (October 1994): 894–904.

25. One of the most important case studies in the PLA text that the authors used to justify the concept was the U.S. action in the Security Council in justifying its actions in Iraq in 2003 on UN Security Council Resolution 1368 (2001), "Threats to international peace and security caused by terrorist acts, http://daccess-dds-ny.un.org/doc/UNDOC /GEN/N01/533/82/PDF/N0153382.pdf?OpenElement; and UNSC Resolution1373 (2001), with the same title, http://daccess-dds-ny.un.org/doc/UNDOC/GEN /N01/557/43/PDF/N0155743.pdf?OpenElement. Also see Xu Ou and Tong Yunhe, "Cong Yilake Zhanzheng Kan Guoji Fa Zai Weilai Zhanzheng de Zuoyong" [From the standpoint of the Iraq War, examining the utility of international law in future warfare], in Liu and Liu, *Xin Junshi Geming yu Junshi Fazhi Jianshe*, 475–79.

26. Zhang et al., *Zhanyi Xue*, 205–7.

27. Liu and Liu, *Xin Junshi Geming yu Junshi Fazhi Jianshe*, 581.

28. See Alexander L. George, *The Chinese Communist Army in Action: The Korean War and Its Aftermath* (New York: Columbia University Press, 1967).

29. See Cheng and Wortzel, "PLA Operational Principles," 173–97.

30. Zhang Shanxin and Pan Jiangang, "Fazhizhan de Hanyi yu Yunyong" [The utility and implications of legal warfare], in Liu and Liu, *Xin Junshi Geming yu Junshi Fazhi Jianshe*, 428–34.

31. Le Hucheng and Zhang Yucheng, "Faluzhan Zai Junshi Douzheng Zhunbei Zhong de Diwei he Zuoyong" [The utility and position of legal warfare in the preparation for military conflict], in Liu and Liu, *Xin Junshi Geming yu Junshi Fazhi Jianshe*, 355–62. See also Liu Zhongshan, "Ziweiquan yu Zhuquan" [Sovereignty and the right of self-defense] *Zhanlue yu Guanli* [Strategy and management] no. 1 (2002): 50.

32. The concept of "lawfare," or using the international legal system to lay the ground for and to justify military operations, is discussed in Qiao and Wang, *Chaoxian Zhan*. When the book was first published and discussed in the United States, many American "China watchers" dismissed it because the two authors were senior colonels in the General Political Department of the PLA. Over the years, however, the concepts have been reinforced in other Chinese publications. Qiao Liang has been promoted to major general and as of 2010 was a professor at the PLA's Air Force Command College.

33. Rajaswari Pillai Rajagopalan, "China's Missile Defense Test: Yet Another Milestone?," *IDSA Comment,* Institute for Defence Studies and Analysis, February 1, 2010, http://www.idsa.in/idsacomments/ChinasMissileDefenceTest_rprajagopalan_010210.

34. State Council Information Office, *China's Peaceful Development Road* (Beijing: State Council Information Office, 2005), www.chinadaily.com.cn/english.doc/2005-12/22/content_505678.htm.

35. Yan Xuetong, Wang Zaibang, Li Zhongcheng, and Hou Ruoshi, eds. *Zhongguo Jueqi: Guoji Huanjing Pinggu* [The international environment for China's peaceful rise] (Tianjin: Tianjin People's Press, 1998).

36. Ibid., 2.

37. Ibid., 234–35.

38. The concept can be found in a speech by Zheng Bijian archived at the Brookings Institution. See Zheng Bijian, *China's Peaceful Rise: Speeches of Zheng Bijian, 1997–2004* (Washington, DC: Brookings Institution, 2005), http://www.brookings.edu/fp/events /20050616bijianlunch.pdf. Also see Zheng Bijian, "Zhongguo Heping Jueqi Fazhan Daolu You Liyu Zhong-Mei Guanxi" [China's peaceful rise is conducive to the Sino-U.S. relationship] *Luntan Tongxun* [China reform forum newsletter], September 28, 2004, 3–6.

39. Zheng Bijian, "China's Peaceful Rise," *Foreign Affairs* 84, no. 5 (Summer/Fall 2005): 18–24.

40. Zheng Bijian, in discussion with author, Beijing, August 23, 2005.

41. The Center for International and Strategic Studies (CSIS) in Washington maintains a regular program of exchanges with the Central Communist Party School of China and its China Reform Forum. A compilation of Zheng Bijian's speeches on "China's peaceful rise" can be found on the CSIS website, www.csis.org. See also Zheng, "Zhongguo Heping Jueqi Fazhan Daolu You Liyu Zhong-Mei Guanxi," 3–6.

42. "Remarks of Chinese Premier Wen Jiabao, 'Turning Your Eyes to China,'" *Harvard University Gazette,* December 10, 2003, http://www.news.harvard.edu/gazette/2003 /12.11/10-wenspeech.html.

43. Hu Jintao, speech in celebration of the 110th anniversary of Mao Zedong's birth, December 26, 2003, ibid.

44. Ibid.

45. Ibid.

46. PLA officers in discussion with author, May 2004 and August 2005.

47. Zheng Bijian, in discussion with author, August 23, 2005.

48. Wortzel, "China's Peaceful Rise."

49. USCC, *2011 Report to Congress*, 166–72.

50. USCC, *2010 Annual Report to Congress,* chapter 5, "China and the Internet," http://www .uscc.gov/annual_report/2010/Chapter5_Section_1(page221).pdf.

10. Challenges Posed by the Chinese Military

1. The author used trade and investment information from the Central Intelligence Agency's *World Fact Book* as the basis for these statements, https://www.cia.gov/library /publications/the-world-factbook (accessed on January 8, 2013). The CIA maintains *The World Fact Book* as an online resource available to the public and updates it weekly.

2. European Commission, "Trade: China," December 3, 2012, http://ec.europa.eu/trade /creating-opportunities/bilateral-relations/countries/china/.

3. Xinhua, "China-ASEAN 2011 Bilateral Trade to Hit Record High," ASEAN-China Centre, November 17, 2011, http://www.asean-china-center.org/english/2011 -11/17/c_131252005.htm.

4. Bao Chang, "ASEAN, China to Become Top Trade Partners," *China Daily,* April 20, 2012, http://www.chinadaily.com.cn/cndy/2012-04/20/content_15094898.htm.

5. An excellent explanation of a "hedging strategy" with China is Thomas J. Christenson, "Chinese Realpolitic," *Foreign Affairs* 75, no. 5 (September/October 1996): 37–52. See also Greg Yellen, "Holding the Tiger by the Tail: Chinese Maritime Expansion and the

U.S. 'Hedge' Strategy," *The Monitor* 16, no. 2-3, (Summer 2011): 31–49, http://web.wm.edu/so/monitor/issues/16-2/3-yellen.pdf.

6. USCC, *2012 Report to Congress,* 243–57.

7. Larry M. Wortzel, "PLA 'Joint' Operational Contingencies in South Asia, Central Asia, and Korea," in Kamphausen et al., *Beyond the Strait,* 327, 355–59.

8. East Asia Security Act of 2005, H.R. 3100, 109th Congress.

9. Office of the Secretary of Defense, *Annual Report to Congress, 2011,* 34.

10. Wendell Minnick, "New U.S. Law Seeks Answers on Chinese Nuke Tunnels," *Defense News,* January 5, 2013, http://www.defensenews.com/article/20130105/DEFREG02/301050003/New-U-S-Law-Seeks-Answers-Chinese-Nuke-Tunnels.

11. Desmond Ball et al., *Crisis Stability and Nuclear War* (Ithaca, NY: Cornell University Press, 1987), 62.

12. USCC, *2011 Report to Congress,* 205.

13. Ibid.

14. Krekel et al., *Capability of the People's Republic of China.*

15. Stokes et al., "The Chinese People's Liberation Army Signals Intelligence."

16. USCC, *2009 Report to Congress* (Washington, DC: Government Printing Office, 2009), 167–68.

17. David Kennedy, "Weekly Intelligence Summary: 2012-12-16," *Verizon Security Blog, March 16, 2012,* http://securityblog.verizonbusiness.com/2012/03/16/weekly-intelligence-summary-2012-03-16.

18. Richard Esposito and Lee Ferran, "International Plot to Smuggle U.S. Stealth Technology to China Foiled: Feds," ABC News, April 25, 2012, http://abcnews.go.com/Blotter/arrested-alleged-plot-smuggle-us-military-tech-china/story?id=16210937#.T5lLy4ImZ8F.

19. James W. Cartwright, testimony before the USCC, hearing on "Developments in China's Cyber and Nuclear Capabilities," George Mason University Prince William Campus, Manassas, VA, March 26, 2012. http://www.uscc.gov/hearings/2012hearings/transcripts/March_26_2012_USCC_Hearing_Transcript.pdf.

20. *National Defense Authorization Act for Fiscal year 2000,* 106th Congress, S. 1059.ENR, http://thomas.loc.gov/cgi-bin/query/D?c106:6:./temp/~c106G2dB8T.

21. *National Defense Authorization, Fiscal Year 2001,* Public Law 106-398, 106th Congress, October 30, 2000 (114. S3ct. 1654), http://www.gpo.gov/fdsys/pkg/PLAW-106publ398/pdf/PLAW-106publ398.pdf.

22. Larry M. Wortzel, *Why Caution Is Needed in Military Contacts with China,* backgrounder no. 1340 (Washington, DC: Heritage Foundation, 1999), 6.

23. Jane Perlex, "New Chinese Leader Meets Military Nuclear Officers," *New York Times,* December 5, 2012, http://www.nytimes.com/2012/12/06/world/asia/chinese-leader-xi-jinping-meets-officers-of-military-nuclear-unit.html?_r=0.

SELECTED BIBLIOGRAPHY

Bai Zhonggan, Zhou Ying, Wang Guoyu, and Wang Liandong. "SAR Qipian Ganrao de Xu Guan Yindao Suanfa Yanjiu [Study on Sequentially Booted Information on Platform Location for SAR Deception Jamming]." *Xiandai Leida* [Modern radar] 29, no. 1 (January 2007): 77–79.

Blasko, Dennis J. *The Chinese Army Today: Tradition and Transformation in the 21st Century.* New York: Routledge, 2006.

Cai Fengzhen, and Tian Anping, eds. *Kongtian Yiti Zuozhan Xue* [Integrated aerospace operations]. Beijing: PLA Press, 2006.

———. *Kongtian Zhanchang yu Zhongguo Kongjun* [The aerospace battlefield and China's Air Force]. Beijing: PLA Press, 2004.

Center for Technology and Security Policy. *Coping with the Dragon: Essays on PLA Transformation and the U.S. Military.* Washington, DC: National Defense University Press, 2007. http://www.ndu.edu/CTNSP/docUploaded/CopingwithDragon.pdf.

Chang Xingqi. *Junshi Hangtian Xue* [Military astronautics]. 2nd ed. Beijing: National Defense Industries Press, 2005.

Che Rucai, and Zhang Honghua. "Zhui Zing Xing Gen Zong Kongjian Fei Hezuo Mubiao de Xiangdui Guidao Sheji" [Relative orbit design of a chaser tracking a non-cooperative target in space]. *Hangtian Kongzhi* [Aerospace control] 24, no. 5 (October 2006): 40–45.

Che Yajun, and Xue Xinglin, eds. *Zhanchang Huanjing yu Xinxihua Zhanzheng* [The battlefield environment and informationalized warfare]. Beijing: National Defense University Press, 2010.

Chen Qiang. "Chinese Practice in Public International Law." *Chinese Journal of International Law* 3, no. 591, 2003: 17–28.

Chen Yong, and Sun Zhixin. "Zhicheng Guojia Liyi Tuozhan de Zhanlue Xing Guanjian Jishu Fazhan Sikao" [Support national interests expand the strategy of key technological development concepts], "Zhanlue Luntan" [Strategy forum]. *Guofang Keji* [National Defense Science and Technology]. November 2006, 17–21.

Cheng Yong, and Guo Yanlong. "Fan Weixing Jiguang Wuqi Fazhan Xianzhuang yu Dongtai Fenxi" [An analysis of present-day trends in antisatellite laser weapons].

Dimian Fangkong Wuqi [Ground air defense weapons] 312, no. 4 (2004): 51–54. www.cnki.net.

Chizum, David G. *Soviet Radioelectronic Combat.* Boulder, CO: Westview, 1985.

Cliff, Roger, Mark Burles, Michael S. Chase, Derek Eaton, and Kevin Pollpeter. *Entering the Dragon's Lair: Chinese Antiaccess Strategies and Their Implications for the United States.* Santa Monica, CA: Rand Corporation, 2007.

Cole, Bernard D. *The Great Wall at Sea: China's Navy Enters the Twenty-First Century.* Annapolis, MD: Naval Institute Press, 2001.

Dai Xu. "Taikong: Da Guo Jueqi de Xin Jiyu [Space: A Rising Power's New Opportunity]." *Huanqiu Shibao* [World daily], December 21, 2006, 11.

Ding Bangyu, ed. *Zuozhan Zhihui Xue* [The study of command and control operations]. Beijing: Military Science Press, 2006.

Erickson, Andrew S., and Lyle J. Goldstein, eds. *Chinese Aerospace Power: Evolving Maritime Roles.* Annapolis, MD: Naval Institute Press, 2011.

Fan Jinrong, and Zhao Wenping. "Jiguang Wuqi Ji Qi Zai Kongfang Tian Tixi de Zuoyong" [Research on laser weapons technology in air and space defense systems]. *Xiandi Fangwei Jishu* [Modern defence technology] 34, no. 5 (October 2006): 13–18.

Fisher, Richard D. *China's Military Modernization: Building for Regional and Global Reach.* Westport, CT: Praeger Security International, 2008.

Friedberg, Aaron L. "The Future of U.S.-China Relations: Is Conflict Inevitable?" *International Security* Vol. 30, no. 2 (Fall 2005): 7–42.

Gao Qingjun. "Characteristics and Limitations of Space Reconnaissance in High-Tech Local War." *Zhuangbei Zhihui Jishu Xueyuan* [Journal of the Academy of Command and Technology] 16, no. 1 (February 2005): 52–56.

Ge Dongsheng, ed. *Guojia Anquan Zhanlue Lun* [On national security strategy]. Beijing: Military Science Press, 1006.

Ge Xinliu et al. "Xinxi Zhan Zhong Daodan Budui Mianlin de Wenti yu Duice" [The real problems in information war encountered by guided missile forces]. In Military Science Editorial Group, *Wo Jun Xixi Zhan Wenti* [Research on questions about information warfare in the PLA]. Beijing: National Defense University Press, 1999.

Goldstein, Avery. *Rising to the Challenge: China's Grand Strategy and International Security.* Stanford, CA: Stanford University Press, 2005.

Guo Wujun. *Lun Zhanlue Zhihui* [On strategic command and control]. Beijing: Military Science Press, 2002.

Han Xiaolin, ed. *Gao Jishu Zhubu Zhanzheng Lilun Yanjiu* [Research and theory on limited war under high technology conditions]. Beijing: Military Friendship and Literature Press, 1998.

He Qizhi. "Legal Progress of Space in China." *Air and Space Law* 18, no. 6 (1993): 261, 289–291.

Hu Jintao. "Renqing Xin Shiji Xin Jieduan Wojun Lishi Shiming" [Understanding the new historic missions of our military in the new period of the new century]. Speech to the Central Military Commission of the Chinese Communist Party,

December 24, 2004. http://gfjy.jiangxi.gov.cn/htmnew/11349.htm (accessed November 17, 2009).

Hu Shangli. *NMD yu Fanzhi NMD* [National missile defense and countermeasures to national missile defense]. Translated by Mi Jianjun. Beijing: National Defense University Press, 2001.

Huang Chaohui. "Duikang Tiaojian Xia SBIRS Dui Zhanlue Daudan Tufang Nengli Yingxiang Yanjiu" [Study on strategic missile penetration capabilities influence by SBIRS under countermeasures]. *Xiandai Fangwei Jushu* [Modern defence technology] 34, no. 6 (December 2006): 36–38.

Huang Luwei, Bi Yiming, and Yang Jifeng. "Daodan Budui Wangluo Zhongxin Zhan Wenti Yanjiu" [Research on network-centric warfare and the missile forces]. *Zhihui Kongzhi yu Fangzhen* [Command, control and simulation] 28, no. 2 (April 2006): 18–21.

Huang Shiqi, and Liu Daizhi. "Fan Chengxiang Weixing Zhencha Jishu yu Fangfa Celue Yanjiu" [Study anti-imaging spy satellite technology and tactical methods research], *Xitong Gongcheng yu Dianzi Jishu* [Systems engineering and electronics] Vol. 28, no. 7 (2006): 104–7.

Huang Zhideng. "Taikong Wuqihua yu Taikong Weishe" [The weaponization of space and space threats]. *Guoji Jishu Jingji Yanjiu* [Studies in international technology and economy] 9, no. 1 (January 2006): 24–28.

Jencks, Harlan. *From Muskets to Missiles: Politics and Professionalism in the Chinese Army, 1954–1981.* Boulder, CO: Westview, 1982.

Jiang Luming et al. *Xiandai Guofang Jingjixue Daolun* [*Guide to Modern National Defense Economics*]. Beijing: National Defense University Press, 2002.

Jiang Yamin. *Yuan Zhan* [Long distance operations]. Beijing: Academy of Military Science Press, 2007.

Jiang Yongwei. "E Jun Wu Ren Ji Zai Shizhan Zhong Jishu Yong" [The utility of Russian unmanned aircraft technology in actual combat]. *Xiandai Junshi* [Contemporary military affairs] 5 (June 13, 2005). http://www.military.china.com/zh_cn/xdjs/05/11033359/20050613/12396.

Joffe, Ellis. *Party and Army: Professionalism and Political Control in the Chinese Officer Corps, 1949–1964.* Cambridge, MA: Harvard University Press, 1971.

Kamphausen, Roy, and Andrew Scobell, eds. *Right-Sizing the People's Liberation Army: Exploring the Contours of China's Military.* Carlisle, PA: Strategic Studies Institute, 2007.

Kamphausen, Roy, David Lai, and Andrew Scobell, eds. *The PLA at Home and Abroad: Assessing the Operational Capabilities of China's Military.* Carlisle, PA: Strategic Studies Institute, 2010.

Lawrence, D. B. "Soviet Radio-Electronic Combat." *Air Force Magazine* 65, no. 3 (March 1982). http://www.airforce-magazine.com/MagazineArchive/Pages/1982/March%201982/0382radioelectronic.aspx.

Lennox, Duncan. "Space Warfare: Part Two; In War and Peace." *Jane's Defence Weekly,* March 28, 2007.

Lewis, John Wilson, and Xue Litai. *Imagined Enemies: China Prepares for Uncertain War.* Stanford, CA: Stanford University Press, 2006.

Li Bingyan. *Da Moulue yu Xin Junshi Biange* [Grand strategy and the new revolution in military affairs]. Beijijng: Military Science Press, 2004.

Li Daguang. "Taikong Zuozhan de Zhidao Sixiang" [Thoughts on aerospace operations command and control]. *Guoji Taikong* [International aerospace], no. 3 (2004): 27–30.

Li Jijun. *Junshi Zhanlue Siwei* [Thinking about military strategy]. Beijing: Military Science Press, 2006.

Li Naiguo. *Xinxizhan Xinlun* [A new discussion on information warfare]. Beijing: National Defense University Press, 2004.

Li Rongchang, Cheng Jian, and Guo Lianqing, eds. *Kongtian Yiti Zinxi Zuozhan* [Integrated, informationalized aerospace war]. Beijing: PLA Academy of Military Science Press, 2003.

Li Rongchang, Cheng Jian, and Zheng Lianqing, eds. *Kongtian Yiti Xinxi Zuozhan* [Integrated aerospace information operations]. Beijing: Academy of Military Science Press, 2003.

Li Xiaobing. *History of the Modern Chinese Army.* Louisville: University of Kentucky Press, 2007.

Li Ying, and Zhou Binyu. "Ground High-Power Laser Anti-Satellite Reconnaissance Technology." *Guangdian Duikang yu Wuyuan Ganrao* [Optoelectronic warfare and passive jamming] 14, no. 2 (2002): 9–12

Li Yong, Wang Xiao, Yi Ming, and Wang Long. "Threats to Spaceborne Optoelectronic Imaging and Telemetry Systems and Countermeasures Technology." *Hongwai yu Jiguang Gongcheng* [*Infrared and Laser Engineering*] 34, no. 6 (December 2005): 631–35, 640.

Liu Jingbo. *21 Shiji Chu Zhongguo Guojia Anquan Zhanlue* [China's national security strategy in the early 21st century]. Beijing: Shishi Chubanshe, 2006.

Liu Jinjun, and Chen Bojiang. *Lu-Kong Xietong Zuozhan Gailun* [An introduction to combined ground-air warfare]. Beijing: PLA Press, 1996.

Liu Jixian. "Junshi Hangtian Lilun de Yanjiu yu Chaungxin-dui 'Junshi Hangtian Xue' de Renshi yu Pingjia" [Study and originality in military space theory: Understanding and commentary on "military space theory"]. *Zhongguo Junshi Kexue* [China military science] 19, no. 6 (June 2006): 144–48.

Liu Jixian, and Liu Zheng, eds. *Xin Junshi Geming yu Junshi Fazhi Jianshe* [The new revolution in military affairs and building a military legal system]. Beijing: PLA Press, 2005.

Liu Mingtao, and Yang Chengjun, eds. *Gao Jishu Zhanzheng Zhong de Daodan Zhan* [Ballistic missile combat in high technology wars]. Beijing: National Defense University Press, 1993.

Lin Yuchen. "Shijie Qian Kong Daodan Fazhan de Xianzhuang" [The state of the world's development of stealth missiles]. *Xiandai Junshi* [Modern military affairs]. http://military.china.com/zh_cn/xdjs/03/11033357/20060117/13039.

Lu Jiuming, and Zhu Kai. "Junshi Tongxin Weixing Ji Qi Xinglian Lu Xingneng Yanjiu" [Research on military communications satellites and the performance of downlinks]. *Xiandai Fangwei Jishu* [Modern defence technology] 34, no. 3 (June 2006): 48–51.

Ma Junguo, Fu Qiang Xiao Huaitie, and Zhu Jiang. "Leida Kongjian Mubiao Zhibie Jishu Zongshu" [Survey (summary) of radar space target recognition technology]. *Xiandai Fangwei Jishu* [Modern defence technology] 34, no. 5 (October 2006): 90–93.

Mao Guohui. *Xinxi Shidai Zhanzheng Fali Yanjiu* [Research on legal aspects of information age warfare]. Beijing: Military Science Press, 2006.

Mao Yuan. "'GeGe Diqiu' Yinfa de Sikao" [Thoughts prompted by "Google Earth"], *Huojianbing Bao* [Rocket soldiers daily], June 1, 2007, 2.

Meng Lang. *Weilai Zhanzheng Shemma Yang* [What is happening on the future battlefield], May 1, 2001. http://www.people.com.cn/GB/junshi/62/20010108 /372946.html.

Military Science Editorial Group. *Wo Jun Xixi Zhan Wenti Yanjiu* [Research on questions about information warfare in the PLA]. Beijing: National Defense University Press, 1999.

Min Zengfu. *Kongjun Junshi Sixiang Gailun* [An introduction to air force military thinking]. Beijing: PLA Press, 2006.

Mulvenon, James, and David Finkelstein, eds. *China's Revolution in Doctrinal Affairs: Emerging Trends in the Operational Art of the People's Liberation Army.* Washington, DC: Rand, 2005.

Mulvenon, James, David Finkelstein, and Andrew N. D. Yang, eds. *The People's Liberation Army as an Organization: Reference Volume 1.0.* Santa Monica, CA: Rand, 2002.

Nie Yubao. "Daji haishang di da jian jianting biandui de dianzi zhan zhanfa" [Combat methods for electronic warfare attacks on heavily fortified enemy naval formations]. In Military Science Editorial Group, *Wo Jun Xixi Zhan Wenti Yanjiu* [Research on questions about information warfare in the PLA]. Beijing: National Defense University Press, 1999.

Pan Xiangting et al., eds. *Gao Jishu Tiaojian Xia Meijun Jubu Zhanzheng* [*American Limited* [(Local)] Warfare under high technology conditions]. Beijing: People's Liberation Army Press, 1994.

Pan Youmie. "Zhuoyan Kongtian Yitihua Tansuo Guojia Kongtian Anquan Zhanlue" [Focus on Air-Space Integration and Exploring a National Air-Space Strategy]. *Zhongguo Junshi Kexue* [China military science] 19, no. 2 (2006): 60–66.

Pan Zhenqiang, ed. *Guoji Caijun yu Junbei Kongzhi* [International disarmament and arms control]. Beijing: National Defense University Press, 1996.

Peng Guangqian, and Yao Youzhi, eds. *The Science of Military Strategy.* Beijing: Military Science Press, 2005.

Qiao Liang, and Wang Xiangsui. *Chaoxian Zhan: Dui Quanqiuhua Shidai Zhanzheng yu Zhanfa de Xiangding* [War without limits: Thinking and rules of war in a globalized age]. Beijing: PLA Arts and Literature Press, 1999.

Ren Xiafeng. "Zhuanyu Jingjiqu Junshi Liyong de Falu Wenti: Zhongguo de Guanjiao" [Legal issues regarding military and intelligence gathering activities in the EEZ and adjacent airspace: A Chinese perspective]. http://vip.chinalawinfo .com/newlaw2002/slc/slc.asp?db=art&gid=33557856.

Ryan, Mark A., David M. Finkelstein, and Michael A. McDevitt, eds. *Chinese Warfighting: The PLA Experience since 1949*. Armonk, NY: M. E. Sharpe, 2003.

Shambaugh, David. *Modernizing China's Military: Progress, Problems and Prospects*. Berkeley: University of California Press, 2002.

Shang Jie. *Xiandai Dimian Zuozhan Liliang de Yunyong he Fazhan* [The use and development of modern ground warfighting power]. Beijing: People's Liberation Army Press, 1994.

Shen Genhua. "Lun Xinxi Shidai de Hexin Junshi Nengli [On core military capabilities in the information age]." *Zhongguo Junshi Kexue* [China military science] Issue 116, no. 2 (August 2011): 44–52.

Shen Shilu, Feng Shuxing, and Xu Xuefeng. "Tian Ji Dui Di Daji Dongneng Wuqi Zuozhan Nengli yu Kexing Xing Fenxi" [The analysis of the operational capability and feasibility of space-to-ground kinetic weapons]. *Zhuangbei Zhihui Jishu Xueyaun Xuebao* [Journal of the Academy of Command and Technology] 17, no. 1 (February 2006): 33–37.

Shen Weiguang, Jie Xijiang, Ma Ji, and Li Jijun eds. *Zhongguo Xinxi Zhan* [China's information warfare]. Beijing: Xinhua Press, 2005.

Shu Rui, Zhou Yanping, Tao Kunyu, and Jiang Yijun. "The Study of Infrared Spectrum of Space Targets." *Guangxue Jishu* [Optical technique] 32, no. 2 (March 2006): 196–99.

Si Laiyi. "Lun Xinxi Zuozhan Zhihui Kongzhi Jiben Yuanze" [On basic principles for command-and-control information warfare]. In Military Science Editorial Group, *Wo Jun Xixi Zhan Wenti Yanjiu* [Research on questions about information warfare in the PLA]. Beijing: National Defense University Press, 1999.

Stokes, Mark A. *China's Strategic Modernization: Implications for the United States*. Carlisle, PA: Strategic Studies Institute, 1999.

Stokes, Mark A., and Dean Cheng. *China's Evolving Space Capabilities: Implications for U.S. Interests*. Arlington, VA: Project 2049 Institute, 2012. http://www.uscc.gov /RFP/2012/USCC_China-Space-Program-Report_April-2012.pdf.

Sun Yiming, and Yang Liping. *Xinxihua Zhanzheng Zhong de Zhanshu Shuju Lian* [Tactical data links in information warfare]. Beijing: Beijing Post and Telecommunications College Press, 2005.

Tang Yuyan, and Huang Peikang. "Jiaohui Duijie Zhong Leida Celiang Xinxi de Zui You Guji" [Optimal estimation of radar measurement information in Rendezvous Docking]. *Xiandai Fangwei Jishu* [Modern defence technology] 34, no. 6 (December 2006): 98–102.

Tao Benren. "Dui Dimian Junshi Dianzi Xinxi de Tianji Fanghu Xitong" [Space defense system for ground military electromagnetic information]. *Hangtian Dianzi Duikang* [Aerospace electronic warfare] 22, no. 4 (August 1, 2006): 15–1.

Tao Zhonghua. *Xin Gainian Yinfa Weilai Fangkong Wuqi Biange* [New concepts bring forth a revolution in future air defense weapons]. http://military.china.com /zh_cn/critical/25/20050518/12322568.html.

Thomas, Timothy L. *Decoding the Virtual Dragon: Critical Evolutions in the Science and Philosophy of China's Information Operations and Military Strategy.* Fort Leavenworth, KS: Foreign Military Studies Office, 2007.

———. *Dragon Bytes: Chinese Information-War Theory and Practice.* Fort Leavenworth, KS: Foreign Military Studies Office, 2004.

———. *The Dragon's Quantum Leap: Transformation from a Mechanized to an Informatized Force.* Fort Leavenworth, KS: Foreign Military Studies Office, 2009.

Tian Taoyun. "Yingjie Xin Tiaozhan: Zhongguo Junshi Zhuanjia Tichu Junshi Hangtian Lilun" [Meeting a new challenge: China's military experts propose military aerospace theory]. *Xinhuawang*, December 13, 2002. news.xinhaunet.com/newscenter/2002-12/13/content_659248.html.

Tseng Ming-Yi. "Chung Kung Ting Hsiang Neng Wuch'I Yanfa HsienK'uang Shen Ts'ai" [Taiwan investigation of PRC's "directed energy" weapons research]. *Kuofang Tsa-chih* [National defense magazine], Vol. 21, No. 6 (January 2007): 26–31.

U.S. Department of Defense. *Quadrennial Defense Review Report.* Washington, DC: Department of Defense, 2010.

Van Tol, Jan, with Mark Gunzinger, Andrew Krepinovich, and Jim Thomas. *AirSea Battle: A Point-of-Departure Operational Concept.* Washington, DC: Center for Strategic and Budgetary Assessments, 2010.

Wang Guobo, and Yang Chen. " 'Gege Di Qiu' Yinfa Guanbing Re Yi ['Google earth' prompts heated discussion among grassroots level military personnel]." *Kongjun Bao* [Air Force daily], April 19, 2007, 2.

Wang Houqing et al. *Zhanyi Fazhan Shi* [Campaign development history]. Beijing: National Defense University Press, 2001.

Wang Lidong. *Guojia Haishang Liyi Lun* [On national maritime interests]. Beijing: National Defense University Press, 2007.

Wang Pufeng, ed. *Mao Zedong Junshi Zhanlue Lun* [On the military strategy of Mao Zedong]. Beijing: Military Science Press, 1993.

Wang Wenrong et al., eds. *Zhanlue Xue* [The science of military strategy]. Beijing: National Defense University Press, 1999.

Wang Zhengde, ed. *Jiedu Wanglou Zhongxin Zhan* [Interpretation of network centric warfare]. Beijing: National Defense Industries Press, 2004.

———, ed. *Xinxi Duikang Lun* [Information confrontation theory]. Beijing: Military Science Press, 2007.

Wang Zhigang. *Dianzi Xinxi Jishu* [Electronics and information technologies]. Beijing: Military Literature Press, 1998.

Wang Zhiyuan et al., eds. *Lianhe Xinxi Zuozhan* [Joint information operations]. Beijing: Academy of Military Science, 1999.

Wang Zhongquan. *Meiguo He Liliang yu He Zhanlue* [American nuclear (weapons) strength and nuclear Strategy]. Beijing: National Defense University Press, 1995.

Wortzel, Larry M. *China's Military Modernization: International Implications.* Westport, CT: Greenwood Press, 1988.

————. *China's Nuclear Forces: Operations, Training, Doctrine, Command, Control, and Campaign Planning.* Carlisle, PA: Strategic Studies Institute, 2007.

————, ed. *The Chinese Armed Forces in the 21st Century.* Carlisle, PA: Strategic Studies Institute, 1999.

————. *The Chinese People's Liberation Army and Space Warfare: Emerging United States–China Military Competition.* Washington, DC: American Enterprise Institute, 2007. http://www.aei.org/paper/26977.

Wu Chunqui. *Da Zhanlue Lun* [Grand strategy: A Chinese view]. Beijing: Military Science Press, 1998.

Xiang Wujun. *Lun Zhanlue Zhihui* [On strategic command and control]. Beijing: Military Science Press, 2002.

Xiao Chaoren et al., eds. *Zhonggong Dangshi Jianming Cidian* [A concise dictionary of the Chinese Communist Party's history]. Beijing: Jiefangjun Chubanshe, 1986.

Xiao Xingbo. *He Zhanzheng yu Renfang* [People's air defense and nuclear war]. Beijing: People's Liberation Army Press, 1989.

Xin Qin. *Xinxihua Shidai de Zhanzheng* [Warfare in the information age]. Beijing: National Defense University Press, 2000.

Xu Xiaofeng, Zhu Xiaosong, and Liu Liyuan. "Jiyu Mou Weixing Tongxin Xitong de Ganrao Yanjiu" [Jamming analysis based on a certain satellite communications system]. *Hangtian Dianzi Duikang* [Aerospace electronic countermeasures] 22, no. 5 (October 2006): 28–29, 45.

Xue Xinglin. *Zhanyi Lilun Xuexi Zhinan* [A guide to the study of campaign theory]. Beijing: National Defense University Press, 2002.

Yan Xuetong. *Guoji Zhengzhi yu Zhongguo* [International politics and China]. Beijing: Peking University Press, 2005.

————, ed. *Zhongguo Guojia Liyi Fenxi* [An analysis of China's national interest]. Tianjin: Tianjin People's Press, 1997.

Yan Xuetong, Wang Zaibang, Li Zhongcheng, and Hou Ruoshi, eds. *Zhongguo Jueqi: Guoji Huanjing Pinggu* [The international environment for China's peaceful rise]. Tianjin: Tianjin People's Press, 1998.

Yang Hua, Chen Changming, Ling Yongshun, and Ma Donghui. "Tian Ji Daodan Yujing xitong ji Dui Qi de Gongji he Ganrao Fenxi [Analysis of Jamming of Spaceborne Missile Early Warning System]." *Hangitan Dianzi Duikang* [Aerospace electronic warfare], no. 4 (2001): 5–7, 37.

Yang Jinhui, and Chang Xianqi. "Kongjian Xinxi Duikang Wenti Yanjiu" [Research and problems of space information warfare]. *Wu Xiandian Gongcheng* [Radio engineering] 36, no. 11 (2006): 7–9.

Yang Yonghui, and Xiao Siwei. "Weixing Ce Kong Lian Lu Ganrao Jishu Yanjiu [Jamming Technique against Satellite TTC Channel]." *Hangtian Dianzi Duikang* [Aerospace electronic countermeasures], Vol. 22, no. 5 (2006), 22–24.

Yao Yunzhu. *Zhanhou Meiguo Weishe Lilun yu Zhengce* [Post war American deterrence theories and policies]. Beijing: National Defense University Press, 1998.

Ye Zheng. *Xinxihua Zuozhan Gailun* [An introduction to informationalized operations]. Beijing: Military Science Press, 2007.

Yu Kunyang, Mao Zhaojun, and Li Yunzhi. "Mei, E', Hangtian Budui Zuzhi Tizhi Fenxi Ji Qishi" [Analysis of U.S.'s and Russia's Space Organization Systems and Their Inspiration]. *Zhuangbei Zhihui Jishu Xueyuan Xuebao* [Journal of the Academy of Equipment Command and Technology] 16, no. 6 (2005): 70–75. www.wangfangdata.com.cn.

Yu Yongzhe, ed. *Gao Jishu Zhanzheng Houqin Baozhang* [Ensuring logistics in high technology warfare]. Beijing: Military Science Press, 1995.

Yuan Jun. "Guowai Weibo Wuqi ji Qi Fazhan" [Foreign Microwave Weapons and Their Development]. *Zhongguo Hangtian* [China aerospace], no. 5 (2001). http://www.space.cetin.net.cn/docs/ht0105/ht0010511.htm.

Yuan Zelu. "Taikong Zuozhan Yinlun" [Essay on aerospace operations]. *Dimian Fangkong Wuqi* [*Ground Air Defense Weapons*] 311, no. 3 (2004): 44–48. www.cnki.net.

Zhang Hualiang, and Song Huaren. "Luelun Xinxihua Zhanzheng Zhu Zhanchang Xiang Taikong Zhuanyi de Biranxing" [Discussion on the inevitability of the main battlefield in information war transferring to outer space]. *Zuangbei Zhiui Jishu Xueyaun Xuebao* [Journal of the Academy of Equipment Command and Technology] 15, no. 5 (October 2004): 14–17.

Zhang Jingbao et al., eds. *Dangdai Zhanshu Zhinan* [Guide to contemporary military tactics]. Beijing: National Defense University Press, 1994.

Zhang Kaide, and Zhao Shubin. "Shimin Daji Zhihui Kongzhi Jishu Chutan" [The command and control technology of time-critical strikes]. *Zhihui Kongzhi yu Fangzhen* [Command, control and simulation] 28, no. 2 (April 2006): 1–5.

Zhang Liying, Zhang Xixin, and Wang Hui. "Fan Weixing Wuqi Jishu Fanfa Cuoshi Qian Xi" [Preliminary analysis of anti-satellite weapon technology and defensive measures]. *Feihang Daodan* [Winged missile journal], no. 3 (March 2004): 28–30.

Zhang Shude. "Xun Jiao He Yi-Liantong Weilai Zhanchang de Qiaoliang" [Combine Training and Teaching: The Bridge to Integrating the Future Battlefield]. http://www.chinamil.com.cn/site1/jsslpdjs.2006-08/15/content _5551.

Zhang Wannian, ed. *Dangdai Shijie Junshi yu Zhongguo Guofang* [*China's national defense and contemporary world military affairs*]. Beijing: Military Science Press, 1999.

Zhang Xingye, and Wang Chaotian, eds. *Zhanyi Sixiang Fazhan Shi* [The history of the development of campaign thought]. Beijing: National Defense University Press, 1997.

Zhang Yongwei. "Xiao Weixing zai Junshi Zhong de Yingyong" [The military uses of small aatellites]. *Xiandai Junshi* [*Modern military affairs*]. http://military.china.com/zh_cn/xjds/05/11033359/20051025/12782.

Zhang Yuliang, ed. *Zhanyi Xue* [The science of military campaigns]. Beijing: PLA National Defense University Press, 2006.

Zheng Shenxia, and Liu Yuan, eds. *Guofang he Jundui Jianshe Guanshe Luoshi Kexue Fazhan Guan Xuexi Tiyao* [Study materials for completely building the military and national defense]. Beijing: PLA Press, 2006.

Zheng Tongliang. "Status of Development of Safety Protection Technology for Military Satellite Systems." *Hangtian Dianzi Duikang* [Aerospace electronic warfare], no. 2 (2004): 5–9.

Zhongguo de Jiguang Wuqi Shi Taiji Haishi Jiaoao? [Are China's laser weapons trash or arrogance?]. Zhonghua Wang Junshi [China military online network] September 28, 2003. http://military.china.com/zh_cn/critical3/27/20030928/11547884.html.

Zhou Wenjiong, Xiao Yuxiang, and Wu Shiqi. "Wei Xiao Weixing Zhuan Fashi Qipian Ganrao de Shiyan Fenxi he Fangzhen" [Delay analysis and simulation of micro-satellite repeater deception jamming]. *Dianzi Xinxi Duikang Jishu* (Electronic information countermeasures technology] 21, no. 6 (November 2006): 27–30.

Zhou Yanping, Zhao Xue, and Long Weijun. "SAR Xing de Kedui Kangxing Yanjiu" [Study of possible countermeasures against SAR satellite]. *Zhuangbei Zhihui Jishu Xueyuan Xuebao* [Journal of the Academy of Equipment Command and Technology] 14, no. 5 (October 2003): 33–37.

Zhu Mingquan. *He Kuosan: Weixian yu Fangzhi* [Nuclear proliferation: Danger and prevention]. Shanghai: Science and Technology Literature Press, 1995.

Zhu Wenquan. "Wo Jun Weilai Zhanchang Xinxi Zhan Chutan" [Exploring the future information warfare battlefield in the PLA]. In Military Science Editorial Group, *Wo Jun Xixi Zhan Wenti Yanjiu* [Research on questions about information warfare in the PLA]. Beijing: National Defense University Press, 1999.

Zhu Youwen, Feng Yi, and Xu Dechi, eds. *Gao Jishu Tiaojian Xia de Xinxi Zhan* [Information warfare under high technology conditions]. Beijing: Military Science Press, 1994.

INDEX

ABOUT THE AUTHOR

Dr. Larry M. Wortzel is a leading authority on China and Asia, with many years of experience in intelligence issues, international trade and economics, foreign policy, national security, and military strategy. He had a distinguished thirty-two-year military career, retiring as a colonel in 1999. Wortzel was director of the Asian Studies Center of the Heritage Foundation and then its vice president for foreign policy and defense studies. He is a commissioner of the congressionally appointed U.S.-China Economic and Security Review Commission, as well as president of Asia Strategies and Risks, LLC, consulting on security, political, and military affairs in China and Asia.

Following three years in the U.S. Marine Corps, Wortzel enlisted in the U.S. Army in 1970. His first assignment with the Army Security Agency took him to Thailand, where he focused on Chinese military communications in Vietnam and Laos. Within three years he had graduated Infantry Officer Candidate School, as well as both the Airborne and Ranger schools.

After serving four years as an infantry officer, Wortzel shifted to military intelligence and traveled regularly throughout Asia while assigned to the Intelligence Center Pacific (part of the U.S. Pacific Command) from 1978 to 1982. He then attended the National University of Singapore where he studied advanced Chinese and traveled in Asia. Wortzel next worked for the under secretary of defense for policy, developing counterintelligence programs to protect America from foreign espionage. He also managed programs to gather foreign intelligence for the Army Intelligence and Security Command.

From 1988 to 1990, Wortzel was assistant army attaché at the U.S. embassy in Beijing, where he witnessed and reported on the Tiananmen Massacre. After assignments as an army strategist and as an intelligence personnel manager, he returned to the embassy in China in 1995 as the army attaché.

In December 1997, Wortzel became a faculty member of the U.S. Army War College, serving as director of the Strategic Studies Institute for two years until his army retirement.

Dr. Wortzel's books include *Class in China: Stratification in a Classless Society* (Greenwood, 1987) and *Dictionary of Contemporary Chinese Military History* (Greenwood, 1999). He is editor of *China's Military Modernization: International Implications* (Greenwood, 1988) and *The Chinese Armed Forces in the 21st Century* (Strategic Studies Institute, 1999). He has edited six other books on China and contributed chapters to books on Chinese military history, Chinese war-fighting doctrine, and Asia-related strategic issues. His views on China and Asia are often sought by such publications as the *Wall Street Journal*, the *Washington Times*, the *New York Times*, the *San Diego Tribune*, the *International Herald Tribune*, the *Orlando Sentinal*, *National Journal*, *Asahi Shimbun*, and *Sankei Shimbun*. Wortzel has appeared on *PBS NewsHour*, the History Channel, Fox News, CNN, MSNBC, BBC, and Al Jazeera. As an expert on China and policy matters, he continues to regularly publish articles on security matters and be part of radio and television broadcasts. He is a member of the Council on Foreign Relations and the International Institute of Strategic Studies.

A graduate of the U.S. Army War College, Wortzel earned his BA in history from Columbus College and his MA and PhD in political science from the University of Hawaii.